TRADING

Other books by Susan Goldenberg

THE THOMSON EMPIRE
CANADIAN PACIFIC: A PORTRAIT OF POWER
MEN OF PROPERTY: THE CANADIAN DEVELOPERS
WHO ARE BUYING AMERICA

TRADING

Inside the World's Leading Stock Exchanges

Susan Goldenberg

Harcourt Brace Jovanovich, Publishers
San Diego   New York   London

LIBRARY OF CONGRESS CATALOGING IN PUBLICATION DATA
Goldenberg, Susan.
   Trading : inside the world's leading stock exchanges.
   Includes index.
   1. Stock-exchange.   I. Title.
HG4551.G65   1986   332.6'42   85-17570
ISBN 0-15-191005-7

Designed by Francesca M. Smith
Printed in the United States of America
First edition
A B C D E

TO MY PARENTS

Contents

Preface

"S"   "X"   "XON"   "DMP"   "How's XYZ?"
"At the market"   "At 1/8"   "Fill or kill"
"Off the bid"   "GTC"   "Take them"   "Sold me"

Every weekday in the United States and Canada thousands of these trading instructions are written, yelled, flashed, and signaled with hand and finger motions on stock exchange floors.*

Across the Atlantic, on the floor of the London Stock Exchange, instead of pandemonium, the atmosphere is stately and dignified. Some members wear top hats. Traders saunter around the floor, shopping for the best deal, inquiring about price by quietly murmuring, "What are XYZ?"

Across the Pacific in Tokyo traders jostle and yell on a packed floor, indicating company names with sweeping pantomime gestures: wiggling hands represent fishing firms; driving signals, automobile manufacturers; and rowing motions, shippers.

*For the record, the ones given here mean: Sears, U.S. Steel, Exxon, Dome Petroleum, What's the price?, Prevailing price, one-eighth of a dollar (full price is omitted), Kill order if terms unavailable, I withdraw, Good till canceled, I'll buy (for "Take them" or "Sold me").

In Zurich stocks are read aloud, one by one, and the traders scream their bids in a cacophony after each name.

The trading methods vary, but the end result is the same: Instantaneously fortunes are made or lost; corporations raise money to expand their operations or are grabbed by takeover sharks; and pension funds, insurance companies, and banks increase or decrease the values of their holdings.

There are now 130 stock exchanges in fifty-four countries around the world, with more springing up practically every day as additional nations and cities embrace the notion that an exchange can bestow prestige on their economy. And as John Phelan, Jr., chairman and chief executive officer of the New York Stock Exchange (NYSE), the world's largest, remarked: "Each of the major stock exchanges not only has its own rules and procedures, but its own personality as well."

This book, the first of its kind, deals with the world's leading stock exchanges—New York, American, Midwest (Chicago), Pacific (San Francisco and Los Angeles), Tokyo, London, Zurich, Paris, Frankfurt, and Toronto. NASDAQ (the U.S. National Association of Securities Dealers Automated Quotation System in over-the-counter securities) and four smaller exchanges—Amsterdam, Geneva, Philadelphia, and Montreal—are also covered because of their impact on the first group, and because exchanges do not operate in a vacuum, I have depicted their distinctive backgrounds and some securities houses that belong to them. I have also included the world's leading commodities and options exchanges in Chicago, considering their importance in today's investment scene.

At no other time in their long history have the exchanges undergone as gut-wrenching a self-evaluation and evolution as they are now experiencing from increased competition at home and from abroad. All want to expand the number of listed companies and to broaden their product ranges away from the traditional stocks and bonds. They are anxious for more investment by individuals, whose role in the marketplace is being eclipsed by institutional pension fund, bank, and insurance company investors. Some exchanges are opening their doors to membership by foreign brokers; others are investigating the market potential for domestic and international linkages to permit twenty-four-hour trading.

Trading systems are also undergoing unprecedented change. Certain exchanges in Europe are moving from a roll call system to the simultaneous, continuous method used in the United States for all stocks. And the U.S. securities industry is debating whether to re- place the traditional stock exchange floor—where traders shout and flail their arms—with a younger, extremely successful computer box method. *Who* can trade is under conversion, too. The U.S., U.K., and Canada are edging toward the universal bank systems of Switzerland and West Germany, where since the banks also act as brokers, there are no separate brokerage houses. The result of this upheaval at the exchanges and within the trading community could well be that the distinct trading customs that give each exchange its unique person- ality will fade into gray, faceless homogeneity, just as the skylines of the major cities of the world are losing their individuality.

For this book, I traveled to Europe, Asia, and the United States. To interview in Toronto, I simply took the subway since I live in a suburb. This is an independent book, but I am exceedingly grateful for the interviews and frequent, gracious hospitality I received from the exchanges, securities industry, banks, government regulatory agencies, the European Commission in Brussels, and a number of professors. I also wish to express my appreciation to those officials at the Canadian Department of External Affairs and the Department of Industry and Trade in the province of Ontario who assisted me by setting up the schedule for my meeting many of the people with whom I had secured interviews outside Canada. My thanks as well to Al- fons Cortés of Liechtenstein for his manifold help.

And finally, I would like to thank Harcourt Brace Jovanovich for understanding and encouraging what I wanted to do.

S. G.

September 1985

THE WORLD'S LEADING STOCK EXCHANGES
(As of year-end, 1984)

EXCHANGE	VOLUME (millions of shares)	DOLLAR VALUE (Stocks only. In billions of U.S. dollars. Foreign currencies converted at 1984 average rate of exchange.)	NUMBER OF MEMBERS	SEAT PRICE (high-low range) $	NUMBER OF TRADED COMPANIES	OTHER PRODUCTS TRADED
UNITED STATES						
New York	23,071	764.7	1,366	375,000–290,000	1,543	Options, financial futures
NASDAQ	15,159	153.5	5,726	Not applicable	4,097	Options
Midwest (Chicago)	1,852	59.9	444	58,000–29,000	1,788	—
American	1,545	21.5	817	255,000–160,000	796	Options
Pacific (San Francisco and Los Angeles)	1,010	27.9	516	65,000–24,000	835	Options

Philadelphia	453	13.6	417 (dual membership in equities and options)	75,000–60,500	1,169	Options, financial futures
CANADA						
Toronto	2,124	20.5	79	65,000–45,000	933	Options, financial futures
Montreal	401	5.4	75	20,000–15,000	443	Options, commodity and financial futures
ASIA						
Tokyo	108,825	300.1	83	6,600,000	1,444	—
EUROPE						
Amsterdam	*	24.9	141	Not applicable	514	Options
Frankfurt	*	14.4	351	Not applicable	381	Options, foreign currencies

continued

THE WORLD'S LEADING STOCK EXCHANGES (*cont.*)

EXCHANGE	VOLUME (*millions of shares*)	DOLLAR VALUE (*Stocks only. In billions of U.S. dollars. Foreign currencies converted at 1984 average rate of exchange.*)	NUMBER OF MEMBERS	SEAT PRICE (*high-low range*) $	NUMBER OF TRADED COMPANIES	OTHER PRODUCTS TRADED
Geneva	*	64.6†	17	$70 entrance fee; $105 for new technical and electronic equipment	367	—
London	*	48.9‡	4,525 individuals.	As of 1986, minimum of 50 shares in the exchange, purchased at market value	2,568	Options

Paris	*	10.8	78	Not made public; members buy shares in the exchange at a negotiated rate from departing members	1,017	—
Zurich	*	119.8†	24	Not applicable	354	—

*European exchanges do not compile statistics on volume.

†The Geneva and Zurich exchanges do not separate their figures for stocks and bonds. Zurich estimates two-thirds of its volume is in stocks and one-third in bonds. Also, there is no statistical breakdown for the exchange alone; instead, the only available statistics covered all transactions in the cantons in which Zurich and Geneva are located. Sometimes, both buy and sell transactions are included, making the total appear higher than at exchanges which count them singly.

‡London counts its sales and purchases as two separate transactions; most other exchanges count them as one. Therefore, the figure supplied by London has been halved to bring it in line with those of other exchanges.

Source: All statistics based on exchanges' data.

TRADING

1

Tokyo

The Japanese have earned a reputation for imitation. There are strong similarities between Tokyo's subway system and London's older underground in the layout of the track lines and in the street signs that indicate subway stations. People drive on the left, as in England. Many department store mannequins have blond hair and a Western appearance. In restaurants the gorgeous pastries are French in style, and gourmet cooking means a French, not a Japanese, meal. The Japanese writing system is derived from the Chinese. And the nondescript office towers housing the *shoken gaisha* (securities firms) in the Marunouchi financial district are similar in style to those in any major U.S. city.

The Tokyo Stock Exchange (Tokyo Shoken Torihikisho—TSE), located two subway stops from the lively neon signs of the Ginza shopping district, at first also seems a carbon copy, rather than an original. The design of its new trading floor building, opened in spring 1985, is a commonplace Western box style. The Grecian-style architecture with Corinthian pillars of the exchange's former quarters, located next door, bore a striking resemblance to the New York Stock Exchange's building.

Just as the New York exchange is the heart of the Wall Street financial district, the Tokyo exchange is the core of Kabutocho. (*Kabuto* means "helmet" and *cho* means "block." The story goes that in the eleventh century a Japanese general placed his helmet on a rock where the exchange is now located and prayed for victory.) Kabutocho was the site of Tokyo's first bank and first post office, and it also was where the warehouses for rice, Japan's major agricultural crop, were once located. Before Japan became an industrial country, its economic clout was based on who produced the largest rice crop; thus rice was the first commodity in which the Japanese developed trading techniques.

The Tokyo exchange is the world's second-largest, after the New York Stock Exchange, and does more business than London, Amsterdam, Paris, and Frankfurt all put together. Despite stock manipulation (regarded as the worst among major exchanges), lack of investor protection and information, low dividends, and few foreign listings, the TSE is thriving—a mirror of the vigorous Japanese economy.

The market should remain healthy. Even though the rate of growth in Japan's economy has slowed to half what it was during the 1970s, it is still substantially higher than that of most other industrialized countries, including the U.S. By the year 2000 Japan is expected to have a higher per capita income than the U.S. Moreover, analysts see a substantial increase in the amount of pension money invested in the stock market since the Japanese population is aging close to four times faster than the populations of other industrialized nations. By the 1990s pension funds are predicted to total $250 billion, four times the current level. Tokyo also has the good fortune of being an obvious participant in the trend toward twenty-four-hour trading because of its time zone position between New York and London.

The Tokyo exchange has come a long way from its origin in 1878 as a marketplace for the sale of bonds by the former samurai feudal lords. During his reign between 1868 and 1911 Emperor Meiji, who was responsible for the start of industrialization in Japan, established the bonds as compensation for the abolition of the samurai feudal system. The stock market grew slowly, from 1911 to the outbreak of World War II, pinched by the reluctance of big companies to be listed publicly and by government controls imposed during the 1937 Sino-

*The former home
(until mid-1985)
of the Tokyo Stock
Exchange, with its
Corinthian col-
umns, imitates the
style of the New
York Stock Ex-
change building.*

Japanese War. At the beginning of World War II the exchange was
replaced by the Japan Securities Exchange, a quasi-governmental
agency into which regional exchanges were absorbed. There was little trading during the war.

Trading on Japan's exchanges was suspended by U.S. occupation
forces in 1945. Indeed, they converted the Tokyo exchange into a
billet, using the trading floor as a gymnasium. When trading resumed in 1949, the occupation forces had revamped its system on
the American style. The stock market's remodeling was part of an
overall American attempt to reshape the Japanese economy. The
Americans also dissolved family-owned zaibatsu conglomerates (which

dominated the economy) and redistributed ownership of farmland from landlords to the tenants who farmed it.

They also delayed Japan's entry into futures—contracts to buy or sell a commodity at a specified future date at a price established at the time of the trade. The occupation forces stated that "futures transactions are not to be conducted" when they reopened the Tokyo market.

The reborn postwar Tokyo exchange resumed activity slowly, with only 256 million shares traded in 1949. But a decade later the volume had passed 10 billion, and in 1972, the year before the worldwide oil crisis, it had multiplied tenfold. The market sagged to half its 1972 level during the 1974–1976 economic squeeze in Japan, but since then it has been strong.

The Tokyo exchange is open from 9:00 A.M. to midafternoon, and as in the U.S., trading is done throughout the day in all stocks. Unlike U.S. exchanges, Tokyo is open on Saturdays except for the second Saturday of the month, when financial institutions in Japan close, giving workers a two-day weekend. As the country sought to recover economically after the war, the exchange, like most Japanese businesss, was open every Saturday. In 1973 this situation changed in response to union pressure. While the unions at Japanese banks and securities houses are weak, the Tokyo Stock Exchange's union is strong partly because many in management used to be union members. Like clockwork, the union stages a half day strike two or three times a year to reinforce negotiations over salaries and spring and winter bonuses. The strikes are set so that they do not interfere with trading activity and are held, as one union leader says, "to protect the situation."

Two thousand people are jammed onto the floor of the Tokyo exchange. Nowhere else in the world is a stock exchange floor so crammed. Congestion is so heavy that the securities houses hire as their floor traders tall, husky former school athletes, capable of pushing through the crowd. Their height also makes them more visible to their firm's representatives in the booths encircling the floor. The floor traders wear blue jackets, the exchange's staff, black ones, and the *saitori*, Tokyo's counterpart of the U.S.'s specialists—the middlemen between buyers and sellers on American floors—are in brown. Like the specialists, the *saitori* trade specific stocks allocated to them, but unlike the Americans, they cannot trade for their own personal accounts. They can act only as intermediaries for transactions between floor representatives of the securities firms.

The rectangular pillar-free floor has two clocks at one end—a circular-numbered one at ceiling level and a digital clock halfway down the wall. The director of floor operations sits at a desk beneath the clocks and scrutinizes the activity through binoculars. Hourly he writes trading volume on a chalkboard beside his desk. Foreign stocks are traded in a corner near him. The rest are grouped by industry—at narrow, rectangular tables (trading posts) with green surfaces in the old building and natural-toned wood one-piece, horseshoe-shaped units in the new building. Alongside the wall are elevated rows of attached cubicles, where the securities firms' clerks receive orders from their offices by telephone. They signal to their firms' floor traders to come for their orders with different tonal levels of various sounds such as *Aa* or *Oo*.

Otherwise, communication is by descriptive hand signals for the various stocks. For the Honda Motor Company, a finger is pointed toward the cheek since *Ho* means "cheek" in Japanese; the signal for IBM, the most heavily traded of the foreign stocks, is pointing to one's eye and then writing the letters *B* and *M* in the air; for companies the names of which begin with Fuji (Fuji Bank, Fuji Car, Fuji Oil, Fuji Photo, etc.), traders purse their lips and blow lightly on their hands, producing the sound *fu*. Sony is easy—an *S* outlined in the air. The Tokyo exchange has the singular custom of greeting the opening and closing sessions of each year with clapping. It is unique also in that traders enter the information into the latest computer terminals after first calculating the sums on an abacus.

As in the U.S., Tokyo has a stock market index showing upward and downward trends, but knowledgeable investors follow another indicator—the stock market performance of Heiwa Real Estate Company, Ltd., the main business of which is leasing the stock exchange building to the exchange. If Heiwa's price rises, traders view it as an omen that the volume is rising, whereas a drop usually means the market is weakening.

Unlike Western exchanges, Tokyo has no female traders. Although 40 percent of Japanese women now work, most remain "tea servers" in this tradition-bound society where men walk in front of women to enter and exit from elevators and subway cars and where girls, rather than boys, are golf caddies. The few females on the exchange's floor are limited to being clerks for the male traders.

The exchange is made up of two tiers, as if the New York and American exchanges' stocks were combined in one place with two sections. The first tier is like the NYSE and houses 1,000 of the most marketable stocks. Of these, the 250 stocks in which trading is most active are traded in the conventional hand signal manner, and the remainder, begun in 1985 in the new building, are traded through a computerized system, resulting in reduction of the specialist posts from fourteen to five. Called CORES (Computer-Assisted Order Routing and Execution System), it was first tried out for three years in the second section, which is akin to the American Stock Exchange (Amex) in its trading of stocks of newer growth companies. There are close to 440 stocks in Tokyo's second tier; Amex had 796 as of the end of 1984.

The opening of the second tier in 1961 contributed significantly to the collapse of the Tokyo stock market in 1965, the worst crisis it has undergone since World War II. The exchange had pressured securities dealers to buy second-tier stocks to develop that market and maintain it during a major sell-off by investors in 1963, saddling the firms with too many shares in stocks that were plunging in price. Yamaichi Securities Company Ltd., then the largest dealer, would have gone bankrupt if the Bank of Japan had not bailed it out with an emergency loan. The market recovery enabled Yamaichi to repay the loan far sooner than the ten-year deadline, but it has never regained its leadership and remains in fourth spot.

Ironically, despite Japan's reputation for innovation in electronics, CORES is a copy of the Toronto Stock Exchange's system, considered the pacesetter among major exchanges. At first, Tokyo even called its system, introduced in 1982, by Toronto's name—Computer-Assisted Trading System (CATS)—but later decided to change it. The system replaced a conventional display board showing stock price movements, which also originated in Toronto. That board was developed in 1974 by Toronto-based Ferranti-Packard Ltd., a manufacturer of electrical equipment, which, after submitting fourteen quotes, won the competition to design the board over a Japanese telecommunications firm, Fujitsu Ltd. According to Ferranti-Packard President Barry Hercus, Fujitsu was so anxious to win the contract it offered to provide a board free. The exchange rejected this proposition on the ground that it was unethical to get something for nothing, but it put pressure on Ferranti-Packard to quote a substantially lower price than it otherwise would have.

Japan also lags behind other countries in another burdensome, behind-the-scenes task: the processing of share ownership transfer. In Japan stock certificates are still physically delivered and withdrawn in transactions, whereas elsewhere the exchange records the transfer information in a certificateless, computerized system. Japan will switch to such a method by year-end 1986, but TSE officials predict it could take up to ten years to wean Japanese investors away from their preference for the actual share certificates.

Tokyo ranks second in volume among world exchanges partly because of government regulations that encourage large orders. Recent changes in Japan's commercial code squeezed out odd-lot trading of uneven, usually small amounts in favor of round lots of larger, even-numbered units.* But small investors can still afford to buy inasmuch as the minimum par value per share is low—only fifty yen.† Also, the exchange does not face the competition that U.S. exchanges do from other types of markets and investment products.

Unlike the over-the-counter (OTC) market in the U.S. those in Japan do little business. The main one in Tokyo derives the bulk of its trading from government bonds rather than from stocks. The Tokyo exchange stamped out any hopes the Japanese over-the-counter markets had of attracting fledgling high-technology companies by reducing its listing requirements in late 1983 to be competitive with those of the OTC.

Compared with the U.S., Japan offers a limited menu to investors. The U.S. has more than 200 different products; Japan has under 10, traditional fare, such as bank accounts, term deposits, stocks and bonds. Until recently investors could not buy gold; only dentists could,

---

* Odd lots are less than the usual unit of trading, normally 100 shares. Round lots are 100-share units and multiples of that amount.
† From January to the end of July 1985, the average rate of exchange was 252 yen to the U.S. dollar.

for fillings. The slowness of the exchange to introduce new products, such as the financial futures and options* now prevalent in the U.S., stems partly from the innate Japanese reluctance to change something until it has been studied almost to death and drowned in the nation's penchant for statistics.

The delay in introducing futures and options also has a political genesis: the fierce rivalry between two powerful government ministries. The stock market has traditionally been regulated by the Ministry of Finance (MOF). But because financial futures are regarded as a commodity, they also come under the purview of MOF's main opponent, the Ministry of International Trade and Industry (MITI). However, since one government department is rarely happy to give up power and authority to another division, when the Japanese securities houses applied to MITI for approval to join futures exchanges in North America, they had to wait for months until they received the go-ahead.

The exchange finally branched into financial futures in a limited way in late 1985 through the sale of futures related to domestic government bonds. This was more a necessity than a sudden burst of innovation. Futures are regarded as one way of making bonds more attractive despite a glut of bonds on the market and their low interest rate. The Tokyo exchange may soon become more involved in futures and options, for its new floor is easily adaptable to their trading, which is customarily done in pits.

The Tokyo exchange can afford not to introduce new products because unlike the American exchanges, it faces virtually no domestic competition. The seven regional exchanges are negligible. Tokyo gets 85 percent of the business. So poor are the prospects for the others that although the charter of Osaka, the number two exchange, permits fifty-eight members, it has only fifty-four. Indeed, Osaka is in the paradoxical position of substantially increasing its business, doing twice its 1982 volume in 1983 and outpacing the American, Toronto, and Paris exchanges, while losing ground more and more to Tokyo. Trading in a few companies tends to be heavier on the Osaka ex-

---

*Futures, explained on page 00 of this chapter, and options are dealt with in detail in Chapter 3 on Chicago. Briefly, options are contracts to buy or sell three to nine months in the future fixed amounts of a stock at a preset price.

change because the firms are located nearby. Osaka has also introduced or plans several measures to attract more trading, including a second tier similar to Tokyo's and a trading start ten minutes earlier than Tokyo.

Still, none of Osaka's activity is expected to stop further market share decline in the shadow of Tokyo, which holds several unbeatable aces. Computerization of the Tokyo exchange is drawing an increased order flow in shares listed both on it and Osaka away from Osaka. An even more important factor in Tokyo's favor involves a disadvantage Osaka and U.S. regional exchanges alike face: Institutional trading on exchanges is becoming more of a twenty-four-hour international business, and Tokyo is the Far East choice of these investors.

At most exchanges takeovers, accomplished through one company's buying the controlling block of shares of another, are a common activity. Tokyo is a notable exception. The official line in Japan is that takeovers are in bad taste largely because to a person who established a company, that company is his "life," and he does not want to sell his life. The Japanese regard takeovers as a loss of face, an embarrassment which is reflected in their word for *acquisition, baishu,* also meaning "bribery," and that for *takeover, notbri,* also meaning "hijack."

"The typical U.S. style is John Wayne challenge and conquer, but the Japanese are more conservative and place more emphasis on discipline and endurance," says Yoshio Terasawa, the New York-based chairman of Nomura Securities International, Inc., the U.S. division of the Nomura Securities Company Ltd., Japan's largest securities dealer. Still, these words belie what sometimes happens.

Takeovers do occur—but quite discreetly. Yamaichi Securities claims to be the pioneer in this field, having set up a merger and acquisition department in 1974. In one of the peculiarities that pepper the Japanese financial system, Yamaichi has prepared a bright red brochure on its takeover division which says that "it has been Yamaichi's policy to avoid any form of publicity." Another peculiarity is that takeovers are less a loss of face if the purchasing company is non-Japanese. In such a takeover, management at the acquired company can retain its position. If a Japanese firm were the buyer, management is not let go but is reduced to the discomfiting role of "people by the window"—salaried with a desk, but away from the activity at the center.

As in the U.S., the percentage of shares held by individuals in Japan has eroded. Although the number of individual shareholders is almost 20 million, close to 17 percent of Japan's population, their holdings have declined as a percentage and now account for only 28 percent of all issued shares. One reason for the shrinkage is the institutionalization of the market. Although the zaibatsu conglomerates were outlawed by the American occupation army, they did not fade away. Instead, they metamorphosized into extensive mutual shareholding among companies in the same commercial or industrial group or between companies with close business connections.

These portfolios are regarded primarily as an instrument of good business relations rather than as an investment. In 1949 corporations accounted for 5.6 percent of total shareholdings; now they account for 26 percent. Similarly, ownership by financial institutions has also jumped—from 10 percent in 1949 to approximately 38 percent. As a result of this concentration, about 60 percent of the stock of listed companies is virtually never traded, limiting the availability of shares to the public.

To make the market more attractive to individuals, the Tokyo exchange has proposed stock splits (the division of a number of shares into a larger quantity) and an end to the taxing of dividends after companies have paid corporate taxes, so investors would get bigger dividends. The securities houses are also actively pursuing individuals, aiming their campaigns at housewives because even though in public women seem to be in second place to Japanese men, at home they control the family finances. Since the Japanese dote on their children, Yamaichi, for example, recently ran a promotion designed to win over mothers through their children: a painting competition for kindergarten children at 9,000 schools. In a gimmick that Madison Avenue could envy, Yamaichi promoted the campaign by placing yellow-, blue-, and pink-hatted plastic penguins, called Tuxedo Sams, in their offices, along with front-window posters of attractive girls in black stockings and a tuxedo jacket, holding the birds.

The exchange's suggestion of fatter dividends appeals to investors but not to companies that now get away with paying extremely low dividends. In the 1960s the dividend yields on Japanese stocks were higher than in the U.S., but that position has since reversed. In Japan a company issues dividends as a percentage of the par value (the face value, as distinguished from book or market value) of the stock, which normally is 50 yen rather than of earnings, even if the share price is soaring. It is not uncommon to get a dividend of 10 yen on a share worth more than 10,000 yen.

The imbalance between the price and earnings of a share stems from favorable tax breaks aimed at promoting Japan's industrial growth. Companies can declare more depreciation than in the U.S. and do not have to consolidate the financial statements of the subsidiaries with those of the parent, a procedure that often drags down earnings. Also, Japan's big firms are mostly comparatively young growth companies that tend to pay low dividends. "In the U.S. growth companies can have fifty to sixty times price:earnings ratios and pay no dividends, and nobody says boo," says Darrel Whitten, associate director of research at Bache Securities (Japan) Ltd. (a division of Prudential-Bache Securities, Inc. of the United States).

Still, many Japanese avoid the stock market because of the numerous questionable practices that make it a hazardous place for the novice investor. For example, clapping is customarily used as a prod to push prices higher. "If the composite stock price index is nearing a thousand [regarded as a sign of strength in the market], the traders start to clap, and with that energy the index reaches a thousand," says Masayuki Osaki, public relations manager for the exchange. The stock exchange believes it has rules for "a fair and orderly market" that reflect the Japanese emphasis on spotless hands, analogous to the way diners wipe their hands with hot towels before eating and the way taxi drivers, airport workers, and police officers wear white gloves. But the rules are ignored. What the market lacks in excitement without options and takeovers, it makes up for in its untamed atmosphere, which has made the Japanese conservative about where they put their money. They are among the world's leading bank customers, even though interest rates are just 5 percent or less. When they do decide to gamble, they are more apt to bet on horse races, a popular pastime, as a safer proposition than the market.

Tokyo is the only major world financial center in which a newspaper publishes a weekly column of horror stories about the exchange based on a mixture of fact, conjecture, and rumor. Every Tuesday the *Mainichi Daily News*, an English-language paper, runs "The Kabutocho Scene," which flails away at "manipulation of information as a means of influencing prices," the very cozy relationship between the Japanese financial press and the Ministry of Finance, and "market scams to cover corporate deficits, fatten directors' bonuses, augment capital investment budgets, and generate political contributions."

There is no Securities and Exchange Commission (SEC), as in the United States. One was established by the U.S. Army occupation forces after World War II, but it fell into disuse a few years later. Instead of an SEC independent from the government, there is a small watchdog office, the transaction market division, in the Ministry of Finance. It has little bite because it has just 16 employees (out of a total of 2,000 in the ministry) and because it restricts itself to watching market trends. It has never canceled the license of a securities firm, even when some employees have been caught rigging stock prices, on the ground that the whole company should not be responsible for the bad behavior of one branch. The government's oversight of the market is further cast into doubt by allegations it has never denied: that it finances election campaigns by buying certain stocks and then artificially ballooning their prices.

Prices of dormant stocks can sizzle suddenly not because of investor interest but because companies decide it is time for them to climb. For instance, there was a peculiar coincidence of the share prices of all Japanese bank stocks' doubling in early 1984. By contrast, in North America, even if good news affects an industry, the share prices of all companies in that field do not rise by the same amount because some firms are not as strong as others. According to *Nihon Keizai Shimbun* (*Nikkei*, in everyday parlance), Japan's leading business newspaper, the bank stock rise was prompted by Nomura's suggesting to Sumitomo Bank that the bank's shares were undervalued in light of its financial performance and that the valuation should be left to the market. While this is normal in North America, Japanese companies sometimes prefer their share prices not to rise. However, in this instance, the banks needed the money to upgrade their operations, so they would be in fighting shape to meet the expanded foreign banking participation in Japan. The government, in response to overseas pressure, especially from the United States, is permitting foreign banks to engage in many activities that were exclusive formerly to domestic banks.

In a country where losing face is the cardinal sin, the other banks wanted to catch up to Sumitomo. Employees considering selling their shares in order to buy homes were persuaded to keep them through special loans. This action artificially promoted the price. That such stock manipulation is permissible was indicated by the fact that top officials were willing to be quoted by name in *Nikkei*—and nobody denied the article. Several months later Akitoshi Furuhata, deputy general manager in the international department of the Industrial Bank of Japan, the country's largest long-term credit bank, gave me a novel explanation: "From time to time this type of reevaluation occurs. The last time was in 1973. It's true that eleven years between evaluations is a long time, but people were expecting capital increases by certain banks, which happen cyclically."

The government requires all Japanese companies listed on the Tokyo exchange to issue annual reports. The companies comply with this by providing several versions. The firms invite major shareholders—the banks and insurance companies—to a special meeting and give them a detailed picture. But individual shareholders receive all bones and no meat. The skimpy reports they get bear no resemblance to the thick American versions. There are no glossy covers or pictures, no footnotes explaining financial items, little information on the company's performance, and only annual and semiannual statements rather than quarterly ones as in North America.

Inside the thin annual reports the differences between American and Japanese reports abound. The Japanese supply results for only the parent company, not for the subsidiaries, whereas a U.S. report covers everything. Just two paragraphs are devoted to a description of the Japanese business, capital investment, and outlook, compared with the pages this takes in U.S. corporate reports. There is a Japanese counterpart of the U.S. 10K form, a more detailed version of an annual report that publicly traded companies must file with the U.S. Securities and Exchange Commission, but that is sketchy, too.

Shareholders are often in the dark about the true value of a company's assets because companies declare their real estate assets at the original purchase prices rather than the current market prices—

and there can be a vast difference. For example, the Mitsubishi Corporation, the largest Japanese conglomerate, owns most of the Marunouchi financial district in Tokyo but carries this prime real estate on its books at the original cost of many years ago. In other areas, though, companies provide a superabundance of details in their reports. For example, they provide a biography for each director, including when he joined the firm, in what capacity, and each of his tiny steps up the corporate ladder. There are no outside public directors on the boards of Japanese companies; instead, they all come from management.

The attention paid to the directors reflects the importance, now lessening but still greater than in North America, attached to lifetime employment at one firm in Japan. Less emphasis is placed on a particular year's results, which the Japanese regard as too short a term in the company's development. Unfortunately the fuller form of corporate disclosure is of little value to individual shareholders because they cannot obtain it free simply by contacting the company, as they would in the United States. Instead, they have to go to the stock exchange or the Ministry of Finance to see the reports—convenient only if they live in Tokyo.

Shareholders fare no better at the brief annual meetings. It is true that annual meetings in North America can also be incredibly brief, but in Japan there is a special dimension besides management taciturnity. Few Japanese dare speak up because of the *sokaiya*, gangsters the companies hire to silence dissident shareholders. The *sokaiya* get this job in return for their pledge not to release dirt they have dug up on key members of the board of directors or corporate problems. Payments to the *sokaiya* are frequently disguised in the form of the equivalent of $200,000 in subscriptions to "magazines" that are a mere two pages in size. *Sokaiya* function with impunity despite the revision of Japan's Commercial Code in 1982 that made deals between them and companies illegal.

There is not much help elsewhere for individual investors. Bond rating services, on the credit worthiness of public and corporate bonds, are a new development. In 1979 *Nikkei*, which has a circulation of 2 million, established the Japan Bond Research Institute after four years of preparation, including training of some staff in New York by Standard & Poor's rating service, owned by McGraw-Hill, Inc. But

Nikkei has what many view as too close a relationship with government and business, and in 1984 a rival rating service was started by Akio Mikuni, a financial consultant who had worked in the corporate planning department of Nomura Securities from 1963 until 1975. Mikuni says his service is the first "independent" one in Japan. He has an impressive roster of clients, including Citicorp, First Boston, Inc., Morgan Stanley, Inc., and Salomon Brothers Holding Company of the United States and the Swiss Bank Corporation and Crédit Suisse Bank of Europe. In 1985 Moody's Investors Service became the first U.S. debt-rating agency to open a Japanese subsidiary.

Nor can investors necessarily count on investment analysts' advice being untainted. The Big Four securities houses—Nomura, Yamaichi, Daiwa Securities Company Ltd., and Nikko Securities Company Ltd.—produce in-depth research material for foreign investors, but the quality of the research analysis provided domestic investors is generally poor. "The analysts are all reading from the same sheet of music and sound so similar you would think they had held a conference," says Charles Rummel, vice president of the Canadian securities house of Richardson Greenshields of Canada Ltd. Rummel lived in Japan for sixteen years and worked in Nomura's research department before returning to Canada to head Richardson's quest for business in Japan. "There is a strong tendency by analysts to take what companies say at face value and not assess it from a different angle or source. This is partly due to the Japanese predilection for consensus thinking and their education system, in which studies are learned by rote." It also stems from the rapid rotation of employees from department to department. The purpose is to acquaint them with the entire company, but unfortunately the result often is that people who are not strong in analysis wind up in the research department.

Not only do Japanese research reports on stocks for domestic consumption tend to be short in quality, but they also tend to give too rosy a picture of stocks out of fear that "sell" recommendations would lose them underwriting business. Still, if individual investors get burned too often, they will take their business elsewhere, and the securities houses do not want that either. So they have "saver stocks" to bail out favored individual clients. "For everything bad they do, the Japanese houses will repay investors with something good," says a Westerner who is in the retail division of the international department of a medium-size Japanese broker. He claims his firm is "honest" and adds, "The dealers have a reputation for selling good, average, and bad stocks and investors must turn elsewhere for advice as to which stock falls into which category. Saver stocks are those that are manipulated upward or new offerings given at preferential rates."

The firm blamed most for pushing a stock of the week is Nomura. "The accepted rule of thumb under this practice is that investors will lose about thirty percent of their money with Yamaichi, half with Daiwa and Nikko, and end up owing Nomura money," says the research director of the Tokyo office of a major British securities house.

Nomura, however, maintains this is no longer true. "When I started with Nomura twenty-three years ago, every branch would have a wall poster recommending two or three stocks for that week to individual investors who wanted to buy stocks but were not familiar with the market," says Hitoshi Tonomura, now president of Nomura's London subsidiary and previously Tokyo-based general manager of Nomura's overseas division. "But this stopped over ten years ago." However, all that seems to have ceased is the overt promotion. Recently departed Nomura salesmen say they had to generate ten times their salary in gross commissions.

When the Big Four securities houses, especially Nomura, employed their high-pressure tactics overseas, they angered American portfolio managers, but financial analyst Akio Mikuni puts their aggressiveness into a logical perspective: "High-pressure salesmanship has been part of Japan's economic growth. For example, the car companies at first used such methods when selling to first-time owners who knew little about cars. Now that customers know more, car manufacturers stress design rather than just saying, 'Buying a car is a good thing to do.' The same principle applied to the securities firms as they sought to make foreigners knowledgeable about Japanese stocks. Indeed, they could be criticized for not being sufficiently forceful at the outset because if they had been, foreigners would have obtained shares before prices rose."

The exchange has decided not to depend entirely on North America and Europe for future business. While the NYSE is seeking to forge a working relationship with the London Stock Exchange with a view to positioning itself securely in the internationalized world of trading, the Tokyo exchange has been looking instead to other Far

East exchanges and quietly building up ties with them over the past ten years.

It sent staff to Thailand and Indonesia to assist them in each step of developing a stock market. Then in 1981, Tokyo took a further step toward a loose Far East partnership when it began informal conferences with representatives of the exchanges in the Japanese cities of Osaka and Nagoya, as well as in Korea, Hong Kong, Taiwan, the Philippines, Thailand, Singapore, Malaysia, and Indonesia. Ultimately these exchanges may form a federation similar to the Paris-headquartered International Federation of Stock Exchanges, which counts among its members most of the world's major exchanges, including Tokyo, and which discusses industry-wide topics. Tokyo is convinced its size would make it the undisputed kingpin in such a federation since Hong Kong does only about 4 percent of the volume of Tokyo and Singapore does less business than Hong Kong. However, unification this year of the Hong Kong market's four exchanges—Hong Kong, Far East, Kam Ngan, and Kowloon—and the installation of computer technology will add muscle to the Hong Kong market. The People's Republic of China has also done its utmost to assure investors that it will not interfere with Hong Kong's financial system when it takes over the colony in 1997 from Britain.

In its desire to attract more overseas business, the Tokyo exchange mirrors the increasing international thrust of Japan's economy. The exchange's international ambitions have led to the appointment of senior management with a global outlook. According to the exchange's constitution, its governors are supposed to elect its president. In practice, the governors have no say, and the president does not have a securities industry background. Instead, he is an *amakudari* (descendant from heaven), a former senior government official shifted into industry, as is customary when top civil servants near retirement age. The incumbent, Michio Takeuchi, and his three predecessors all were deputy ministers of finance. Between 1978 and 1982, when he became president of the Tokyo exchange, Takeuchi was president of the Export-Import Bank of Japan; he was responsible for the bank's initiating loans to China for the development of natural resources.

Takeuchi is fluent in French, having been based in France for several years by the Ministry of Finance. Once, when a member of the Japanese cabinet visited Paris, he saw the wavy-haired, Western-in-appearance Takeuchi conversing in Japanese and asked who was the Frenchman speaking Japanese so well. Takeuchi has a playful sense of humor. He has been known to break the stuffiness among a group of dignitaries waiting at airports by sending a wound-up toy animal scurrying across the floor. Another time, when he lost a golf match, Takeuchi whipped out a toy dog that, in the tones of a sore loser, growled, "Congratulations."

The chairman of the exchange, a position which rotates among the four largest securities houses (although theoretically open to any member of the exchange), is a figurehead. Still, it is of significance that the current chairman, Yoshitoki Chino, who is also chairman of Daiwa Securities, was one of the first in the securities industry to recognize the importance of international business as the best avenue for growth open to Daiwa because Nomura was unshakable in the domestic market. The TSE's foreign department is multilingual in English, French, and German. Since 1973 the exchange has sent employees from the foreign division to the U.S., the U.K., France, and Germany to learn the languages plus the characteristics of the local securities businesses.

Tokyo alone among Japan's eight exchanges trades foreign stocks. Its open door dates back just to 1973, and few foreign companies have joined. Of the seventeen that had by fall 1985, just two were non-American: Robeco N.V. of the Netherlands and the National Australia Bank. Early American joiners were Dow Chemical, General Motors, IBM, Citicorp, First Chicago, Chase Manhattan, Bank-America, IU International, and International Telephone & Telegraph. Sears, Roebuck joined in 1984, and Walt Disney, American Express, Security Pacific, 3M, and Philip Morris in 1985.

Foreign companies initially were attracted to the exchange for the public relations benefit, because they either were already doing or hoped to do business in Japan, and by the prospect of raising funds in the Japanese market. But Tokyo has turned out to be barren territory for foreign listings. The foreign section of the exchange, which conducts trading between 10:30 A.M. and 11:00 A.M. and between 2:30 P.M. and 3:00 P.M., is the only quiet spot in the midst of the bedlam on the trading floor. Day after day the stock pages in the newspapers reveal the reason for the stillness: trading usually occurs in just the two best known stocks—IBM and General Motors. Even the trading in these is negligible, amounting to under 1 percent of their volume on the New York Stock Exchange. The other stocks do far worse. Trading in Chase Manhattan, which attracts the least business, does not even amount to one one-thousandth of its trading on the NYSE. By contrast, there are more than 140 U.S. corporations listed on the London exchange, and even the Paris Bourse, which is one of the smallest European exchanges, has more than 40 U.S. companies listed.

The Japanese hope for a substantial rise in international volume, at the expense of New York, in their high-technology stocks. Companies traded on the Tokyo exchange include producers of the world's fastest supercomputers, most advanced optical fiber and semiconductor chips, and leading home entertainment playthings, such as digital audio discs. Japan was also the world's top new drug developer between 1980 and 1983. The market has a long way to go to reach this target; between 1980 and the end of 1982 Japanese investment in foreign securities climbed by $2 billion, while foreign investment in the Japanese market fell by close to $1 billion.

Foreign companies avoid listing on the Tokyo exchange because of expensive and complicated requirements. A listing on Tokyo's exchange of the non-North American exchanges can cost as much as $250,000, compared with $150,000 in Paris, the second most expensive, and $80,000 in London. Indeed, accompanying expenses for listing fees, translating, and accounting and legal fees are ten times more expensive in Tokyo than in Paris and thirty times more costly than in London.

Until recently the prime factor in the high cost of a listing was dual accounting. A Japanese accountant had to certify the financial statements of foreign firms. U.S. companies believed this procedure was unnecessary since U.S. financial disclosure is much more substantial than that of Japanese companies. They were further angered that Japanese companies listed on U.S. exchanges do not have to conform with U.S. accounting and disclosure rules requiring segmented geographic and product information since this is not the practice in Japan.

All this spurred the exchange to take remedial action. In 1984 it persuaded the government to eliminate the dual audit requirements, and shortly afterward Sears, the other American newcomers, and the Australian bank joined. The list of foreign applicants is almost as long as the number of foreign firms now traded. They include McDonald's; telephone companies in the U.K., Canada, and Spain; several Swedish firms; and a large German bank, the Dresdner.

For years, until a breakthrough in late 1985, foreign securities dealers wished the Japanese were as willing to open up membership to them on the exchange as they were to get overseas listings. Membership on the exchange actually was open to foreigners since 1982, and they were eager to join despite their criticism of stock manipulation. But it was impossible to gain entry because the Tokyo exchange had only 83 seats, compared with 1,366 at the New York Stock Exchange, and none had become vacant or were for sale.

Most of the more than ninety foreign securities firms in Japan were content with not being members since the exchange made a major concession in 1982 in order to placate them: an attractive special commission rate for foreigners. Because the foreigners were not exchange members, they had to place orders via the Japanese firms that do belong. Until 1982 there was a fifty-fifty split of the commission between the foreign and Japanese firms. In 1982 this was changed to give the foreigners 73 percent. In effect, though, the foreigners fared even better. Since they were not members of the exchange, they did not have to pay for the staff and equipment of a trading floor operation.

The exchange "studied" the foreign membership issue for more than a year after the financial liberalization agreement between Japan and the U.S. in the spring of 1984. The solution was the creation of ten new seats, many of them earmarked for foreign firms in the exchange's first membership expansion since the end of World War II. Floor trading by the new members is expected to begin in April 1986. The exchange dragged its feet partly because the foreign membership question once again aroused pressure from excluded domestic firms to become members. There are 247 Japanese securities houses, but only 140 belong to any of the country's eight exchanges. Because 85 percent of the trading occurs in Tokyo, more Japanese firms want to become members. The domestic lobbyists got the upper hand in a December 1984 bidding war for the first available seat in years. The winner, the Utsumiya Securities Company of Hiroshima, an affiliate of Yamaichi, paid $6.6 million. The seat price of $5 million was a record for any exchange (the NYSE's all-time top price was $625,000 in February 1929). As is usual, the seller received a premium—$1.6 million in this case. The ten new seats were expected to cost up to $5 million.

Only one foreign firm bid—Merrill Lynch & Company, Inc. It is not used to losing. Roger Birk, chairman at the time (he retired in mid-1985) flushed bright red when I asked him if the firm would try again to buy a seat. The answer was understandably yes, for Merrill Lynch has the longest on-location connection with Japan of any foreign securities house. It opened an office in Tokyo in 1962 and in 1972 became the first foreign firm to obtain a license to open a branch operation. (Branches can participate directly in the securities business, whereas representative offices are only liaisons with home offices.) Merrill Lynch is the only firm to have two Japanese branches, with its second one located in Osaka.

Merrill was willing to pay millions of dollars for a seat since it was dissatisfied with splitting commissions. It also was furious that there had been no reciprocity, as expected, for Nomura's becoming a member of the New York Stock Exchange in 1981 for only $285,000. "Although five million dollars is small potatoes to a firm the size of Merrill Lynch, it's a matter of principle that we not pay that amount, compared with what Nomura paid," Walter Burkett, senior vice president and general manager of Merrill Lynch's Tokyo office, told me a few months before Merrill Lynch bid for the vacant seat.

"In order to have a viable income, it is necessary to receive a hundred percent commission," Burkett continued. "An institutional customer is entitled to an up to twenty percent discount; therefore, out of the seventy-three cents on every dollar that we get in commission, we have only fifty-three cents left, which is not enough money to telex an order to New York."

Burkett dismissed the exchange's argument that proportionately, on the basis of the number of seats in New York and Tokyo, a TSE membership is the equivalent in price of a New York seat. He pointed out that because Tokyo does one-third of New York's volume, a member does not get the same value for his fee as in New York. One avenue the firm could have taken to obtain membership was to have bought a firm that was a member, but Merrill was hesitant after its ill-starred purchase of 25 percent of Hong Kong's largest stock-broker, Sun Hung Kai Company, in 1982. It paid $75 million, a peak price, just before the market went into a tailspin. Japanese securities firms that went to the U.S. had the option of joining regional exchanges as a prelude to joining New York's. But this alternative of regional membership is unattractive in Japan, where the biggest regional exchange in Osaka does only 10 percent of the total business in the nation.

Even with Tokyo's doors now truly open to foreign membership, most likely there will be no rush of applicants. Unless the entry fee is lowered, a tremendous volume of business would be necessary to justify joining. "Although this would eliminate the split commissions, the money that would come from the twenty-seven percent that hitherto went to the Japanese intermediary broker might not be enough to pay for floor operations," says James Cathrow, manager of the Tokyo office of Richardson Greenshields of Canada.

Membership on the Tokyo exchange is only one of the bottlenecks foreign securities firms have encountered. Another is obtaining a branch license from the Ministry of Finance. Only ten firms—seven American and three British—are licensed to operate branches. The American companies are Merrill Lynch, Prudential-Bache (under the name of Bache Securities), Smith Barney, Salomon Brothers, Kidder, Peabody, Goldman, Sachs, and Morgan Stanley. The British branches are Jardine Fleming,* Vickers da Costa, and S. G. Warburg. Warburg and Morgan Stanley received their licenses in 1984. There are also more than eighty foreign representative offices—from the U.S., Canada, the U.K., France, West Germany, Switzerland, the Netherlands, Italy, Belgium, Denmark, Singapore, and Australia. (The United States and U.K. are the main rivals, with about the same number of representative offices.) Theoretically there is no limit to the number of foreign firms that can open branches, but the government generally licenses only two per year as a way of controlling foreign inroads into the Japanese market. Just as theoretically the representative of-

---

* In February 1985 Jardine Fleming, reputed to be the largest foreign investor in the Japanese equity market, became the first foreign financial institution to enter a Tokyo-based joint venture with a Japanese trust bank, Yasuda Trust. Jardine will guide Yasuda in its pension fund management and is expected to diversify this investment more into foreign equities.

fices say they do not act as branches, but in practice that is exactly what those with large staffs of thirty or more people are doing.

A visitor to a foreign firm, whether it is managed by a Westerner or Japanese, is struck immediately by the differences in style from the traditional conventions and manners practiced at the Japanese firms. At a Japanese firm the female clerks wear uniforms, usually skirts and buttoned vests. The receptionists jump to their feet and bow to visitors. They bow the visitors to a meeting room, neat but hardly elaborate, and bring cups of green tea, bowing their way in and out of the room. A team of people appears for the interview. The overall appearance of the quarters is grim and utilitarian, with tiled floors, dim light, gray steel desks overflowing with paperwork—all in stark contrast with their lavish overseas offices. When visitors depart, the receptionists race to the elevators to push the button and hold the door open for them.

At Western firms females do not wear uniforms and some wear jeans. The receptionists remain seated. Appointments are in the manager's office, and he conducts the interview alone. The furnishings are more elaborate. Instead of adjacent clerical desks, the workers have some space. The floors are usually carpeted, and there are often lots of plants.

Merrill Lunch is a foremost proponent of this Western image. "We are an American-based international company," Walter Burkett stresses. He has learned just enough of the language to manage in a cab and conducts all conversations with the Japanese members of his staff in English. Salesmen are sent for introductory training to Merrill Lynch's head office in New York. Burkett recruited a number of Japanese from the international side of the Big Four because like many Japanese, they do not want to relocate overseas away from their families.

Although it has been in Japan for more than two decades, Merrill has only just started to turn its attention to selling Japanese stocks overseas. Previously, it concentrated on selling U.S. stocks and bonds and Eurobonds.* But breaking into the Japanese market takes time. Burkett tells an illustrative story: "Shortly after I arrived in Tokyo in

---

*Eurobonds are issued by governments, public agencies, and corporations on the international capital markets in a currency other than that of the country of origin. They are of either medium- or long-term duration.

1981, I received a call from the treasurer of a Japanese trading company, who said that my predecessor had visited him in 1979 and had then sent material regularly. The treasurer told me that based on finding our information consistently good, his firm would like to do some investing through us, but he limited it to just the first quarter of the year."

Merrill Lynch has taken a unique step among foreign securities firms to improve its contacts. As a wedge into the community, it has hired a retired Japanese ambassador, who had been based in Canada, Korea, and Singapore, to "get us into potential corporate clients at a high level. Although in Japan, middle management and not chairmen make investment decisions, chairmen can get people at the proper level to be receptive to meeting you," Burkett says. Since the ex-ambassador is on a government pension, Burkett says his fee is "relatively inexpensive, covering a chauffeured car, membership in a golf club where he meets senior Japanese officials, and a nominal salary." The company also hired an ex-Ministry of Finance official "to take the temperature" of possible changes in regulations that would favor foreign firms.

Because Merrill was slow to pursue the Japanese market, it provided an opportunity for other foreign firms. Those regarded as the leaders are Vickers da Costa and Jardine Fleming from England and the U.S.'s Prudential-Bache. Both da Costa and Bache have employed Japanese managers. Shoji Oshima, da Costa's general manager, says the firm wanted a Japanese to head its Tokyo office because "a manager who cannot speak the local language and has to use an interpreter is not as effective, nor is he as respected by his juniors." The growth of da Costa since Oshima became manager in 1980 is representative of the increase in foreign branch operations in Japan. "In 1980 there was the manager, his assistant, an interpreter, chauffeur, secretary, and telex operator, and the office was just a liaison one. Now we do research, sales, settlements, corporate finance and market U.K. securities. We have forty employees, and our revenue has increased more than tenfold."

Among U.S. houses in Tokyo, Prudential-Bache claims to have the largest research department following Japanese stocks. Hisamichi Sawa, vice president and director of research, says Bache has done well against Japanese houses in selling Japanese stocks in the U.S.

because it has "a more extensive base of contacts in New York than Nomura. It has two hundred people there, and we have close to four thousand."

The business style at a Japanese securities house reflects the national emphasis on lifetime employment at the same company and on consensus-by-management in decisions. Heavy cycles of layoffs of several thousand people, to which Merrill Lynch, for example, resorts periodically when profits slump, are rare at a Japanese securities house. Nearly fifteen years of working in the U.S. have given Nomura's Yoshio Terasawa (Terry to his American friends) a faint American accent as well as perspective on the diametrically different ways of conducting business.

Sitting in his office at the foot of Manhattan with a grand view of the East River and switching easily from Japanese in telephone conversations to English, he good-humoredly ticks off the differences.

"About ten years ago, when Donald Regan [now White House chief of staff in the Reagan administration] was still head of Merrill Lynch and it was laying off about one-third of its staff in response to having a difficult time, I asked him, 'Don, why are you laying off so many people?' He replied, half-jokingly, 'You know, Terry, that's what the Harvard Business School teaches you.'* In the U.S., whenever profit declines, the first remedy considered is layoffs. In Japan, when profit declines, we do not immediately decide to fire people who have been loyal for years because when the business picks up, these people are its assets, and it is difficult to recruit such people again. Instead, we figure not every day will be rainy, but that it will probably be sunny again and so we deal with a decline by paying lower salaries for a temporary period which can last up to twenty months."

This paternalistic attitude has its roots in Japan's management-training system which fosters a closer relationship than the en masse approach in the U.S. Nomura operates on an apprenticeship basis, with about two junior employees assigned to a slightly older manager, a few rungs above them, for two years. They silently accompany the senior executive to meetings with clients or listen to his telephone conversations and learn by osmosis. After work the three go to a bar, where the apprentices quiz their instructor further on

---

* Japan has no U.S.-type business schools.

how to make money. "It's important to be able to read balance sheets and understand various technical terms, but this is basic knowledge; to the Japanese it is more important that employees learn the culture of their company," Terasawa says.

He adds that Nomura outshines Merrill Lynch in profits because the Japanese practice of collective decision making prevents costly mistakes. "In the U.S. Mr. X is elected chief executive officer at the shareholders' meeting and can make decisions on his own, although he can be fired at the next board meeting if his performance is viewed as unsatisfactory. His goal is to increase earnings per share because if he does, he can buy back his stock option at the lower price set a few years earlier, retire to Palm Beach, and purchase a big boat. In the U.S. it's 'he'; in Japan it's 'they,' and if something goes wrong, nobody is fired, although his salary may be cut by thirty percent to indicate displeasure.

"Because decision making in Japan is by *ringisho* [a collective ring of people] and everybody must give his *hanko* [stamp of approval], we likely would not make a mistake like Merrill did in its money-losing investment in that Hong Kong firm."

As in the U.S., competition within Japan's securities industry is fierce, but the Japanese firms do not face the added competition from other financial sectors. Before World War II, banks were allowed to participate in the securities business, but the U.S. occupation forces split the two areas on the pattern of the separation in the U.S. There is talk about opening exchange membership to the banks, as is allowed in parts of Europe, but no sign of action because the trust banks do not relish the much bigger securities firms in turn gaining access to their pension business. They are not as worried about the seventy-five foreign banks that have less than a 5 percent market share as a base from which to start.

Unlike North America, Japan still has fixed commission rates, which allow Japanese securities firms to ring up profits that are among the fattest, worldwide, in the investment industry. In 1985, in an effort to brunt criticism of these profits by institutional investors, who called at the same time for negotiated rates, the industry agreed to provide discounts on big volume orders. If Japan follows the U.S. precedent, this compromise will unleash demands for discount rates for every-body. Meanwhile, the securities firms remain Japan's fastest-growing financial sector and continue to rack up record profits that surpass those of many big Japanese banks. The large firms also derive more income from their minority ownership of medium-size and small dealers. For example, Nomura owns 3.3 percent of Sanyo Securities Company, Ltd.

Except for Nomura, which is named after founder Tokushichi Nomura, the firms have names that deliberately project strength. *Nikko* means "expanding"; *Daiwa*, "big harmony"; and *Yamaichi* "first mountain." Now they seek the same power overseas. By the end of this decade each expects to derive 30 percent of its profits from outside Japan, compared with 5 percent in 1980. All now have an international network of offices and are developing more reference material for Western investors. The four firms all have developed computer on-line data base services for use by domestic and international investors, with current and historical information on Tokyo exchange prices and the financial performance of about 1,500 Japanese companies. The annual fee to clients ranges from Yamaichi's $15,600 to $26,000 for Nomura's more extensive coverage. Moreover, the Japanese have taken the initiative to translate their research into English, whereas the Westerners, with limited exceptions, have not translated their reports on Western companies into Japanese for potential Japanese investors in Western-traded stocks.

The Big Four's determination to succeed overseas is illustrated by one of Yamaichi's two company mottoes inscribed in the pocket datebooks carried by employees: "Build up Yamaichi as a truly international business." Yamaichi is not alone. Employees in Daiwa's international division boast of working from 8:45 A.M. until 11:00 P.M., whereas the domestic side leaves around 7:00 P.M. Those international employees who finish earlier hesitate to leave because they "would not feel comfortable."

Hideki Watanabe, manager of the planning section of Daiwa's international planning and administration department, tells a story that further displays this dedication to realizing company quotas. "A Daiwa salesman got sick on a trip to the Middle East and asked his boss if he could return to London to recuperate. The boss said, 'Decide yourself,' but when the man returned, the boss got very angry. Other employees have been sent to a country and told not to return to Tokyo until they have a mandate from the potential client."

The internationalization of the Japanese securities houses has provided a golden opportunity for young Westerners attending Japanese universities who speak Japanese and want to stay in Japan to find jobs despite a lack of experience in the investment business. They stay for a few years and then jump to the Tokyo offices of Western firms, where their backgrounds enable them to demand salaries of up to $200,000.

Of the thirty foreigners (all male) working for the Japanese houses, one-third are employed by the eighth-largest firm, Sanyo Securities, which views the foreigners as a key tool in its goal to enlarge its international business from its present 10 percent of company revenue. The Sanyo Westerners, most of them in their twenties, constitute one-third of the firm's international research staff and are actively involved in collecting research for distribution to non-Japanese investors, whereas at other firms the Westerners serve merely as translators. Although it has more foreign staff than its competitors, even Sanyo has a quota permitting only half of its international research staff to be foreigners. Circumventing the quota system is possible through fancy maneuvering, such as having a foreign branch of a securities house hire the Westerner and lend him permanently to the Tokyo office.

After a while the Westerners tend to sour on working for the Japanese houses. They become disenchanted with the low wages and the first-time-ever experience of feeling like second-class citizens—confined mostly to translating and paid on a less favorable scale than the Japanese. There is a two-tier salary system in Japan. Regular workers, employed after graduation from university, have lifetime jobs at full pay. But foreigners are classified as part-time workers, although they work regular hours. They have no chance for overtime pay unless their contracts stipulate it. Moreover, the salary of the Japanese at securities houses, in comparison with the U.S., is low ($50,000 maximum supplemented by bonuses at least equal to the salary). This two-class salary system is expected to end within a few years, but in the meantime, various perks are dangled to retain foreigners. These include company assistance toward payments for accommodation, which is then deducted from the salary to reduce income tax payments; inclusion in the company pension plan; and help in funding their children's education, which for private kindergarten alone comes to $5,000.

An even greater difficulty to resolve is the discrimination that the Westerners say they encounter. "The working environment can be very unpleasant because the Japanese have many ways of saying 'you' from a slighting to a respectful form of addressing a person, and they often say it in a derogatory way to the foreigner," says one Westerner who departed from a Japanese firm after two years. Furthermore, the road to promotion is blocked because Japan is still a closed society to outside management. "Until 1975 the Ministry of Education did not grant a full professorship to a non-Japanese, and for a long time those Japanese who were educated overseas never slid smoothly into the system but instead were derided as 'reeking of butter,' " says Charles Rummel. "No foreigners have become managing directors of a Japanese subsidiary or even got halfway up the hierarchy of the parent company, whereas there are many instances of nonnatives heading North American operations. The Japanese argue that a non-Japanese cannot understand their management system or speak Japanese well enough, but there are Westerners who are fluent in Japanese, and managers at American companies also work long hours."

The securities houses fit into this mold. There are no Western managers at their overseas operations. Instead, the Japanese prefer to send over their own people. They are first groomed as salespeople, subsequently sent at company expense to leading business schools in North America or London, and then assigned to an overseas office. Westerners employed by the overseas offices are kept financially happy by being put on the usual commission system, rather than the flat Japanese salary, but they are not part of the hierarchy. Staff meetings overseas are held in Japanese.

Symbolic of the nowhere trail for Westerners to date is that of a Harvard graduate who joined Nomura's New York office in 1968. In the company's Christmas photo the staff is posed by rank, and the Harvard man was third in 1968. But by 1981 he had slipped to about the fiftieth spot, replaced by young people in their twenties brought in from Tokyo. The Japanese say they plan to employ Westerners as overseas managers, but as yet they have not. Rummel cites an analogy to illustrate the Japanese attitude: "There once was a nomad in a tent in a desert. A camel at first put its nose in the flap of the tent, and before the nomad knew what was happening, the whole camel was in the tent, and there was no room for the nomad."

The Tokyo stock market is racing toward internationalization and a rainbow of new products to compete against New York and London, its two major rivals. While the administration of the exchange and Ministry of Finance officials advocate a cautious go-slow approach, the industry—through its overseas offices—has tasted the riches that throwing wide the doors can bring, and it will not give up pushing for more. As one Westerner working for a Japanese securities house points out, exchange and government officials are in the same helpless position "as King Canute trying to hold back the tide."

2

London

To walk along Threadneedle Street to Old Broad Street and the 213-year-old London Stock Exchange is to stroll through some of England's most colorful history. From the time of Henry VIII to the seventeenth century, Old Broad was a fashionable residential street, where many lord mayors of London lived. Henry VIII's adviser Thomas Cromwell, who lived opposite the exchange's site, high-handedly ordered his neighbor's house moved twenty feet away, so Cromwell could extend his garden. The exchange is partly on the site of the birthplace of John Henry Cardinal Newman (1801–1890), an Anglican who converted to Catholicism and tried to bring the Church of England and the Roman Catholic Church closer together.

The London Stock Exchange is an integral part of the City (as the financial district is known), a square mile bordered by the London Wall (remnants of a stone wall built when London was the capital of a Roman colony) on the north, the Thames River and London Bridge on the south, the Tower of London on the east, and St. Paul's Cathedral on the west. At the core is the Bank of England, the U.K.'s central bank, which playwright Richard Brinsley Sheridan, who wrote *The School for Scandal*, nicknamed the Old Lady of Threadneedle

Street and which is still guarded by a gatekeeper dressed in a black hat, a pink jacket, black trousers, and a velvet cape. Nearby in the zigzagging streets, the names of which change at almost every stoplight, are the headquarters of the United Kingdom's four largest banks, the world's largest concentration of foreign banks (including more U.S. banks than in New York), and Lloyd's of London, the international insurance group. Compact in size, the City is enormous in impact, annually contributing about $6 billion in foreign exchange earnings to the economy.

Although its present building is only fourteen years old, the stock exchange has been at this site since 1802, when it was formally constituted. Informally it dates back to the seventeenth century, when traders met at coffeehouses in the district. The earliest records of daily price lists are from 1698. In 1773 "New Jonathan's" Coffeehouse became the de facto stock exchange, and since that time the exchange has retained the flavor of a convivial coffeehouse. "There used to be a lot of larking about and practical jokes," recalls James Dundas Hamilton, a member since 1946 and senior partner of the brokerage house of Fielding Newson-Smith & Company. "Once, when Donald Bradman, a famous Australian cricketer and a stockbroker, visited the exchange in the 1950s, members set up three wickets on the floor and gave him a child's bat and a tennis ball, which he batted off the floor. Another time somebody set ablaze a newspaper my partner was holding and yelled, 'Fire!' " Some members, sticking to tradition, still wear black silk top hats,* and messengers and porters, clad in blue jackets with red collars, are called waiters, a throwback to the exchange's coffeehouse past.

Today the exchange is again making history through what its chief executive, Jeffrey Knight, describes as "frenetic change of the kind that has never happened to any other exchange at any time." While the government has given it until December 1986, the exchange expects by the early fall or sooner to complete the overhaul of its system, officially established in 1908 and unique among major exchanges, in which order taking and execution are separated between two types of members: *brokers*, who buy and sell stocks for clients,

---

*The story is that messengers originally wore top hats so each bobby (policeman) could watch over them and the valuables they carried until they reached the line of vision of the next bobby.

Wearing the traditional top hat, a member leaves the London exchange.

and *jobbers*, who perform the actual transaction. Several jobbers offer competing prices in the same stock, unlike the U.S. specialist system in which one person sells a stock exclusively. Brokers are paid by commission; jobbers make their profits on the *turn* (spread) between what they pay to buy shares and the price at which they then sell.

The new rules will allow firms to continue in single capacity or perform the dual functions of brokers and jobbers. Outsiders—both British banks and foreigners—will be allowed to own 100 percent of the exchange's member firms for the first time and are expected swiftly to supplant the original members as the major players. Already they have bought the City's two dozen largest broking and jobbing firms, paying far above the true value in their eagerness to gain entry to the marketplace. Trading in government securities, which is done on the exchange's floor, will be opened to foreigners as well as to more domestic dealers. Merchant banks, the British version of U.S. investment banks, will be permitted to deal in securities; they now manage portfolios and arrange corporate financing. Because this package also encompasses replacing the brokers' fixed commissions with negotiated rates, the financial community calls the whole process the Big Bang, the label the U.S. securities industry gave its 1975 switch to negotiated rates. However, the U.S. Big Bang did not also include a restructuring of the entire market system, as is the case in London. What worries the stock exchange is that the foreigners may choose not to cross the welcome mat. In late 1985 many major international dealers began to crystallize plans to regulate their own business activities; if realized, these plans could drain away much of the international business that the exchange expected the Big Bang would attract.

The expression *Big Bang* has two possible origins. The first is that it derives from the military term for the bombing of Hiroshima and Nagasaki in 1945: Some on Wall Street believed negotiated commissions would cause the same devastation to their industry. The second explanation is that the changes would produce a new world, just as some scientists theorize that the universe was created by a big bang.

As at the New York Stock Exchange, ownership will remain in the hands of individuals. The London exchange wanted to shift proprietorship to firms but narrowly lost a June 1985 vote because smaller members were worried about losing influence in the exchange's governing council to an influx of big newcomers. Exchange officials fretted that the large outside banks and securities firms on which they were counting to inject much-wanted new volume would be deterred by the lack of a say in forming policy. But most outsiders were unconcerned, convinced that since they actually owned many of the members' firms, they would still be able to determine the exchange's activities, albeit indirectly, similarly to what happens at the NYSE. The reformulated exchange will be a hybrid of U.S. and British customs. The swift-paced, best-deal orientation of the U.S. will erase the easygoing, old-school-tie mannerisms of the U.K. Like the U.S., the U.K. will have negotiated rates, but in the U.K. the regulatory climate will remain less restrictive: There neither is nor will be a securities and exchange commission, and the barrier between banks and brokers, which the U.S. still has but which continental Europe has not had for generations, will be gone. The elitist nature of the market, buttressed by the lack of an extensive branch network system to bring the lure of trading to the public at large, should also wane. If the U.S. precedent is followed, as is probable, discount rates (arising from the new right to haggle over commissions) as well as storefront brokerages are on the horizon. Even a year before the Big Bang, a few sidewalk brokerages were opened in London, including one in Debenham's, a major department store.

The metamorphosis is regarded as vital if London is to gain optimum advantage from its fortunate geographic time-zone location between New York, continental Europe, and Tokyo and to nail down its position as Europe's premier exchange in the emerging global securities market. London used to be the world's financial capital and has more overseas listings than New York or Tokyo. Without these listings, London would be a much smaller exchange. As of year-end 1984, 77 percent of its aggregate market value came from foreign stocks; they also made London equal to 59 percent the size of the NYSE's aggregate market value. On the basis of U.K. listings only, London's market value was only 13 percent that of the Big Board. London exchange officials and members are worried that modern communications are eroding the exchange's grip on international business by enabling investors, traders, and multinational corporations to move quickly in and out of the money markets in the U.S., the Far East, and Switzerland. Domestic interest trails that in the U.S.: London exchange officials estimate three to four million Britons (or about 5 to 7 percent of the population) own shares directly compared with forty-eight million Americans (or about 20 percent of the U.S. population).

"London has been a major capital for banking, insurance, commodities, gold, Eurobonds, and shipbuilding, but its securities market has been parochial and arrested in its development," says a senior official* of the Bank of England, which, as the chief government body overseeing the exchange, was a major force in its restructuring. "The scarcest resource in the London securities market has been capital. In 1983 the Bank surveyed the U.K.'s largest institutional investors to ascertain what proportion of portfolio management in North America was funneled through U.K. brokers and found that under five percent was."

Members placed the blame for this outflow and for the development of most Eurobond business outside the exchange on the single capacity system (the separation of jobbing and broking functions), which they said made it impossible to compete in international markets. They also charged that fixed commissions were driving U.K. investors to the U.S. and its discount rates. More than 120 U.K. companies are traded on U.S. markets in the form of American Depository Receipts (ADRs)—substitute certificates for stock in a foreign company that are held in trust by a U.S. bank which issues receipts that are then traded in the U.S. marketplace. The procedure circumvents the expensive British commissions. This decline in domestic investment worried the Thatcher government; its denationalization strategy for firms such as British Telecom and its tax incentives for stock investment depended on attracting ordinary citizens to the market. Revision of the trading system was deemed crucial for handling the expected surge in volume.

The exchange had indirectly acknowledged that its customs were antiquated back in 1970 by allowing members to perform as both jobbers and brokers overseas so they would be on an equal footing with local firms. These companies then clamored to have the same privilege at home, but smaller firms were content and secure with the less competitive status quo. In 1979 the entire securities industry became frightened when the abolition of the U.K.'s foreign exchange controls prompted an invasion of foreign securities houses that came prowling after the U.K.'s expanding overseas business. The majority of members pleaded for dual capacity, and the exchange heeded since it was eager to revive international business that had been sapped by the controls.

* It is the Bank of England's policy not to allow any official to be quoted by name.

It was also apparent that rich foreigners could gain the upper hand against the severely undercapitalized U.K. firms. "There is a popular saying that an Englishman who makes five million dollars retires to the country, but an American tries to make another five million," says Michael von Clemm, chairman of the London-based Crédit Suisse First Boston, a large merchant bank. British brokers rarely have capital bases exceeding $20 million. In the U.S. twenty-five brokers top $100 million in capital, and the largest firm, Merrill Lynch, has $2 billion. A large London securities firm has 800 employees; despite extensive layoffs in 1984, Merrill Lynch has 40,000. "Big organizations will need fifty million pounds* to do well in the new system," explains John Robertson, senior partner of Wedd Durlacher Mordaunt, one of the City's two largest jobbers. He speaks from personal experience. In "a hard business decision" he sold his firm (he is a great-nephew of one of the founders) to Barclays Bank because "to survive in the restructured system, our firm needed a much larger capital base."

All major participants claim credit for the Big Bang. The government and the Bank of England say they are responsible; the exchange maintains it would have acted on its own. All agree that the first shove occurred in 1976, when the Labour government then in power extended the jurisdiction of the Restrictive Trade Practices Act to include not only supplies and goods but also the service industries. The stock exchange came under this umbrella, but banks and insurance companies did not.

The government's Office of Fair Trading, which administers the act, is empowered to take any restrictive agreement to court unless the agreement is economically necessary. The exchange was obliged to compile a list of what it viewed as restrictive practices. It listed seventy-six, to which the Office of Fair Trading added seventy-one. Mindful that the U.S. had switched to negotiated rates the previous year, the government focused its attention on three main areas of restrictive behavior: the single-capacity split between brokers and jobbers, fixed commissions, and access to membership. (Only existing members could decide who could join, and there was no means of appeal.) Priority was assigned to eliminating fixed commissions. But

---

*From January to the end of July 1985, the British pound averaged $1.21 U.S.

it was clear that once the commissions were deregulated, the rest of the system would topple, too, because single capacity could thrive only in a protected environment of set rates.

The case was scheduled for October 1983, but in July 1983 the exchange's chairman, Sir Nicholas Goodison, and the (by then) Conservative government settled out of court. With pretrial legal fees of £1 million, the case was threatening to become the costliest in history, so Sir Nicholas promised the exchange would reform if the government withdrew its charges. Exchange executives argue that defending the exchange's practices legally was undermining its ability to make changes, a stand that causes government officials to snort derisively. "That argument is based on flimsy legal advice and ex post facto rationalization," says Colin Lowry, a senior Office of Fair Trading official involved in the case. "If the exchange had wanted to do so, it could have come out and said so and arranged a deal earlier." Lowry adds that more likely, the looming court case played the pivotal role.

Under the July 1983 pact, the Bank of England, in its capacity as overseer of the City, was assigned the task of ensuring that the exchange adhered to the agreement. To underscore the message, Prime Minister Margaret Thatcher appointed a loyal Conservative as the Bank's new governor when the five-year post became vacant in July 1983, coincidentally the same month as the exchange's agreement with the government. Her choice, Robin Leigh-Pemberton, formerly chairman of National Westminster Bank, is the first clearing bank executive to be made governor since the 292-year-old Bank was nationalized in 1946. The position had been unofficially the prerogative of the merchant banks. (Clearing banks take deposits and provide loans and export financing to business and personal customers. Merchant banks raise capital for industry and government, manage institutional and private investment portfolios, and advise about mergers and takeovers.)

The grandiose Bank, with its vase court (board of directors') room containing three fireplaces, massive chandeliers, and a Royal Wilton rug woven in 1939 for £1,200,* is only one block from the exchange, and Leigh-Pemberton quickly piled on the pressure through several

---

*There also are two sets of doors to provide secrecy; however, they are unlocked so a director can quickly have access to the cloakroom (washroom).

speeches. In April 1984 the exchange issued a Green Paper on how the restructured market would work. Clumsily or haughtily, depending on one's view, it had neglected to consult smaller member firms; they reacted with dismay since they feared being overrun by the merged banks and big jobbers and brokers. Some doomsayers in the City predict that within four years of the Big Bang, as few as 12 to 15 of the 214 pre-Bang broker and 17 jobber firms will control 70 percent of the business. Matters were not helped by the fact that Sir Nicholas and Jeffrey Knight lack rapport with many members. Knight, a former chartered accountant and a talented organizer, who has realigned the exchange's 1,200 employees into functional divisions in preparation for the Big Bang, sincerely means to be pleasant. Unfortunately what often comes out is unintentionally abrasive, and staff members readily admit he "has a public relations problem." Sir Nicholas, a graduate of classics and architecture from Cambridge University and an expert on the history of furniture, clocks, and barometers, is a gifted negotiator, but even his most fervent admirers say he can seem like a cold fish.

The simmering resentment exploded into open rebellion in the spring 1984 elections for the Council (governing body) of the exchange. Three of Sir Nicholas's opponents were elected, with one, Jeremy Lewis, obtaining more votes than Sir Nicholas. Lewis is a partner of Seymour Pierce & Company, a century-old broker specializing in securities for the water industry and with a history of cautiousness. Hanging on the boardroom wall is a framed excerpt from a 1902 article on founder Charles Arthur Pierce, describing him as "looking askance at new-fangled fashions and manners of modern exchange life."

"I felt insufficient heed was being paid to the interests of smaller brokers," Lewis told me shortly after his election. "Of the two hundred and fourteen broking firms at the exchange, I felt seventy-five percent would be at a disadvantage. Under the present system all brokers are on an equal competitive footing regarding prices quoted on shares. We have to compete for customers in other areas such as research and service.

"But under the new system smaller firms could be elbowed out. Institutional business will go to bigger firms whose size will enable them to offer bargain rates. The banks will direct either all their business or their most worthwhile business through their merchant bank subsidiaries.

"Smaller brokers will have to fall back on private-client business, and this will become more competitive, too. Until now such business has been insufficiently profitable for larger brokerage firms to pursue, but with institutional business likely becoming less profitable under negotiated rates, they will turn to business generated by individuals. All this will cause partners at smaller firms either to retire early or seek a merger with a stronger firm." That, he argued, could be bad for small investors. "Smaller firms lubricate the market by encouraging investment by small private clients. If the market becomes one of just a few firms, it could be harder for firms to raise money, and individual investors might feel there is no place for them."

Although Knight portrayed the dissidents as "reactionaries," their number included some past exchange reformers. For example, H. R. E. Bradshaw, senior partner at the brokerage house of Vivian Gray & Company, was a leading proponent in the 1970s battle over female participation. The exchange had allowed women as members, but not on the trading floor. "That was similar to Victorian era parlormaids who were permitted into the drawing room to serve when the bell rang," Bradshaw says. To his delight he discovered that the Manchester regional exchange had admitted two women, and since the six "country" exchanges merged with London in 1973, those women could, by virtue of their Manchester membership, automatically join London's floor. A Vivian Gray employee, Susan Shaw, was the first woman on the floor.

While the spring 1984 revolt did not give the rebels the upper hand, it did jolt the exchange into pacifying their fears of being shoved aside in the new regime. After the Big Bang all stock exchange firms *may* have dual capacity as jobbers and brokers, but this will not be compulsory.

An easing of ownership regulations was scheduled in advance of the Big Bang to permit participants to reorganize in time. In December 1983 nonmembers were permitted to acquire 49 percent of "international dealers," companies formed by members of the exchange for pursuing overseas securities business. In June 1985 the exchange authorized 29.9 percent ownership of both a jobber and a broker; previously an owner of 29.9 percent of one type of firm could have only 5 percent of the other. The 29.9 percent level dated back to 1982; formerly outsiders were limited to 10 percent ownership. As of March 1986, British and foreign banks as well as foreign securities dealers will be able to own up to 100 percent of brokers and jobbers.

Negotiated commission rates will replace set ones, but the 15 percent value added tax plus the 1 percent stamp duty tax will remain. Until November 1983 the stamp duty, which applies to all legal documents covering purchases, was 2 percent. Each year the government obtains from the duty about £1 billion, one-third of which comes from stock exchange transactions.

The exchange's new format is modeled largely on that of the United States' National Association of Securities Dealers Automated Quotation (NASDAQ) system of many *market makers* offering competitive price quotations in the same stock. Dual-capacity firms will have to register as market makers and broadcast their prices to all member firms through the exchange's electronic automated quotation system (known as SEAQ), which will be similar to the NASDAQ network. Exchange officials are encouraging the installation of SEAQ screens by banks and department stores to attract more Britons to the market. The system will record share price changes throughout the day, enabling monitoring against abuses. All details will be reported to regulatory officials immediately, probably within ninety seconds, as at NASDAQ. All dealing slips will be time-stamped, but there will be no immediate publication of last-trade data (the latest price, high and low prices for the day, and volume) since some fear this would scare off potential market makers. Such reporting is probable, though, if London continues to ape NASDAQ. NASDAQ's members at first opposed and then, to their pleasant surprise, found last-trade reporting benefited their images and business among investors.

For the time being the electronic system will coexist with the floor. But the Young Turks at the exchange are pressuring for the floor to be replaced within five to ten years by a floorless, computer-linked system like NASDAQ's. By adopting a NASDAQ type of system, the exchange will not have to enlarge its floor, now jammed with thirteen hexagonal-shaped stalls, called pitches, where the jobbers make their pitch in quoting buy and sell prices.

London studied both NASDAQ and the NYSE auction market, in

which one specialist creates a continuous market in stocks assigned by the exchange if there are imbalances in supply and demand. The exchange ruled out an auction market because it requires a high frequency of two-way orders, and the bulk of the securities listed in London are not traded frequently. London preferred NASDAQ's market maker system because it is similar to London's jobbing method: Both are quote-driven, and several price makers compete for an order. London's officials hope this system will placate jobbers and small regional firms about their future after the Big Bang since the automated quotation system simultaneously displays prices to everybody.

Members also believe such a system lends itself to today's institutionalized, international market. "Neither the auction nor the jobbing market is suitable for institutional investment because they militate against taking large positions," says Andrew Smithers, senior partner at S. G. Warburg & Company, a leading U.K. merchant bank. "Moreover, the auction market is not suitable for twenty-four-hour, global trading since it requires people on the floor."

London differs from the U.S. in trading government securities (*gilts*) through the stock exchange. For the past 200 years, since Prime Minister William Pitt the Younger (1759–1806) created the position, the government has appointed one person as its broker at the exchange. From the outset the government broker has been picked from the firm of Mullens & Company. Four times daily the current broker, Nigel Althaus, wearing the same silk top hat his father and grandfather once wore, chats with brokers and jobbers and then reports their mood to the Bank of England. Using this sounding board, the Bank's staff and Althaus devise the government's financings. He has raised up to £15 billion a year for the government. For this responsibility Althaus receives a nominal £2,000 annually, the same amount as the first government broker. His main income is from his position as a partner at Mullens.

Although the government broker has become a fixture, Pitt originally regarded the position as a temporary adjunct to his goal of erasing the national debt. "This goal was almost achieved under Prime Minister William Gladstone,* but then there were various wars, and now the economic thinking is that national debt is a good way to

* Gladstone was Prime Minister four times between 1868 and 1894.

control the supply of money," Althaus says. Pitt's Commission to Reduce the National Debt still exists, but it has not met since the celebration a decade ago marking the centennial of its previous meeting.

Unofficially the government broker and his one assistant hold their posts for ten years, and Althaus's term runs to 1989. However, he will be absorbed into the staff of the Bank of England in 1986, when the restructuring of the gilts market will cause his job to disappear. From Althaus's viewpoint, the switch will not necessarily mean an improvement "because the government will no longer have its broker out on the street as its eyes and ears as to what the ordinary stockbroker is doing."

As part of the Big Bang the Bank has adopted the U.S. system of appointing primary dealers to make markets in gilts in return for special dealing and borrowing rights with the Bank. U.S. primary dealers conduct their business over the telephone; the London exchange is retaining the trading of gilts on its premises for economic reasons. Gilts account for close to 80 percent of the turnover at the exchange. Furthermore, it was hoped that since only exchange members are eligible to be primary dealers, new firms would join and subsequently branch into other trading activity. The Bank has selected twenty-nine British, European, and U.S. companies as primary dealers, but there are doubts as to whether business will be sufficient for all to do well and for the heavy costs incurred by staff expansion and the installation of requisite communications systems to be offset.

The British also believe better investor protection is possible through exchange supervision of gilts trading. Institutions dominate the U.S. government securities market and are expected to be sufficiently knowledgeable to safeguard themselves. There is little regulation, and some of the seeming experts have suffered heavy losses. The bulk of U.K. gilts volume is generated by individuals, and the British have reasoned that if in the U.S. large institutions were vulnerable, retaining gilts trading under the supervision of the exchange would best protect small investors in the United Kingdom.

The exchange's recasting also triggered a debate over keeping the status quo of self-regulation or creating a U.S.-style securities and exchange commission. The British recognized that the existing self-regulatory body, the Council for the Securities Industry, was, as a critical government-commissioned report stated, "a fifth wheel on the coach with little prospect of ever becoming more useful." But the government also dislikes what Colin Lowry of the Office of Fair Trading describes as "nannying." The exchange's members pride themselves on living up to its motto: "Dictum meum pactum"—My word is my bond.

"In the U.S. people do what they think they can get away with, and if there is a problem, they may go to court; but in the U.K. there is more of a judgmental, qualitative approach," says the Bank of England official. "The British believe that observing the spirit of the law is better than following the letter of the law because this usually trails what is actually happening." The compromise solution, called the Securities and Investment Board, was what securities firms characterized as a halfway house between industry self-regulation and a SEC. The chairman of the new board was appointed by the Department of Trade and Industry, but he also had to be approved by the governor of the Bank of England. The board's temporary headquarters are at the Bank, and the governor also has the authority to appoint the other members.

After the Big Bang, members may trade subject to personal, rather than corporate, liability if a securities firm cannot meet its commitments. The occasion is known as hammering and dates back to when a waiter would pull out a mallet from his wooden desk at the end of the day and hit the desk three times to signal trouble. "I regret to inform the members that ——— firm cannot comply with its bargains," the waiter would say in a gloomy tone. The firm's partners had to place all their personal wealth at the disposal of the exchange in order for clients to be compensated. Not surprisingly this practice was unpopular. It prompted many members to form limited liability companies so their companies, rather than they themselves, would be liable in the event of hammering.

Symbolic of their profession, the chief recreations of exchange members are shooting grouse and stalking deer. Their hunting instinct surfaced as they sat in quaint, dimly lit offices or what Prince Charles has denounced as "giant, glass stumps better suited to Chicago" and searched for corporate mates. Von Clemm of Crédit Suisse First Boston (which has stayed aloof) describes the outcome as a "feeding frenzy" by U.K. and U.S. banks willing to pay premiums way above the real value for U.K. brokers and jobbers. "Americans feel they can get along with everybody, but they are paying a very high price on the assumption that they can assimilate the British," von Clemm says. This may be why the biggest welter of alliances has involved U.K. commercial and merchant banks, although several large continental European banks and an Asian bank have also taken the plunge. The purchasers include Switzerland's largest bank, Union Bank of Switzerland, which bought into Phillips and Drew, a broker known for the quality of its research. Banque Bruxelles Lambert acquired Williams de Broe Hill Chaplin, a broker. The Hong Kong and Shanghai Banking Corporation obtained a 200-year-old broker, James Capel & Company. In considering applications from foreign firms to buy into U.K. companies or to gain membership on their own, the exchange is giving preference to those whose countries extend reciprocity of access—an attempt to nudge the Tokyo exchange into accepting foreign members.

The British banks acted swiftly. On the same day in 1984 that Barclays Bank, Britain's largest clearing bank, bought into de Zoete & Bevan, a large broker, and Wedd Durlacher Mordaunt, one of the two largest jobbers, Midland Bank, the number three clearing bank, did likewise with W. Greenwell, a gilts broker. National Westminster, the number two clearing bank and already the country's biggest insurance company in personal lines of business, has acquired Bisgood Bishop, the leading jobber on the exchange's Unlisted Securities Market (USM—for junior stocks), and Fielding Newson-Smith.

The merchant banks have not wasted time either. Kleinwort Benson Ltd., Britain's largest merchant bank, which underwrote the sale of British Telecom in 1984, the world's biggest-ever share issue, bought into Grievson Grant & Company, a broker with a large gilts business. S. G. Warburg & Company, one of the City's most elite and unquestionably its most eccentric merchant bank, put together a blue-chip assortment. It bought interests in the jobber firm of Akroyd & Smithers, chief rival of Wedd Durlacher Mordaunt, as well as in Rowe & Pitman, a broker whose clients include the royal family, and in Mullens & Company, supplier of the government broker.

Whether the clearing or the merchant banks will be the victor is not easy to call since each has strengths. The clearing banks boast they have more capital available to build their securities business. (The biggest merchant banks have capital equal to just one-third that of Merrill Lynch.) Also, the clearing banks have international contacts from their activities throughout the world. Conversely, the merchant banks maintain they have the upper hand because they are more accustomed to the special rhythm of the securities business. "The basic business of clearing banks is to take money from depositors and lend it to clients, with the banks taking the short-term financing credit risk, whereas in the long-term capital market in which merchant banks specialize, the investors assume the risk," says Warburg's Andrew Smithers.

Observers are entranced by the warfare. "London's investment community automatically thinks internationally and has been willing to allow foreigners to ascend the heights of the British establishment," says Manfred Adami, managing director of Crédit Suisse First Boston Investment Management Ltd. "Consequently, every U.K. merchant bank has been started by foreigners, mostly from Germany and the U.S. Yet an amazingly provincial outlook exists side by side with the international, like a sweet and sour dish or a hot and cold baked Alaska."

Says the manager of a foreign (not U.S.) bank, based in the City for more than a decade: "The clearing banks have a spotty history in the securities business. National Westminster is the most switched-on, but Barclays did not think out in advance how it would meld de Zoete and Wedd Durlacher into one piece. The senior executives at the U.K. clearing banks have narrow training and little experience in the securities business. By contrast, the merchant bankers, with few exceptions, are shrewd, talented, and hardworking."

Barclays has overcome problems with its Barclays Merchant Bank, the division that acquired de Zoete and Wedd Durlacher. Before its present chairman, Lord Camoys, was hired in 1978, the bank was not structured as a traditional merchant bank. There was mostly duplication because two teams doing the same work split the United Kingdom between them. Camoys reorganized the bank on strictly functional lines, and profits subsequently doubled. Typical of the banks, Barclays bought rather than created its own in-house securities shop since it thought it would be cheaper in the long run than a cram course in a new field for employees. Also, the time-consuming process of nurturing contacts was leapfrogged.

National Westminster has a longer background in merchant banking than Barclays. It also was familiar with the securities business through subsidiaries that are members of the Swiss and Dutch stock exchanges. While Barclays wanted the biggest securities firm, Nat West opted for Bisgood Bishop, even though that firm ranks Number Five in size among jobbers, because of a mutual interest in the exchange's fast-growing young Unlisted Securities Market. Nat West's merchant bank, City Bank, established in 1970, is a leader in bringing new issues to the unlisted market, and Bisgood Bishop has 75 percent of the jobbing business there.

The union arousing the greatest curiosity in the City is the one Warburg patched together with Akroyd & Smithers, Rowe & Pitman, and Mullens. The combination will be larger, in terms of capital, than such big U.S. firms as Morgan Stanley and Donaldson, Lufkin & Jenrette, Inc. Some personal and working ties already existed between the firms. Senior Warburg partner Andrew Smithers is the great-grandson of the cofounder of Akroyd & Smithers. That firm's joint senior partner, Timothy Jones, has a son working at Rowe & Pitman. Both Warburg and Akroyd & Smithers and Akroyd & Smithers and Rowe & Pitman were already associated in ventures outside the U.K.

Warburg, founded in the 1940s by a Jewish German emigrant, Siegmund Warburg, has unusual habits, including requiring potential recruits to undergo handwriting analysis. (Recent successful candidates included two sons of Robin Leigh-Pemberton, the governor of the Bank of England.) In financing techniques, Warburg has been a pioneer. In the 1960s it invented the reverse takeover, under which the stock of the takeover candidate is used by the bidder to acquire the company. Warburg later was the first U.K. merchant bank to do a Eurobond issue at the establishment of this market in 1963. More than $100 billion in Eurobonds have been issued since then, and Warburg has become the leading U.K. merchant bank in this field.

Competitors wonder if Warburg's earnest work ethic style will clash with the hunting and cricket match culture of its acquisitions, but in the eyes of the four firms they complement one another. For Warburg, it enabled immediate readiness for the trading of securities after the Big Bang. "The speed of change was such that we could not do it internally," Smithers says.

The acquired firms also foresaw synergistic benefits. "In the new environment there will be enormous cross benefits for our jobbing firm in having access to the order flow from Rowe and Pitman and from the primary issuing business of Warburg," says Akroyd & Smithers's Timothy Jones. "Rowe Pitman will benefit because under the new system it will be increasingly important to have access to the market, which we will provide since our firm is one of the two largest jobbers. We realized that once U.S. and Japanese investment banks become directly involved in the exchange and fulfill all the functions they perform in their own countries, the competition would be pretty daunting for our firm."

Some prominent U.S. banks have also bought London exchange members. The banks saw two advantages. After the Big Bang in the U.K. they can participate in the issuing of securities, unlike the situation in the U.S., where they are barred from doing so by law. Secondly, they gained indirect entry to the large Japanese market, where banks cannot deal in securities, since the firms they acquired have big businesses there. So tantalizing were these benefits that a large U.S. bank, Security Pacific National Bank of California, beat the British in becoming the first to buy into a U.K. securities firm. Its choice: Hoare Govett, one of the leading foreign brokers in Singapore, Hong Kong, and Australia. (The London exchange does a large volume in Australian stocks.)

William Richardson, head of Security Pacific's capital markets banking group, says the decision to buy into Hoare Govett was part of a game plan "to complement and reinforce our domestic strategy in the U.S. We felt we should acquire an interest in a London broker that was international in scope with a Far East presence." One-third of Hoare Govett's business at the time of its acquisition was in the Far East.

When Security Pacific approached Hoare Govett, it was not calling on a stranger since Hoare Govett had handled the listing of the bank's stock on the London exchange in the 1970s. Hoare Govett's managing director, Richard Westmacott, sold because Security Pacific was willing to invest in his pet project—further expansion of Hoare Govett in the Far East. Security Pacific's capital markets group certainly had the money; it had grown since its inception in 1977 from 2 people and $17,000 to 350 people and $35 million.

The lure of the Far East business similarly incited the largest U.S. bank, Citicorp, to buy into Vickers da Costa, a century-old firm where Winston Churchill's brother, Jack, was once a partner. Da Costa has been in Hong Kong and Japan for more than twenty years and is one of only ten foreign securities firms with branch status in Tokyo. By hesitating for nearly a year after Security Pacific had made its move, Citicorp paid fifteen times the value of da Costa's average earnings over the preceding three years. Early-bird Security Pacific had paid between six and eight times Hoare Govett's average earnings. Citicorp laid out the money because it was convinced the acquisition, code-named Schweppes, had "fizz," says the capital markets vice president and general counsel Robert Dinerstein, who compiled the 300 pages of covering legal documents during eight trips to London. "Both the London and Tokyo markets are growing rapidly as international capital markets become a single global market. Corporations are increasingly indifferent as to where they raise money, so long as the terms are satisfactory."

Vickers da Costa has always had an international thrust. Like Warburg, it was started by a German Jew. During World War II, when the London exchange ordered every member of German origin to resign, all but three da Costa partners—Vickers, da Costa, and Churchill—were affected. "We are unusual among London brokers in making more money overseas than in London and in seeing the world from a Pacific view rather than from just the square mile of the City," da Costa Chairman Sir Kenneth Berrill,* reflected as he outlined his reasons to me for his instigating the deal with Citicorp.

He did so because by world standards da Costa was small in terms of both staff and capitalization and "life would be tough" in the fierce competition the Big Bang would produce. Also, while da Costa was a big fish in the Far East, that market is a small pond compared with the U.S. Sir Kenneth realistically concluded that "The biggest flow

---

* In March 1985 Sir Kenneth was appointed the first chairman for a three-year term, of the new Securities and Investment Board.

of international business is transborder U.S.—between the U.S. and Tokyo and the U.S. and Europe—and the rest is very small."

The problem having been pinpointed, Sir Kenneth's next task was to discover the candidate that would help da Costa the most. His was a process of careful elimination. He ruled out joining another London broker because the combined capital base would still be small. Similarly he rejected linking with a London merchant bank since "they are also small by world standards and are generally more domestic than internationally oriented. Then, too, if we had become part of a merchant bank, the other merchant banks would likely have stopped giving us business, and we do a lot of business with the merchant banks. We spoke to some U.S. brokers, but they tell you how to run your business. None of the U.K. clearing banks were interested, and very few have an international communications setup, which is an essential ingredient. So we ended up looking at international banks, of which only a few rank in size with the American ones."

Subsequently, Sir Kenneth became a marriage broker between Citicorp and Scrimgeour Kemp-Gee, a broker that is active in the Middle East and Europe and whose data-processing procedures are compatible with da Costa's. Citicorp has pledged that neither da Costa nor Scrimgeour will lose its identity and that Citicorp will not replace management with its own executives.

Citicorp followed these purchases by forming a venture targeted at small securities firms that want to provide services similar to those offered by houses now part of big U.K. or foreign banks but that lack the funds to do so. With NMW Computers, the largest U.K. stock-processing house, Citicorp established a settlement facility for customers to pay or receive money from transactions. Citicorp also will supply loans, credit cards, and foreign exchange.

A third large U.S. bank, Chase Manhattan, has bought into two brokerage houses—Simon & Coates, a major player in the Unlisted Securities Market, and Laurie Milbank, which specializes in gilts. But American brokerages are not as interested. Shearson Lehman Brothers, Inc., owned by American Express, bought into L. Messel, another big participant in gilts and strong in research. Months later Prudential-Bache started its own firm, P-B Securities Ltd., securing its initial two employees in a raid on James Capel & Company (admired for its research). Still later, Prudential-Bache acquired both a discounter and a broker. Otherwise, American brokerage firms elected not to buy, convinced they could succeed on their own, especially since many have had representation in the City for years, the earliest dating back to 1904. However, Dean Witter Reynolds Inc., the financial services arm of Sears, Roebuck, is shifting responsibility for its international business to London from New York, a heartening gesture to Londoners who feel this is indicative of London's growing strength, as against the NYSE's, in international trading.

All the Americans have placed research ability high on their shopping lists because research ability is something Wall Street prizes. In the U.K., however, the emphasis on research analysis is only about fifteen years old, and some think it is threatened by the Big Bang. "Analysts grew up as an optional, extra facility. Even today a broker's big salesmen tend to read through the U.K.'s leading business newspaper, the *Financial Times*, or speak to friends to get their bright ideas and only talk to their firm's analysts if all else fails," says James Ferguson, a senior research analyst at James Capel. "Under fixed commissions brokers could charge more than their regular rate if they offered good research, but with a more competitive market some brokers may be tempted to get rid of their research departments in order to cut operating costs."

The much larger U.S. banks conceivably could take away considerable business from both old and new U.K. firms, but the British profess no fear. "Clients feel U.S. firms always think in dollar terms first, and in investment finance it is necessary to be aware of opportunities in all currencies," says Warburg's Smithers. Also, the British believe that for the Americans to succeed, they will have to alter their more insular way of thinking. "Because the U.S. domestic market is so big, the U.S. doesn't take the rest of the world as seriously as the U.K., which has been internationally oriented for centuries and, therefore, has a more objective view as to which are the best markets," says Capel's Ferguson.

Expansion across the Atlantic is two-way. While the American firms are invading the U.K., some British firms are penetrating the U.S. The merchant bank Henry Ansbacher Holdings has acquired Laidlaw Adams & Peck, Inc., of New York, a medium-size broker, and Kleinwort Benson has purchased ACLI Government Securities, Inc., of Chicago, one of the thirty-seven primary dealers in U.S. government securities. Its purchase in April 1984 was the first outright acquisition by a foreign bank of a U.S. primary dealer. Since then, many other major British firms have also ventured into the U.S., again through acquisitions. However, their smaller amount of capital compared to that of the giant U.S. firms has placed them at a disadvantage in the competition for large-scale underwritings.

In addition to the main exchange, securities are traded four other ways in London: an off-floor market in major stocks under the auspices of a big nonmember; an electronic system of Reuters Ltd., the large U.K. news agency; the Unlisted Securities Market (USM) in small stocks (similar in function to the American Stock Exchange); and a small over-the-counter (OTC) market for securities not on the exchange.

The off-floor market was established by a leading London merchant bank, Robert Fleming & Company Ltd., to take advantage of the interim until brokers and jobbers can act in dual capacity. Fleming, which has about £10 million under portfolio management (a large sum for the U.K.) is coowner with Jardine Mathieson, a Hong Kong trading company, in a joint venture of Jardine Fleming—one of the few foreign securities firms with a branch license in Tokyo. What Fleming is doing is similar to the third market in the U.S., which is operated by large nonmembers of the exchanges.

In spring 1985 Reuters gained the non-North American rights to market the New York-based Instinet service, through which large orders are electronically executed in seconds away from the trading floor by computer-linked brokers. That was a logical move for Reuters, which has distributed stock price information over its news wire for years, and it subsequently bought 20 percent of Instinet. The Reuters system, launched in summer 1985, covers U.S. stocks and options and foreign stocks traded in the U.S. in American Depository Receipt form. The long-term goal is to add stocks from other world markets, starting with British ones. As in the U.S., exchange members cannot participate, but there are many other available players among non-U.K. members and foreign dealers in the U.K. Reuters would like to work out an accommodation with the exchange, but that could prove difficult since the exchange is more interested in the success of its automated quotation system. The conflict could prompt the exchange to advance the Big Bang to prevent Reuters from gaining a strong foothold.

The main London market still appeals to companies with pretax profits of £3 million or more. Both the unlisted and over-the-counter markets are attractive to companies with pretax profits of £500,000 or more. Despite its name, the Unlisted Securities Market consists not of unlisted companies, but rather of formerly unlisted companies that are now publicly traded. Family-controlled companies prefer the OTC market because they can retain more control this way than through the USM, which requires a minimum amount of the company's equity to be offered to the public. The OTC also differs from the USM in that it is directed more toward institutional instead of individual investors.

Trading methods differ, too. Both the main market and the USM use brokers and jobbers. The main market is more actively jobbed since at the USM one jobber—Bisgood Bishop—does three-fourths of the work. At the OTC market transactions are done over the telephone on a matched basis between seller and buyer, with the securities firms acting as both jobber and broker. Prices on most stocks are quoted by only one dealer, unlike the competing market maker system in the OTC market in the U.S. and the main London market. As in the U.S., OTC dealers do not charge commissions; they make their money from the spread between the buy and sell prices.

Two rival factions splinter the small OTC market, with each jousting for the Securities and Investment Board to name it the chief self-regulator of this form of trading: the 350-member National Association of Security Dealers and Investment Managers and the tiny British Institute of Dealers in Securities. The latter has only a handful of members, but they include some powerhouse firms.

Since its November 1980 debut the Unlisted Securities Market has been a hit. Starting with only 11 listings, it now boasts 300. Its success has spurred other European exchanges to establish or plan junior markets with similar qualifications for members and issues. A USM candidate need be only three years old—rather than five as is required for the main market—and it need offer the public only 10 percent of the equity, compared with 25 percent otherwise.

Up to £25,000 can be saved in advertising costs for the flotation of the issue since only a small box in the *Financial Times* is necessary, in contrast with the usual full prospectus that often runs as long as four newspaper pages. No initial fee is paid to the exchange, whereas a main market listing can cost as much as £13,700. Annual fees are a flat £1,000; a fully listed company pays £370 to £3,050. In addition, shareholder disclosure requirements regarding the acquisition or disposal of assets are not as tough. Shareholders follow USM stocks in the same fashion as fully listed ones—by reading the stock pages of the *Financial Times*. The paper flags USM firms with a tiny dagger.

The USM originated in 1973, a crisis year for the London exchange. As at other exchanges, share values were plunging in the wake of the steep hike in world oil prices. The falling market, combined with the high interest rates that diluted the worth of new share issues, deterred unlisted companies from going public. Mergers and takeovers, spurred by the bargain share prices, were shrinking the number of listed companies.

Under pressure from the government to encourage the growth of small and medium-size businesses, the beleaguered exchange relaxed its requirements still further. Rule 163(2) had already allowed informal trading in unlisted securities. The 163(2) market previously was regional in nature and consisted of sporting clubs, small breweries, and public utilities. Under this rule the Lawn Tennis Association finances the Wimbledon tennis club through the issue of debentures. The owners derive no income from the debentures, but have the right to center-court tickets at the annual Wimbledon championship matches.

The exchange's more liberal interpretation sparked great interest in the 163(2) market, raising fears over its lack of adequate supervision. Stung by the criticism, the exchange established the USM. It contains some unusual listings, such as the company staging the Miss World beauty contest, a casino, Apinall's of London's exclusive Knightsbridge district, and a disco, Pineapple Dance Studio. The day Pineapple's stock was listed, the company's young, attractive chairwoman, Debbie Moore, appeared in a miniskirt on the exchange's floor, where she was mobbed by enthusiastic male traders. Although this incident gained the USM a hard-to-shake reputation of "anything goes," no scandals have occurred, and only four firms have collapsed.

"Because of the volatility of the USM and the lack of research on many companies, investing in USM stocks is like backing young colts in a race because the investment is based on hope rather than fundamentals," says John Donald, an analyst at broker Phillips and Drew, a leading supporter of the USM. Because most securities firms expected the USM to fail, they virtually ignored it, leaving the field open for hungry, younger firms such as Phillips and Drew and its chief rival, Simon and Coates, also a broker. They had been banging into the proverbial brick wall trying to wrench away corporate finance business from the decades-old alliances between U.K. companies and their longtime investment houses.

The idea for the over-the-counter market was imported to the U.K. by former Conservative Member of Parliament Robin Granville Hodgson, who had graduated from both Oxford University and the Wharton School of Finance at the University of Pennsylvania. He then worked for U.S. and Canadian securities firms, where he became acquainted with NASDAQ. With the zeal of a convert, he decided that since London lacked an OTC market, his firm, Granville & Company, would pioneer one. He also established the National Association of Securities Dealers and Investment Managers (NASDIM), with a role similar to that of the National Association of Securities Dealers in the United States.

The OTC market is a pipsqueak compared with the unlisted and main markets in the U.K. and NASDAQ. It trades only 140 companies, compared with close to 4,100 at NASDAQ. Its twelve market makers are about as many as NASDAQ has for some stocks. There is no automated quotation system. The total capital involved is in the low millions of pounds so that liquidity is generally thin, and the market suffers from fragmentation, with Granville and one other firm, Hill Woolgar, each operating an independent OTC market with its own customers, separately from the OTC market of the other ten market makers.

The London exchange could have been the first in Europe to launch futures and options trading, but it let the opportunity slip through its hands. London has the only financial futures exchange in Europe, the London International Financial Futures Exchange (LIFFE), but the credit for its creation belongs to Michael Barkshire, chairman of Mercantile House Holdings, one of the first U.K. financial firms to have an international outlook. Back in 1967, Barkshire drew up a blueprint of what he believed would happen in financial markets until the end of this century and how Mercantile House should capitalize on these developments. He decided to pattern his firm on full-service U.S. securities houses by acquiring a U.K. broker (Laing & Cruikshank), a U.K. commodities brokerage (Rouse Woodstock), two U.K. discount houses (Alexanders & Jessel and Toynbee & Gillett), and a U.S. investment bank (Oppenheimer & Company).

In 1978 Barkshire spent five months in the U.S. investigating the financial futures market and whether his firm should enter that area. "I decided it was likely such trading would spread around the world and felt the European center should be in London because it is the biggest international money center."

In late 1979 he formed a working committee of a cross section of eight London financial firms and held seminars to ascertain the depth of support for such a market. He expected 500 people but got 5,000. By December 1980 the committee had completed its proposal, which it submitted to the Bank of England. In February 1981 the Bank responded obliquely that it would be improper for it to say there should be a financial futures market in London but that it would not object to its establishment. "International" was incorporated in the name with the hope—so far realized—that other European exchanges would not form competitors and because membership is open to foreign firms. Of the 250 members, half are foreign banks and commodity brokers.

LIFFE moved into the unoccupied Royal Exchange, across Threadneedle Street from the stock exchange. The building is distinguished by a golden grasshopper on the roof, commemorating the insect's role in saving the life of its builder, Thomas Gresham, who as a child had been abandoned in a hayfield by his parents. A grasshopper got lodged in his ear, and help arrived in response to his anguished cries. The building is owned by the City of London, which leases it for £125,000 annually. That amount is not as nominal as it seems. In return, LIFFE had to restore the historic paintings and statues (including one of Abraham Lincoln) and display them to the public, which entailed constructing a costly elevated walkway for viewers.

LIFFE's chief executive, Michael Jenkins, previously developed the stock exchange's computerized settlement system and was joint managing director of the European Options Exchange in Amsterdam. He says LIFFE is better off on its own than associated with the stock exchange. "If a futures exchange had been a division of the stock exchange, nobody would have worried about it being successful. The exchange has had options for seven years and still hasn't got this division off the ground. Nor does it mind because it is a small activity. If a new market is going to succeed, there must be a strong incentive for it to do so. When it is regarded as of marginal importance, it does not get the necessary commitments. Also, stock exchange members generally are not successful at futures trading because it is a different type of market requiring a special mentality."

What Jenkins is alluding to is the unhurried exchange atmosphere, compared with that of the rough-and-tumble futures market. There is also a social gap between the stock exchange members, who attended exclusive schools such as Harrow, Eton, or Rugby and speak with an upper-crust accent and the traders at LIFFE, who were educated at neighborhood schools and speak with a thick East End London barrow boys accent. The easy accessibility to LIFFE membership is their key to becoming rich in a society that is still very much class-oriented.

The success of the Chicago financial futures markets prompted the establishment of LIFFE, but while Chicago has many individuals (*locals*) as members, LIFFE at first recruited institutions in the belief this was the fastest route to robust business. But the liquidity did not come up to expectations, so some institutional investors have transferred their business to Chicago. In addition, U.S. brokerage houses that acquired London houses rerouted their futures trading through their domestic operations in the U.S. to achieve economies of scale.

The U.K. also differs from the U.S. in allowing both the stock and futures exchanges to trade currency options; in the U.S., with the exception of the Philadelphia Stock Exchange, these are traded only at futures exchanges. LIFFE allows trading on *margin* *; the London Stock Exchange, which believes margins leave investors too vulnerable to sudden price swings, does not. In the fall of 1985 the stock

---

* A margin account allows clients to pay a portion of the price of the security and borrow the balance from their broker. The term "margin" refers to the difference between the market value of the stock and the loan which the broker makes against that price.

exchange started trading currency options on an interchangeable basis with the Philadelphia exchange, which pioneered such options. This agreement is the first step toward a twenty-four-hour market—with the Hong Kong Futures Exchange expected to be the other partner—and should give the London exchange more vigor against LIFFE.

As for jurisdiction, there is no British equivalent of the U.S. Commodity Futures Trading Commission (CFTC); instead, LIFFE is supervised by the Bank of England in its capacity as overseer of all London markets. LIFFE is treated as both a commodities and a securities market because the twenty-year government gilts it trades are viewed as a security. Jenkins predicts LIFFE will do better in gilts after the Big Bang increases the number of gilts dealers. He believes the larger number of dealers will expand the need for futures contracts to offset risk.

LIFFE has talked with the Chicago Mercantile Exchange (the Merc) and the CFTC about becoming the third leg in the link between the Merc and the Singapore International Monetary Exchange. This proposal could founder on British reluctance to allow the release of information on investors' trading positions, which the CFTC requires. An act of Parliament would be essential to end this confidentiality.

Procrastination accounts for the London exchange's weak options business. It started its own after dithering over whether to be part of an European options exchange covering several European countries, proposed in the late 1970s by the freshly aggressive Amsterdam Stock Exchange (Effectenbeurs). The much smaller Dutch exchange believed options would help Amsterdam regain its age-old glory as the international powerhouse of finance. Many mansions along the Herengracht ("Gentleman's Row") in the middle of the city were built 200 years ago with money the Dutch made from their astute American investments, spanning the $24 purchase of Manhattan Island from the Indians to the financing of the Louisiana Purchase in 1803 and the building of U.S. canals and railroads during the nineteenth century.

The Amsterdam Stock Exchange, established in 1876, mirrored the international success of the Dutch financial community, but by the late 1970s its influence had waned. Between 1970 and 1980 its

Although the floor of the Amsterdam exchange appears traditional, new policies may help the exchange regain its former glory as an international powerhouse of finance.

number of listings fell 50 percent. To inject new life, the members hired an outsider as full-time chairman for the first time. This choice was Baron Boudewijn van Ittersum. The baron, whose hereditary title* dates back to the fifteenth century, joined the Dutch Ministry of

---

*While his name probably derives from the name of a German town, the baron prefers a more colorful version. "One of my ancestors defeated the king in a fight, and the king called him a stupid man. In order not to arouse the king's animosity, my ancestor replied, '*Id ter sum*—This I am—three times.'"

Finance's monetary policy division in 1967, was later posted to the International Monetary Fund and World Bank in Washington, and then was appointed director of foreign financial relations by the Dutch government.

Van Ittersum has left untouched the main market's structure, which resembles the system of separation of brokers and jobbers, fixed commissions, and prohibition of mergers with banks that London, convinced that the day for this style of trading is gone, will be dropping. These regulations have had the same impact as the similar rules did in London: Members are parched for capital, and institutional investors send their business to the U.S., which has discount rates. With opportunities for change stalemated in the main market, van Ittersum has sought new business in other directions. He started a Parallel Market for junior companies, with less onerous listing requirements than for the main market, similar to London's Unlisted Securities Market. He also developed a simplified trading system in U.S. and Japanese stocks to encourage Dutch institutional investors to keep their business at home. On the promotional front the baron initiated the sale at the exchange of sweatshirts displaying graphs of stock market trends.

Amsterdam had not intended to go on its own in options; it decided to because other European countries spurned its overtures for a common venture in options. "We were too far ahead of our time," van Ittersum says. "Germany opposed the idea of options; France is always very protective; Belgium was not interested. London said the same, but we felt that London's real aim was to watch how we made out and then begin their own options division." That is exactly what London did.

Like London's members, Amsterdam's traders had little faith that options would do well when the Effectenbeurs set up its options division in 1978, and indeed, the subsidiary lost money during its first three years. The parent exchange did its best by introducing new products (it was the first to trade gold options, beating the U.S. exchanges by eighteen months) and then it got lucky as investors latched onto options as a way of making money while the economic slump depressed actual stock prices. Their aspirations pumped life into the options offshoot, and it has made a profit ever since. Recently it became part of the first international options trading network the other members of which include Montreal and Vancouver, in Canada, and Sydney, Australia. The foursome are the first to trade a "fungible" option—an option bought on one exchange and sold on another the same day.

Americans looking across the ocean must have a sense of déjà vu about events in the U.K. and wonder if the outcome of its Big Bang will be the same as in the U.S. Deregulated commissions sparked a huge increase in the volume of business in the U.S. But the other side of the ledger was grim: for the securities industry, a shock wave of mergers, acquisitions, and firms that did not survive. For the exchanges, power over members diminished as off-floor negotiations, especially in big transactions, increased, with the floor used only to formally consummate the deal. Now a similar bloody survival of the fittest is brewing in England, and it is uncertain whether the other side of the equation of the Big Bang will be leadership regained in the global securities market or merely grievous upheaval.

3

Chicago

Once the "second city" in the United States, Chicago recently slipped to third in size among American cities, trailing Los Angeles as well as New York. But it is a champion in the investment world. It is home to the world's two largest commodity markets—the Chicago Board of Trade (CBOT) and the Chicago Mercantile Exchange (Merc)—to the largest options market—the Chicago Board Options Exchange (CBOE)—to the second-biggest U.S. stock exchange—the Midwest—and to the leading U.S. market in small commodity contracts—the MidAmerica. The Board of Trade, Mercantile, and MidAmerica exchanges account for 75 percent of global trading in futures, and the Options exchange accounts for 55 percent of all world trading in options. In late 1985, the CBOT and MidAmerica, whose types of contracts overlap, began to hold merger talks.

The five exchanges are within easy walking distance of one another. The CBOT, CBOE, and Midwest are clustered at the foot of the city's Loop. The MidAmerica is a few blocks west on Jackson Boulevard. It will move into the CBOT's building as part of the consolidation if the proposed merger with the much larger CBOT materializes. The Merc is across the Chicago River on Wacker Drive, near the 110-floor Sears Tower.

Pulsating with the raw energy that characterizes Chicago, the commodities and options exchanges make the regular din of stock exchanges seem like a quiet, refined tea party. Theirs is a dizzying kaleidoscope of fortunes made or lost in seconds, frantic pressure, people pushing and shoving, occasional fights on the huge, congested floors, scientific charts, wild rumors often given the same credibility as the charts, hard drinking, broken marriages. Individuals are no longer major players in the stock market, and the stock exchange floor is the preserve of professional traders. Commodities and options floors, on the other hand, welcome the lone ranger traders—the mathematics professors, lawyers, doctors, former taxi drivers, and car wash owners—each hoping to make a killing.

"Chicago used to be tagged as a stockyard center and as the home of Al Capone, but now it is known internationally for its futures and options markets," says Leo Melamed, regarded as the godfather of the modern futures market. The city recognized the importance of these markets when it selected the Mercantile's president, Clayton Yeutter, chairman of the Chicago Chamber of Commerce for 1984. It was the first time in more than two decades that the head of a Chicago exchange was chosen. Yeutter was named U.S. trade representative in 1985 by President Ronald Reagan.

At the commodities exchanges trading is done on either a *cash* or *futures* basis. Cash sales are for *spot* (immediate) or *forward* (usually within 120 days) delivery. They are arranged privately, whereas futures sales are conducted through regulated trading in public auction. Most of the trading floor is devoted to futures trading.

Both futures and options investors bet on the future direction of the market. Said to date back to ancient Greece, futures are contracts to buy or sell specific quantities of an agricultural commodity such as grain or livestock or of financial instruments like treasury bonds and stock indexes from one to eighteen months in the future at a price established at the time of the trade. Fewer than 5 percent of such contracts result in actual delivery; instead, transactions that nullify the original deals cancel most futures contracts prior to delivery.

Their purpose is to permit *hedging* (protection) against price fluc-

CHICAGO
OPTIONS AND FUTURES EXCHANGES
(As of year-end, 1984)

EXCHANGE	NUMBER OF CONTRACTS (*millions*)	NUMBER OF MEMBERS	SEAT PRICE (*high-low range*) $	TYPES OF CONTRACTS
Chicago Board Options Exchange	123.2	1,802	$270,000–195,000	On 145 of most widely held securities; four U.S. treasury bonds; Standard & Poor's 100 and 500 market indexes and transportation index; foreign currency options
Chicago Board of Trade	74.4	3,170	325,000–228,000	Grains; metals; U.S. treasury bonds and notes; Government National Mortgage Association certificates; unleaded gasoline; crude and heating oil; options on treasury bond and soybean futures; futures on NASDAQ stocks, London stock index, and municipal bond index
Chicago Mercantile Exchange	44.9	2,661	255,000–152,000	Livestock; foreign currencies; Standard & Poor's 100 and 500 indexes; gold bullion; ninety-day U.S. treasury bills; Eurodollar futures
MidAmerica	3.1	1,205	13,200–5,600	Grains; livestock; metals; foreign currencies; U.S. treasury bonds and bills

tuations. Futures prices and cash prices generally follow parallel paths because both respond to changes in supply and demand. This reasonably predictable relationship enables hedging. Investors expecting a price rise in wheat, foreign currencies, or gold go *long* and buy a futures contract; those anticipating a price decline go *short* and sell.

Options are contracts to buy or sell fixed amounts of a stock at a preset price for periods of from three to nine months in the future. Options to buy a stock are *calls;* options to sell are *puts.* The stock involved is the *underlying security,* and the preset price is the *exercise* or *strike* price. When stock prices are weak, demand falls for call options; the reverse applies for puts. Investors can profit if the price of the underlying stock rises above the exercise price of a call option or falls below that of a put.

On an average day the Board of Trade, number one among the world's commodities exchanges, trades $12 billion to $15 billion worth of commodities; at the New York Stock Exchange, $3 billion to $4 billion worth of securities are usually traded daily. Introduced in the 1970s by the Chicago markets, financial futures were the investment world's first new product in more than a century. The fastest-growing segment of futures, they have jumped from a mere 3 percent of total futures volume in 1977 to half the business at the Merc and one-third at the CBOT. As for the CBOE, some days it registers greater volume than in 1973, its first year. Although only 5 percent of U.S. investors use options, on peak days the CBOE does the equivalent of half the NYSE's record daily volume.

In the stock market, investors have a limited menu of stocks or corporate bonds. In futures and options there is a dizzying choice of more than fifty products. They include futures on wheat, corn, sunflower seeds, soybeans, hogs, cattle, potatoes, eggs, chickens, rice, butter, lumber, cotton, plywood, gold, silver, zinc, copper, British pounds, Canadian dollars, Japanese yen, Swiss francs, German marks, mortgage rates, U.S. treasury bills, treasury bonds, treasury notes, sugar, cocoa, coffee, orange juice, gasoline, and stock indexes representative of the complete market or one industry. The CBOE trades options on 145 blue-chip NYSE stocks as well as on a representative stock index and on such industries as computers, oil, telephone, and transportation.

Options and futures are traded together in the form of options on futures, which give the right to buy the futures contract for a set price at any point within a certain time. Options on futures provide hedgers with more choices since they can buy either the future itself to lock in the current price or options on that future to accomplish the same thing. In addition to this product, which straddles two types of markets, the distinction among stock, options, and future exchanges is further blurring as they move into one another's realm. Stock exchanges now trade options and futures, and both the CBOE, and the CBOT are considering the trading of securities.

Chicago prides itself on beating New York in pioneering financial futures and options. The Mercantile Exchange started financial futures in 1972. The American Stock Exchange (Amex) waited until 1978; it did so poorly that it rapidly withdrew. It is now preparing to try again. The New York Stock Exchange took until 1980; it is strongly outpaced in volume by Chicago. Amex launched options trading in 1975, two years after the CBOE; the NYSE delayed until 1983.

"The New York Stock Exchange felt it was everything and looked down its nose at futures trading," says Warren Lebeck, who developed financial futures trading at the CBOT. "Not only was New York financially bankrupt in the 1970s, but it also was bankrupt of ideas about the importance of futures trading." According to census statistics, New York has twice as many brokerage firms as Chicago, but the Windy City has double the number of futures and options traders.

The rewards for futures and options traders are often fast and big: annual income of $300,000, a condominium or house in Florida or California, and another vacation place on Lake Geneva, Wisconsin, near Chicago. The garage on Van Buren Street, running between the CBOE and Board of Trade, is filled with traders' Mercedeses. Some overnight millionaires buy expensive racehorses. Brian Monieson, 1983–1984 chairman of the Chicago Mercantile Exchange, owns two dozen horses. His partner, Myron Rosenthal, at the firm of GNP Commodities, Inc., recently sold a horse for $4.25 million.

Chicago's instant or putative millionaires are so intent on making money that for lunch they grab hot dogs even though there are three private luncheon clubs in the area catering to the industry. The Attic, between the longtime site of the recently moved Midwest Exchange and the CBOT, has starched white tablecloths and motherly waitresses. The Union Club, beside the CBOT, features ornate chandeliers and massive oil paintings. The Metropolitan Club, near the Merc, is so exclusive that there are no menus; instead, the waiters recite the long bill of fare.

But in a flash traders can lose all their money. It is not uncommon to see tough men break into uncontrollable sobbing on such occasions. Or they may react like one unfortunate trader, who had lost his money bidding the wrong way in Japanese yen on the Chicago Mercantile Exchange. A hush fell over the usual cacophony as he shouted: "I think I am [broke], I think I am, I think I am." After the third outburst he threw his trading slips in the air and left the floor.

It is not an isolated incident. Each morning, when asked how they are, many traders respond, "I'm still here." A lot of the survivors seek to soothe their nerves over one day's transactions and the possible disasters of tomorrow by downing drink after drink in the Sign of the Trader, a three-room bar on the ground floor of the Chicago Board of Trade. More liquor reputedly is consumed there than at any other midwestern tavern. When it closes at 8:00 P.M., traders head to Chicago's North Side to drink some more.

Says a veteran member of the CBOT and CBOE: "Our life-style is unique and cannot be understood by people in any other industry. The pressure is so great that there is too much drinking, and attention to families goes downhill to nothing. The divorce rate is very high. I'm one example—I'm on my second marriage. The amount of philandering is mind-boggling. We get so involved with our lives and our opponents' lives that after the close of trading we get drunk together, even though twenty minutes earlier we were screaming, spitting, and shaking our fists at one another."

The trading at the CBOE, CBOT, and Merc is conducted in the style of an auction with a combination of open outcry and hand signals indicating quantity (fingers vertical) and prices (fingers held sideways). Each firm's traders wear different color jackets for faster identification. The atmosphere is frenzied. To circumvent the congestion, one member of a firm, ignoring floor rules prohibiting the action, will fold an order in the form of an airplane and send it flying over the heads of rival traders to a colleague.

At the Midwest Stock Exchange, trading occasionally is so slow that members take time out to watch a ball game on the television set in a lounge adjacent to the floor. At the CBOT, CBOE, and Merc, it is the survival of the fittest. Trading at stock, commodities, and options exchanges occurs in a vast area that, stripped of its equipment, would resemble an airplane hangar. The configuration of the trading booths on the floor distinguishes options and commodities trading from that of stocks. Stocks are grouped, usually by industries, at rectangular or doughnut-shaped booths standing flat on the floor surface. Futures and options are traded in pits, movable, usually octagonal-shaped raised enclosures, with steps descending to the center of each. The design's purpose is to contain the many traders within hearing and sight range of one another. There are sometimes as many as 500 people in a forty-foot-circumference pit, and the crush often bends steel handrails alongside the steps. Designated areas of the steps indicate the months in which contracts come due, and the traders go to the section in which they are interested. Buyers and sellers stand side by side because traders constantly go back and forth between buying and selling.

The prefabricated modular pits are constructed on steel legs and rollers, so they can be raised or lowered, enlarged or shrunk, with the number of steps correspondingly increased or decreased, all within hours. Cooling air is pumped through vents in the steps, and the ducts, being flexible, can be easily transferred if a pit is reconfigured. When trading volume in a product shrinks, the pit's size can be reduced; otherwise, trading can be switched into a smaller pit, or several items can be traded in one pit.

Dozens of telephone lines feed into the traders' booths surrounding the pits (the Merc, for example, can accommodate 128 lines at each of its 1,100 booths), with the network designed to reduce cabling requirements, making possible completion of changes in phone locations within hours.

The trading floor is column-free at the Chicago commodities and options exchanges for an unobstructed view of activity and is set several feet above the building's actual structured floor. This allows the raising of the floor mechanically to improve the range of vision for the up to 3,000 people milling around. The walk-in space facilitates the installation of wires and cables between the original floor and the raised trading floor, making repairs easy. The Merc and CBOE also have faster and wider than normal escalators for shuttling traders to the floor.

The explosion in futures and options created the need for a new type of floor designer. The leader in this field is Space/Management Programs, Inc., of Chicago, established in 1973, the year of the CBOE's birth. The firm designs everything from the trading floor to the desk-drawer dividers in traders' booths. The basic criterion is indestructibility because, as President Charles Kinsey candidly says, "They're animals. They destroy anything. They have no sense of the value of materials. Their whole interest is trading." Compactness also is important inasmuch as the average booth is only thirty inches wide. At least 250 items must be fitted into the trading floor area, from clocks, toilets, and shoeshine booths to the price display monitors bolted around the top rim of the pits.

The exchanges are considering various solutions to clear up the congestion, ranging from sectionalizing the pits to instituting computerized, electronic trading off screens to replace the current public auction method. Traders would give oral price quotations to screens in front of them instead of yelling their quotes at other traders. Experiments have shown that just fifty different word instructions would suffice and that the computer could be readjusted if, say, a person had a cold or if it became necessary to screen out background noise. The words would appear on the screen for verification, and an asterisk would indicate that the computer wanted clarification. The CBOE has built its floor to accommodate such a system, and President Charles Henry believes automated trading could become widespread by 1990.

Automation would drain out the frontier character that gives futures and options trading such zest. Fights over what an agreed price was are not uncommon. There have been altercations in which an angry trader has actually hurled another out of a pit. Traders wear protective glasses, such as those used in racket sports, out of fear that their regular glasses would be broken in a fray. Some even wear helmets. Amazingly, several record-keeping clerks, oblivious of the hullabaloo around them, may be seen reading paperbacks.

The traders stake out their special spots on the steps, and it is an unwritten rule that their territory not be violated. When the Chicago

Mercantile Exchange moved into new quarters in 1983, some members arrived as early as 5:30 A.M., several hours in advance of the opening, to lay claim to the twelve or so inches of space they thought were the best place for them to position themselves. Order size also influences where traders locate. "People with nickel-and-dime orders stand in one part of the pit, and woe betide them if they step over the invisible line. If I take a small order to where the big guys are, they yell, 'Billy, get on the other side of the pit with the peasants,' " says William Carroll, a partner in the Chicago office of Fahnestock & Company and a member of the CBOT and CBOE.

Veterans at the CBOE, Merc, and CBOT tend to freeze out newcomers; they feel more comfortable trading with people they know. Also unpopular are the few traders labeled as "slime" or "scumbags" for forgetting a deal or claiming it was for a different amount. Word of mouth quickly ostracizes such characters, backed by daily bulletin board notices regarding which traders' transactions will no longer be accepted by firms processing orders for independent members.

To keep from going hoarse, traders constantly sip water, coffee, juice, or soft drinks and chew gum or suck on lozenges. The Merc brought in a doctor in response to members' complaints of sore vocal cords, but his advice to refrain from shouting was, of course, impractical. A few members turned to a singing coach for advice on how not to lose their voices, with positive results. Despite the pressure, nobody has yet suffered a heart attack at any of the three exchanges, but some members have collapsed from the heat—the temperature can reach more than 100 degrees Fahrenheit. Each exchange has a team of paramedics in case of emergencies.

Despite the state-of-the-art technology, with terminals everywhere—in libraries, lounges, the board of directors' meeting room—traders rely equally on superstitions. Many park their cars in the same "lucky" row in a garage and pay close heed to often outlandish rumors. The ghost cattle of Nevada is a classic case of a few years ago. The price of cattle on the Chicago Mercantile Exchange initially rose 100 points on the rumor that a large herd was missing; then it fell 200 points when another story had it that the herd was actually a new group of cattle; and finally, the price returned to its original level when it was discovered that no such cattle existed.

The Chicago markets started in humble circumstances. The Chicago Board of Trade, oldest of the five Chicago exchanges, emerged from the chaos in the city's grain markets in the mid-1800s. Chicago was the hub of the midwestern Grain Belt and an increasingly important water and rail transportation center. At fall harvesttime farmers brought their wagonloads of wheat and corn to Chicago for sale and delivery to buyers gathered from across the country. The farmers accepted whatever price was offered because there were insufficient storage facilities. Those unable to sell their crops abandoned them on the streets, and when the crops became spoiled, they were hauled to Lake Michigan and dumped in the water.

In the late spring and early summer the reverse situation developed: Demand outpaced supply because of inadequate warehousing. Prices rose sharply, sometimes fifteenfold. In addition, there were no standard weights per bushel or any standard grades for grain. The chaotic situation clearly required the remedy of a year-round central market with uniform practices. In 1848 eighty-two grain merchants formed the Board of Trade and met at first above a flour store in rooms rented for $110 a year. For the first eight years, in an effort to increase membership, the board served a free lunch of crackers, cheese, and ale at its daily meetings. The lunches were halted in 1856 because so many people turned up that the board's finances were shaken. During the Civil War the board sponsored three Union regiments, and it was first in getting medical supplies to the troops after the crucial Battle of Shiloh.

In 1871 the board's building was destroyed in the famous fire allegedly started by Mrs. O'Leary's cow. The board set up temporary quarters in a ninety-by-ninety-foot wigwam. It then wandered from place to place until 1930, when it moved to its present site at the base of La Salle, Chicago's Wall Street. For many years the forty-five-floor building, appropriately topped by a statue of Ceres, the goddess of grain and harvest, was the city's tallest. Two other agricultural sculptures, one of a bearded man clutching a sheaf of wheat and the other of an Indian holding a stalk of corn, are set at either side of the clock above the entrance.

The sculptures represent the board's focus until the end of the 1960s on trading grains along with cotton and cottonseed. In 1968 it launched its first foray into nonagricultural items and began trading in plywood, an idea that was the brainchild of the board's then executive vice president, Warren Lebeck.

Lebeck had worked at the board for fourteen years but had been passed over for the presidency in favor of Henry Hall Wilson, a former administrative assistant to Presidents John Kennedy and Lyndon Johnson. The Board of Trade has a history of internal feuds among staff and members, and the genial Wilson adeptly soothed ruffled feathers. Wilson lobbied acquaintances to push for approval of the board's taking on new commodities products, and Lebeck did the behind-the-scenes preparatory work. In 1973 he finally received the presidency after both a leading Republican and Democrat were considered for the post. The Republican, sixty-two-year-old Agriculture Secretary Earl Butz, serving in the Nixon administration, was rejected because of his age, and former Democratic National Chairman Lawrence O'Brien declined the job. That left the door open for Lebeck.

Back in 1968 he had proposed diversification into lumber to reduce the CBOT's reliance on grain, especially since the importance of grain was waning as a result of a drop in exports. "Forest products seemed attractive because they were not subject to government influence regarding price, and they were in demand because of booming housing construction," he recalls. "Moreover, the price was extremely volatile, an essential ingredient for successful futures contracts. In the winter of 1968–1969 the price of plywood doubled in anticipation that heavy snows in the Cascade Mountains would be followed by spring flooding, which would make it difficult to get into the area to harvest trees. But access was possible, and the price of plywood fell. People who had signed contracts at the higher price suffered terrible losses and could see the advantages of hedging against this happening."

Lebeck found it easier to convince the board's traders to trade in plywood than to sell the forestry industry on the idea. One reason for the reluctance, he says, was that "larger firms did not want another institution involved in the pricing of products over which they had been the main power broker."

Shortly afterward Lebeck introduced trading in silver and gold futures. The board's subsequent leap into financial futures was a defensive measure. It had lost an important part of its flesh and blood in 1973, when it let the newly formed Chicago Board Options Exchange slip away, rather than retain it as an appendage. To the surprise of many at the CBOT and elsewhere in the securities industry, the CBOE did not fail; on the contrary, it became a resounding success.

Fortunately the CBOT had on its staff a young firebrand, Richard Sandor, one of the earliest advocates of financial futures. Sandor had met Lebeck in 1967, when the twenty-six-year-old Sandor, already a professor for two years at the University of California at Berkeley, invited Lebeck to speak to his business administration class. The likably brash and confident Sandor was hired by the CBOT to set up the first economic research department it had in its more than 120 years.

Sandor, now senior vice president, institutional financial futures, at the Chicago office of the brokerage firm of Drexel Burnham Lambert, Inc., remained at the board until 1975. In his job interview with the board he said he wanted to pursue the possibility of financial futures pegged to insurance and mortgage rates. At first his was a lonely crusade. "I received a lot of cavalier, skeptical remarks, but when interest rates soared during 1973–74, many of these people became believers, and I was thrown out of fewer offices," he says.

Sandor's idea for insurance futures remains stillborn. But in 1975 his concept of financial futures pegged to mortgages—in the form of futures on Government National Mortgage Association (known as Ginnie Mae) mortgage-backed certificates—became the first futures contract on interest rates. The Ginnie Mae futures struck a receptive chord, for although more people buy bread than houses, greater attention is paid to the prices of homes and the interest rates on the mortgages than to bread. Since then the CBOT has begun trading futures in a host of other financial products, most notably U.S. treasury bond futures. It has also branched into crude oil, heating oil, and unleaded gasoline futures.

It was the rival Chicago Mercantile Exchange, though, that initiated financial futures. Started in 1874, the Mercantile, like the CBOT, was going nowhere in the 1960s and was looking for new ways to make money. Initially it diversified into livestock and meat, the first time that futures on perishable agricultural products were traded. This attracted new members, including 1983–1984 Chairman Brian Monieson, who retains his loyalty to pork bellies even though he now does more business in financial futures. The button on his jacket reads: "We will sell no swine before its time." His office is a shrine to pigdom; the desk, windowsill, and credenza are covered with pigs— glass, bejeweled, plush toy, and plastic—and a plaque is inscribed: "Hogs are beautiful."

Pigs did little to rescue the Merc from the oblivion into which it was sliding in the late 1960s. Trading in eggs, which had been the exchange's most reliable product, was drying up because the price was no longer fluctuating, a must for the success of a futures contract. The exchange tried to obtain new business by starting an onion futures market in 1967, but it was a debacle. Price manipulation was so rampant that farmers petitioned for help to Congress, which passed a law banning this contract, the only time it has given an edict directly to the exchanges. Until moments before the vote Congress threatened also to outlaw the trading of potatoes, the only other contract the Merc was then trading. Membership prices were so low that the exchange's board of governors bought memberships to keep the exchange afloat.

This downhill spiral alarmed the Merc's young members, and they staged a putsch in 1969, throwing out the old guard administration. Their leader, Leo Melamed, became chairman. "Leo Melamed is Mr. Mercantile Exchange. He is a bright, progressive thinker, who even today remains the power behind the throne," comments Howard Stotler, president, Stotler and Company, a Chicago brokerage house.

Bristling with electric energy, messianic in his zeal about futures, Melamed is an unpublished author of science fiction and a Life Master bridge champion. (He won some bridge contests with Brian Monieson as his partner.) Melamed sees an analogy between "the analysis required in bridge and that needed for the trading market." Being a broker was not his first career choice, and he jokes that he knew so little about the brokerage business that when he was looking for an afternoon job while attending law school, he applied to Merrill Lynch "because with its then name of Merrill Lynch Pierce Fenner & Smith, I thought it was a law firm."

As with all dynamic people who bulldoze their ideas through, Melamed aroused a mixture of gratitude and resentment among Merc members. They showed their appreciation by electing him chairman of the Merc for four terms, although his vote-getting power declined as the years passed. Subsequently he became a behind-the-scenes power broker in the unpaid position of special counsel, a post especially devised for him. In that capacity in 1982 he created a subdivision, the Index and Option Market, for trading futures on options and stock indexes. The $32 million raised from selling memberships in this division helped the Merc self-finance its Wacker Drive building. (Other Chicago exchanges borrowed for this purpose.) The Index and Option Market's first contract, based on Standard & Poor's 500 stock index, is the most successful futures contract ever.

As the Merc throve, petty jealousies flared up. Members groused about the amount of publicity Melamed received and the attention Merc staff gave him in response to his requests. There was also grumbling that he had too much back room power over the selection of the Merc chairmen who succeeded him. All this discontent came to a head in 1984, when the Merc's new electronic link with the Singapore International Monetary Exchange, which Melamed had pushed hard, did not yield the overnight success to which members had become accustomed with other new ventures. The arrangement made the Merc the first U.S. exchange able to trade after hours through the facility of a foreign exchange. The rumblings of discord contributed to Melamed's scaling down his participation at the Merc to concentrate, he said, more on family and business.

Until the 1970s there was no need for a financial futures market since interest rates affecting the price of money remained stable. This stability ended abruptly because of sudden pressure from several directions: a dramatic increase in inflation, the 1971 devaluation of the U.S. dollar, and a credit crunch in 1973 and 1974. A new norm—volatility—had wiped out the era of flat interest rates, and lenders and portfolio managers were receptive to the idea of financial futures contracts for hedging against the fluctuations.

Sensing this attitude, the Merc launched the International Monetary Market (IMM) in 1972. At the time the Merc had only 6 percent of nationwide business in commodities. "It was clear the Merc could not exist unless it traded diverse products offsetting one another," Melamed says. The IMM now accounts for more than half the volume at the Merc. Although Melamed receives much of the credit, the recommendation originated with E. B. (Everette Bagby) Harris, president of the Merc from 1953 to 1979. He had previously been executive secretary of the Board of Trade and an economist in the U.S. Department of Labor.

Around Christmas 1969 Harris began laying the groundwork by hiring Mark Powers, a young professor in the then-abstruse field of futures at the University of South Dakota, as the first economist at the Merc or any other commodities exchange. Powers, who was reared on a Wisconsin farm, had done his doctoral dissertation on commodities markets, a subject at the time so shunned that previously only two papers had been written. Powers was familiar with the Merc, since his dissertation centered on the Merc's pork belly contract. "In 1969 I was a freak in my interest in commodity futures, and my wife was always embarrassed at cocktail parties when people asked what I did," Powers says. Since 1980 he has headed his own financial consulting firm, Powers Research, Inc., in Jersey City, New Jersey.

Powers's first assignment was to develop a new product to wean

The huge, congested floor of the Chicago Mercantile Exchange makes the usual activity at stock exchanges seem quiet by comparison.

the Merc from its dependence on agricultural futures. For advice he turned to the well-known conservative economist Professor Milton Friedman, then at the University of Chicago, who had participated at the University of Wisconsin while Powers was a student there in a debate on the use of futures in foreign currency trading. "Friedman suggested we start with more exotic currencies, such as the Australian dollar, because he felt the government would prevent trading in prosaic ones," Powers says. The idea sat on the back burner for two years because there seemed no need for such a contract. Foreign exchange rates were fixed by the International Monetary Fund, an organization established in the 1944 agreement reached at the United Nations monetary and financial conference held at Bretton Woods, New Hampshire.

Then, to the joy of Powers, Harris, and Melamed, President Richard M. Nixon announced in August 1971 that he was pulling the U.S. out of the Bretton Woods agreement. But at the same time he announced a general price freeze, striking at the very reason for the existence of commodities exchanges: to be a hedge against price fluctuations. Uncertain whether commodities trading was legal during a price freeze, the Board of Trade did not open the day after Nixon's speech.

When Harris received equivocating advice from government officials about opening, he decided to proceed but ordered Powers "to get us in the money business right away." Friedman was hired as a consultant, and within two weeks after Nixon's announcement the Merc had drafted proposed IMM contracts and companion trading rules. Nine months later the IMM opened. In retrospect, Powers says such speed was possible only because the Commodity Futures Trading Commission (CFTC) did not yet exist, saving the Merc the problem of clearing regulatory hurdles. All it had to do was inform the Federal Reserve Board of its plans.

Although the time was ripe for the IMM, and pork bellies had made the exchange sufficiently wealthy to back the new division, many Mercantile members regarded the IMM as a threat rather than a welcome addition. They were concerned they would lose their clout if, as seemed likely, it caused the lifting of what Powers terms "the steel curtain" on appointments to the Merc's board.

To succeed, the IMM needed the major Chicago banks as members. The banks insisted on board membership, plus a slice of the clearing activity. Up to that time the Harris Bank, which had advised Powers about possible foreign currency contracts, had done all the clearing. Subsequently, Continental Illinois, then the dominant Chicago bank and the clearing bank for the Board of Trade, emerged on top with the bulk of the clearing activity. The Harris Bank and First National Bank of Chicago divided the rest. The IMM received a boost a year after it began, when Illinois passed a law allowing foreign banks to establish branches in the state. More than fifty now have branches in Chicago, altering the city's insular image to that of a major international financial center.

While the Board of Trade and Mercantile exchanges are 100-year-old "overnight" successes, the Chicago Board Options Exchange started at the summit. The CBOE was born from the desperation of Board of Trade members over the decline in wheat and corn futures resulting from the grain surplus in the late 1960s. The discussions were headed by Lawrence ("Larry") Blum, who had joined the CBOT in 1951 on his twenty-first birthday. He now has two sons in the business. An art buff, he is responsible for the $100,000 twenty-foot-high by sixty-feet-long glass mural in the lobby of the CBOE building. Chicago's trademark is massive modern abstract sculptures at office buildings, and Blum did not want the CBOE to be an exception.

With the CBOT dealing in transactions pegged to the future, Blum and his colleagues were certain they could develop a similar market related to stocks. They recalled that the CBOT had ventured into stocks in October 1929 just weeks before the great crash in stock prices. Though the timing was poor, the CBOT registered as a stock exchange in 1934 with the newly formed Securities and Exchange Commission. After 1950 no stocks were traded on the CBOT, and members forgot that it could, if it so wanted, also trade stocks. Then, in 1968, the SEC awakened memories by saying the CBOT should surrender the registration if it was not going to use it. The board, which hitherto could not have cared less about its stock market status, reacted like a tigress protecting her cubs. "It precipitated a feeling that politically the board could not afford to lose its ticket as a securities exchange and that in the face of the ultimatum to use or lose its registration, the board should use it," says Joseph Sullivan, the first president of the CBOE and now president of The Options Group of New York, an investment management consulting firm.

The board might not have taken this stand had its soybean and grain traders not been idly sitting on the edge of the soybean pits, enviously watching the equities boom. It formed a committee to study how to regain its securities business. That this would lead to the formation of the first successful new U.S. stock-related exchange in this century did not occur to anybody.

Sullivan, a former *Wall Street Journal* reporter in Washington, whom CBOT President Henry Wilson had hired as his assistant in 1967, was the sole staff member assigned to the committee. As months passed and expenses mounted, CBOT members realized this was no ordinary committee. By 1971, $3 million had been spent, with no tangible contracts to show for the outlay. The work no longer appeared important because agricultural futures were reviving. "If there had been a vote by the membership in 1971, they would have rejected continuation of the study," Sullivan says. "Some members were even comparing it to the Vietnam War, as an endless endeavor."

Originally the plan was to trade stock futures as another futures contract in an additional pit, similar to trading grain and soybean futures. But the wide disparity between regulations governing securities trading and those for commodities trading made this impossible. It became obvious that the solution was to form a separate CBOE in order to keep the SEC away from the CBOT. The CBOT appointed Sullivan, then thirty-six, as the CBOE's first president.

The CBOE began in a smoking lounge adjacent to the Board of Trade's floor. Soon more space was essential since trading was spilling over into the hallways and even into an unused elevator shaft. At that point the Board of Trade suspended a 19,000-square-foot options floor above its own floor. Again the space became too cramped, and in 1983 the CBOE moved into its own quarters with a 45,000-square-foot floor, located behind the CBOT—a floor so large a jumbo jet could be parked in it.

As the CBOE flourished, so did dissension with its parent. CBOT members griped that their money had been diverted to create a new market in which few of them wished to participate. They preferred their freewheeling atmosphere and disliked the more restrictive SEC rules that the CBOE was obligated to enforce. Also, they believed the CBOE's membership rules discriminated against them.

All CBOT members had the right to join the CBOE for $1,000, a nominal fee compared with the initial outsiders' fee of $10,000. Fewer than 20 percent chose to do so on account of a major catch: They cannot sell their seats, unlike the situation at the Mercantile Exchange, where members can sell their International Monetary Market seats. Without the possibility of similarly making a profit, Board of Trade members were reluctant to join the CBOE. Now that CBOE memberships are worth as much as $270,000, their bitterness is even greater.

A symbol of the edgy relationship: Not until 1985, more than two years after the CBOE had moved across the street, did the two exchanges come to terms on the construction of an overhead connecting walkway, even though each building had a hole in its wall for such a bridge. "The antagonisms between the CBOT and CBOE were like the petty squabbles that cumulatively result in a marriage going on the rocks," Sullivan reflects.

It was not until 1979 that the CBOE got its first full-time chairman, Wall Street veteran Walter Auch. He has presided over tremendous administrative expansion. Since he assumed office, both employees and budget have tripled. Joining the CBOE was not an easy decision for him to make. He had worked at Bache & Company (now Prudential-Bache Securities, Inc.) from 1946—when he started as a trainee, having talked his way as a novice into a six-month trial period—until 1963. He then joined Paine Webber Securities, Inc., as executive vice president of its branch office system. He was contentedly settled in New York, indulging in his hobby of collecting race cars and driving them, sometimes as a guest on the tracks at Le Mans and Monte Carlo. He owned a Jaguar, two Mercedeses, and a fire engine red Cadillac convertible, all of which he was to give up because of lack of garage space at his new Chicago home. Instead, he assembles model cars, many of which line his wall shelves.

Although the CBOE offered him less money than he was earning, Auch decided to follow advice his Scottish grandfather gave him in his youth. "When I came out of the air corps after World War Two, I was talking about my ambitions, and my grandfather said in his heavy brogue, 'That's all very interesting, young man, but I would like to suggest that you live every day in such a way that the line behind the hearse gets longer.' "

Auch lobbied his contacts to widen acceptance of the CBOE within the securities industry. To combat perceptions of the CBOE as a gamblers' den, he sweet-talked well-known public figures such as former Illinois Governor Richard Ogilvie, former SEC Commissioner Steven Friedman, and the chief economist of the Chase Manhattan Bank, Richard Zecher, into joining the board of directors. He dictated that the exchange's offices be furnished in traditional decor to project an image of stability and solidity. It was his suggestion that the administrative floor, located above the trading floor, be designed without columns and with a high ceiling, so it could speedily be transformed to a second trading floor if more space were needed. Auch also recruited as CBOE President, Charles Henry, who as president of the Pacific Stock Exchange, had developed computer systems and options trading at the PSE.

The Merc and CBOE owe much of their success to products based on Standard & Poor's 500 stock index. It represents 80 percent of the market value of NYSE stocks and is one of twelve leading indicators used by the Department of Commerce to gauge economic performance. Portfolio managers also use this index as an evaluation yardstick of a portfolio. Its best-known rival, the Dow Jones industrial average, is a sampling of 30 blue-chip industrial stocks.

According to Roy Anderson, director of Standard & Poor's statistical research and index services, the Chicago Board of Trade competed against the Merc for the use of the S&P 500 index. The Merc got the nod because Standard & Poor's executives regarded it "as more experienced in financial futures." The Merc's three-year exclusive use of the index expired in 1985. Anderson says there are no plans to offer the index to other exchanges since "it would dilute its value, and also, we have a good working relationship with the Merc." That makes the Merc happy for the index has pushed it ahead of the CBOT in volume of financial futures business. The Mercantile spent almost $3 million on advertising the index, including free distribution to members of instructional videotapes and eight-page inserts in financial publications.

The CBOE defeated the American Stock Exchange in arranging

to trade an option on S&P's 100 index, derived from the S&P 500, because S&P executives thought it had a greater chance for success in view of its bigger options business. The CBOE had a similar index, called the OEX 100, but changed to Standard & Poor's in order to end the conflict of interest in calculating and trading its own index. Since all 100 stocks on which the OEX was traded were derived from the S&P 500, there was no change except in name when S&P took over the index.

Robert Cruikshank, president of the Nassau Corporation and a past vice-chairman of the CBOE, promoted the 1983 introduction of the 100 index at wine and cheese parties at which he showed the Mercantile's videotape which he had purchased for $30. The option's popularity is a mixed blessing. On many days it accounts for close to 60 percent of all business, preventing traders from obtaining as large orders and good prices in other options as they did before its inception. What puts the exchange in an even more vulnerable position is that the option's fate is tied to market swings, which could hurt if the stock market slumped.

The flashy success of the Board of Trade, the Merc, and the CBOE has snatched away attention from the Midwest, even though it is the second-largest U.S. stock exchange. Formed in 1882 as the Chicago Stock Exchange, it is the only U.S. stock exchange not trading options or futures or both. In 1893 it moved into a $1.1 million building praised by the *Chicago Evening Post* as "unexcelled in the magnificence of its appointments and decoration by any room used for like purpose in this country." The entrance was a large earth-colored archway. The thirty-foot-high ceiling was of colored glass with skylights which filtered through the natural light. The only supports in the eighty-one-foot-long floor were four huge columns, one in each corner, covered in an artificial marble finish and encircled by brass sconces. Sixty-five colors of paint stenciled on the walls gave the room the semblance of a magnificent Turkish palace.

In 1908 the exchange vacated the site, located at La Salle and Washington streets, and in 1972 the building was demolished despite protests by many Chicagoans. A replica of the floor was built in the city's Art Institute as part of the 1979 centennial celebrations, on the suggestion of the exchange's president at the time, Michael Tolbin, now president of the American National Bank & Trust Company of Chicago. In addition, a facsimile of the arch was placed in the Art Institute's garden.

In 1949, afflicted by losses, the Chicago exchange sought strength in numbers by merging with the exchanges of St. Louis, Cleveland, and Minneapolis-St. Paul to form the Midwest exchange. In 1959 the New Orleans exchange also joined. The inspiration for the merger came from the Chicago exchange's ebullient, popular president, James Day. Members' respect for Day, who died in 1967, is evident from the plaque hung in his memory at the entrance to the Midwest's trading floor. It reads: "A marvellous man. He enjoyed people, solving a problem, building something. Jim Day was unique. He was a giant. This man was loved." The wisdom of Day's idea quickly showed up in the balance sheet of the amalgamated exchanges. First-year volume was 59 percent greater than the combined volume of what the separate exchanges had done a year earlier.

Much of the new business resulted from what Day called his "divide and save strategy." He traveled across the U.S. to convince brokers to split their orders between New York and Chicago. "He would say that if a broker had to buy a thousand shares but only half were available in New York, it would be easier and cheaper to buy the rest at the Midwest because by the time the broker waited until more were available in New York, the price might rise," recalls Norman Freehling, chairman, Freehling & Company, a major Chicago-based broker.

(The one midwestern stock exchange that chose to remain independent was Cincinnati's, one-third of which was bought in 1984 by the B&K Securities Corporation, Inc., of Chicago. B&K, named after its founders, Walter Boyle and Bruce Klein, obtained the part ownership in an unusual swap. It owns a computer operation and agreed to provide computer programming to the Cincinnati exchange in return for the right to sell one-third of the memberships.)

After Day's death the exchange selected Tolbin as president. He stayed until 1978 and was succeeded by the part-time chairman Richard Walbert. At the time Walbert was executive vice president in Chicago of Bache Halsey Stuart Shields, Inc. He had been president of the National Association of Securities Dealers between 1968 and 1970. Associates describe Walbert as the "jolly grandfather type

The Midwest is the second-largest stock exchange in the U.S., and does a larger volume of business than the better-known American.

everyone would love to have, who always has a smile on his face and makes everyone feel important."

Behind that smile is a knack for rigorous cost controls aimed at keeping the exchange prosperous. "When he became chairman in 1976, the stock market was in a down cycle, the exchange was losing money, and seats were selling for as low as two hundred dollars; by the time he retired in 1983 seat prices had risen to fifty thousand dollars, and the exchange was profitable," says Burton Vincent, executive vice president of Prescott Ball & Turben, a past vice-chairman of the exchange and one of the members of the search committee that selected Walbert as president. "Dick improved the exchange's finances by discontinuing unprofitable functions and improving the efficiency in processing transactions."

It was Walbert who decided the Midwest should not be in options. It had dabbled in options in the late 1970s but met with little success against the booming CBOE down the street. Furthermore, its entry was ill timed, for shortly afterward the SEC imposed a moratorium on additional options expansion while it studied the whole options market. Walbert realistically recognized a no-win situation, and the Midwest's sixteen options were sold to the CBOE. Half, including the

Ralston Purina Company and Hughes Tool Company, were later among the most successful on the CBOE. Trading options is not a closed issue at the Midwest; the current chairman, John Weithers, says they might be reintroduced and futures started despite the intense local competition "if we have something special to offer."

The exchange's members were so happy with Walbert they made him the exchange's first full-time chairman in 1980. When he retired in 1983, they did not want to lose his talents. He was put in charge of a stepped-up marketing program, with special responsibility for proselytizing the nation's brokers about the exchange.

John Weithers has spent his entire career at the exchange, starting as a protégé of James Day's. Weithers is credited with originating the idea for the arched windows, reminiscent of the archway in the 1893 Chicago Stock Exchange, at the exchange's new quarters, opened in 1985. "Weithers wanted something special, and we went through four models before he was satisfied," says Robert Wislow, president of U.S. Equities, Inc., of Chicago, developer of the project.

Weithers did not confine his involvement to aesthetic concerns. The exchange is a 10 percent partner in an office tower that is part of the project, so it had more than a casual interest in the rental of space. Weithers was delighted to let U.S. Equities use a conference room adjacent to his office for marketing presentations to potential clients. It was not unusual for visitors to see on display different types of faucets, from which renters could select what they liked.

The Midwest is the nation's number two stock exchange chiefly because it was the first U.S. regional exchange to obtain dual listings in NYSE stocks. It takes less time for dealers to move around and complete trades; with one-third the members of the NYSE, the Midwest's floor is far less congested. This advantage is augmented by high-speed electronic processing of transactions and price-saving features for small-order business. "Since all stock exchanges deal in the same product, an exchange can only differentiate itself by providing faster, more efficient service," Weithers remarks.

The Midwest was the first U.S. exchange to clear transactions by mail for out-of-town members, freeing them from paying Chicago firms for this work. It also was the first to provide a centralized, computerized bookkeeping service, saving members from the paper avalanche that forced the closure of the NYSE for one day a week over several months in 1968. During the past five years the Midwest has spent several million dollars to upgrade its processing system, deliberately gearing its capacity for peak, rather than ordinary, volumes.

The Midwest claims to offer customers a better deal by executing odd-lot orders (units of less than 100 shares) at the price of the last preceding round lot (units of 100 shares) trade. Other exchanges use the price of the next round-lot trade, which may not occur for several hours. Because such transactions account for less than 5 percent of its total volume, the Midwest's method is more public relations than business-generating. Members say customers may not benefit since the early price might be higher.

The Midwest professed nonchalance about the NYSE proposal in early 1985 to take over the Pacific Stock Exchange. It exuded confidence that it was not threatened since it is popular with the institutional investors that account for 70 percent of all U.S. stock market business. According to an eighteen-year Chicago institutional trader, these investors perceive the Midwest practices as "cleaner" than those of some specialists at the Big Board. The critics maintain that the NYSE specialist often impedes the auctioneering intention of the Big Board. They claim he may not allow a trade in which a gain will be made unless he gets a share of the business. They further assert that the NYSE specialist often knows in advance how much stock a trader is handling and that he does not fulfill his role of putting his own money at risk. These institutional investors point out that they often hold thousands of shares until the following day's trading, but that a NYSE specialist, assigned the bluest of blue-chip stocks, is likely to carry only an overnight inventory of a few hundred shares.

The Midwest's advocates also say the electronic Intermarket Trading System (ITS) linking the U.S. exchanges and NASDAQ allows a Midwest customer instant access to New York's floor. Members believe the Midwest's new building gives it an advantage over the congested NYSE and Amex floors, where electronic equipment was shoehorned into areas not designed for such developments.

The Midwest is little known by the general public either nationally or internationally. Weithers's habitually funereal expression grows more doleful as he reads the composite transactions section in the *Wall Street Journal*, which provides results of the previous day's transactions for stocks listed on the seven U.S. exchanges—NYSE, American, Midwest, Pacific, Boston, Philadelphia, and Cincinnati—and for NASDAQ and Instinet, an automated stock-trading system. The table is headed "NYSE-Composite Transactions" with the others listed underneath in fine print.

"On the first day the *Journal* ran this table, it called it the Composite National Market System Tape and mentioned all the exchanges in equal-size type. When it stopped and I asked why, I was told, and I quote, that 'little old ladies in tennis shoes would be confused,' " Weithers says. The *Journal* has ended another procedure that Weithers also believes relegated the Midwest to second-class status. "For a while, for trades that were not done on the New York Stock Exchange, the paper affixed an *m* for the Midwest Exchange, and a *p* for the Pacific. The inference was that they were not as good as New York, especially as New York was not marked with an *n*, even though little old ladies in tennis shoes would have understood if that had been done."

Weithers is also irked that the exchange gets little overseas attention. He is displeased that the International Federation of Stock Exchanges, which has more than one member per country, accepted Amex, which does less volume than the Midwest, along with the NYSE but excluded the Midwest. "We do not feel welcome at the federation, even though most of its members have more in common in terms of size with our exchange than with the much larger NYSE," Weithers says. "The federation takes the same attitude as immigrants who land in New York and stay there, rather than move elsewhere in the United States."

The exchange cannot blame its low profile entirely on others. The Midwest's public relations staff consists of one person, while the Board of Trade, Mercantile, and Options exchanges each have a dozen or so employees in that division. Yet even that one employee is more than the Midwest used to have; until 1981 it relied on an outside public relations firm. Unlike the futures and options exchanges, the Midwest rarely advertises. It has virtually no promotional literature; the other Chicago exchanges have reams. Nor do the media pay the Midwest much attention, though there is daily coverage of the other three exchanges. The Midwest's director of communications, Jack Queeney, had to convince *Registered Representative,* a magazine for stock and commodity traders, that it should write about "more than the NYSE, Amex, and Southern California traders wearing shirts unbuttoned to their navel and gold neck chains and standing beside their Rolls-Royce or Mercedes." The magazine listened somewhat; its story encompassed several regional exchanges.

The Midwest is Chicago's overlooked exchange; the MidAmerica is its forgotten one. Established in 1868, it deals in futures contracts similar to those on both the CBOT and the Merc. The difference is that its contracts in grain, soybeans, livestock, metals, foreign currencies, and U.S. treasury bonds and bills are traded in quantities one-fifth to one-half of those at the other markets. As the only U.S. commodity exchange specializing in minicontracts, its chief customers are medium-size farmers who do not produce the volume of crops to warrant buying regular-size contracts at the CBOT or Merc. The MidAmerica also seeks to attract newcomers to the futures markets by offering an opportunity to experiment at less risk than on the bigger exchanges.

The MidAmerica worked hard to be a big player, but it always lagged behind the other Chicago commodity exchanges in taking the initiative both in the development of new products and in marketing. Like a child wearing too-large hand-me-downs, the MidAmerica used only a fraction of the floor space in its building, whereas the previous occupant, the Mercantile Exchange, found the floor far too small. It did only 10 percent of the business of the Merc, and as a result a Merc membership cost more than ten times the price of one at the MidAmerica. Since the MidAmerica's cornerstone is the smaller farmer, its business shriveled when smaller farmers encountered financial difficulties because of slumping markets. The proposed merger with the CBOT would preserve the smaller MidAmerican contacts, which serve a valuable role for smaller investors, and be a logical fit with the CBOT's products, many of which are large-scale versions of those at the MidAmerica.

The moving bug bit all five Chicago exchanges between 1982 and 1985 as business throve and quarters became cramped. Since the exchanges began planning around the same time, it would have been logical and easier for traders and investors to have them centralized in one place, but intramural squabbling interfered. When U.S. Equities President Robert Wislow bought and then demolished the old

La Salle Street railway station behind the Board of Trade building in 1980, he grandiosely envisaged the Board of Trade, CBOE, and CME as possible joint tenants in his projected new building. But the Mercantile Exchange thought it would be humiliating to be located to the rear of the original Board of Trade building, and the Board of Trade had already decided on an annex to its existing site. Wislow made more headway with the CBOE, which was disenchanted with the CBOT's decision to start charging rent based on the CBOE's volume of business. Helped by astute borrowing terms negotiated by self-described "Mister Mean," Lawrence Blum, then in charge of the CBOE's real estate committee, and by Blum's pushing for completion eight months early, the CBOE building cost $9 million less than budgeted. By contrast, the CBOT annex amounted to two and a half times the original estimate.

Wislow next went after the Midwest Exchange. It had never been on good terms with the Board of Trade; their mutual grievances began with a failed merger in the 1930s. Although the CBOT was not part of the project, the Midwest was about to sign a lease in another building, but then President Kenneth Rosenblum countermanded these negotiations. He believed that physically bringing the Midwest near the CBOE would prompt the latter to do more options trading off Midwest stocks rather than turn to the NYSE. It was decided that the CBOE and Midwest would each flank an office tower, but a temporary setback arose: The MidAmerica wanted to build a floor above the Midwest's. When the Midwest vociferously objected, the MidAmerica bowed out graciously because it got a good deal from the Mercantile. The Merc had been unable to persuade either the Midwest or the CBOE to buy its original building. Caught in a bind since it was on the verge of moving into its new location, the Merc charged the MidAmerica only 15 percent of the original asking price.

The power struggle over the buildings was a short-term trouble. The futures and options markets face problems more difficult to solve, for the inevitable headaches that accompany rapid growth are developing. The combustible growth of trading has created an insatiable demand for administrators, and the demand outstrips the supply. Most of the executives are in their early thirties and have moved from exchange to exchange to get more senior positions. This musical chairs has frequently resulted in undoubtedly bright young people being thrust into areas with which they are unfamiliar because of sudden vacancies. Such instances have helped neither the exchange nor the cause of harmony. In other instances, traders have been appointed to the executive suite, in which they have been ill at ease and often ineffectual.

While options and futures business has flowed to Chicago, the national brokerage houses place their business via electronic communications from New York to save the cost of duplicated administration in Chicago. The lone exception is Drexel Burnham Lambert, which runs its institutional futures department from Chicago. "We believe we should be at the heart of the futures market and that it is essential to serve large customers directly from the floors of the exchanges," says Richard Sandor, who is in charge of the Chicago office.

The exchanges have a wealth of material for the growing rank of prospective traders and investors. Much is glorified promotion, but the Board of Trade has gone a step farther, establishing a twenty-four-person education department headed by Lloyd Bezant, a former member of the Office of Equal Opportunity and the Job Corps. The division has written textbooks for all levels of school as well as academic journals, curriculum guides for agricultural country agents, and information for 4-H groups of young people interested in farming. Its work receives high praise from educators. "Their material is extremely useful, especially the *Commodity Training Manual* on the history and function of the futures market, which I use as a standard reference," says Professor Anne Peck of Stanford University's economics department.

In 1983 the Mercantile Exchange established a $1 million chair in finance at the University of Chicago. Its assignments include developing data bases on historic trends in commodity trading. The CBOE has funded research on formulas for options pricing at the universities of Chicago and California. Universities have also responded on their own to the increased interest. In the early 1970s only a dozen U.S. universities provided courses in futures and options; currently there are more than 100 courses and students are lining up for admittance. For example, enrollment at Northwestern University in Evanston, a Chicago suburb, has more than doubled. Starting in 1983, Drexel Burnham Lambert, in conjunction with Northwestern, began one-week semiannual seminars on futures for people in industry. Participants have come from as far afield as Kuwait, Australia, and Singapore as well as from England, France, and Switzerland.

The educational material is helpful, but the basic problem remains: While on the stock market the same stocks remain fixtures for decades, investors must cope with constant flux in options and futures. "Compared with introducing a new bar of soap, it is relatively inexpensive to introduce a new commodity contract," says Mark Powers. The exchanges are swimming in money from their halcyon days and believe that being beaten by a competitor is costlier than conducting a test run of their own. The result is an avalanche of new products.

Their developers and professional traders, whose lives revolve around the market, take it in stride that some products fail, but the average investor cannot afford to be as sanguine. There is little assurance from the exchanges' track record. One out of every four contracts introduced in recent years has failed. Compounding this confusion is the fact that while a product may succeed on one exchange, it may not on another. It is difficult to predict which will succeed.* Consequently, getting investors to accept the latest options or futures product is not as easy as introducing new shades of lipstick.

Options exchanges have exclusivity for their particular products, picked through a lottery supervised by the SEC. The commission has deviated from this pattern by throwing open trading in options on over-the-counter stocks. If precedent is followed, the exchange with the most liquidity will triumph. But there is no lottery system for futures. The Commodity Futures Trading Commission, a federal agency established in 1974, must approve new futures contracts. A jurisdictional struggle over whether the SEC or CFTC had authority over options on futures was decided in the CFTC's favor in 1981.

The CFTC lacks enthusiastic support from industry or govern-

---

* There are nine other futures markets in the United States and some in Canada and overseas. The U.S. markets are: Commodity Exchange, Inc. (metals, treasury bills); New York Coffee, Sugar and Cocoa Exchange; New York Cotton Exchange and Citrus and Petroleum Associates; New York Mercantile Exchange (metals, potatoes, gasoline); Kansas City Board of Trade (wheat, stock index futures); Minneapolis Grain Exchange; New York Futures Exchange (financial futures); New Orleans Commodity Exchange (rice, soybeans, cotton); Philadelphia Board of Trade (financial futures). The American Stock Exchange is planning a financial futures division.

ment. The exchanges protest that the commission takes too long to approve new contract proposals; regulatory critics maintain it lacks the teeth of the SEC, in part because of a big disparity in the number of employees. The CFTC has a staff of only 500, compared with 2,000 at the SEC and 14,000 in the domestic commodity programs and international affairs section of the Department of Agriculture.

Because futures, options, and stock exchanges are straying into one another's territories in the types of products they trade, it is frequently suggested the SEC and CFTC merge, but several government hearings have rejected amalgamation. SEC and CFTC officials meet quarterly to discuss the areas in which they overlap, such as registration requirements. CFTC Chairman Susan Phillips, the first woman to head a U.S. regulatory commission, says her agency emphasizes prevention of manipulation, while the SEC is more oriented to disclosure and enforcement. Her view is not shared by the head of a congressional committee that oversees the CFTC.

Congressman John Dingell (Democrat—Michigan), chairman of the House of Representatives Committee on Energy and Commerce, which shares jurisdiction over the CFTC with the House Committee on Agriculture, castigates commodities trading as a "cesspool—they regularly do things for which one would lose his or her seat on a stock exchange." In 1984 his committee finally pressured the CFTC into establishing an audit trail regarding transactions and better time-stamping of trades. Futures markets time-stamp in half hours; stock exchanges record immediately.

Phillips maintains that the very nature of commodities trading means it will "always have disgruntled people. For every person who makes money, somebody has to lose in futures trading unlike in the stock market, where everyone can make money if the economy expands. It must be remembered that the primary purpose of futures markets is for hedging and not as an investment vehicle and that those people who go into futures strictly for investment purposes can have difficulties."

Whether the computer box will replace the trading floor is a major issue at stock exchanges. Some experimental electronic trading of futures is under way, but it is likely the electronization will be confined to behind-the-scenes processing. CBOE Chairman Walter Auch is convinced that the special nature of options trading will rule out electronization of options exchanges. "Because trading in a stock is almost a mechanical exercise, in which if a stock is trading at a certain price that is what the customer pays, stock exchanges lend themselves to replacement by automatic execution," he says. "But a fractional change in the price of one option can trigger a chain reaction in a whole series of related options. Having people out on the floor creates the necessary dynamics. If they were just in their offices looking at a screen, they might not notice the price change or care about it."

It has taken Chicago's financial futures and options exchanges only a decade to attain the volume it took more than a century for most U.S. stock exchanges to achieve. Now, as they head into their second decade of trading these products, they face the challenge of maintaining that momentum against the more recently established futures and options divisions at stock exchanges. The Chicago exchanges face a bareknuckles battle to retain their supremacy in the trading world of tomorrow.

4

San Francisco/
Los Angeles
(Pacific Exchange)

The Pacific Stock Exchange (PSE) is notable as the only major world exchange with two trading floors located hundreds of miles apart—400 miles, in this case. This singularity stems from a 1957 merger between the San Francisco exchange, founded in 1882, and the Los Angeles exchange, established in 1899. Recently, the PSE escaped by a hair's breadth the distinction of being the first large world exchange to be absorbed by another. The New York Stock Exchange had wanted to take over the PSE and would have reduced it to the status of a subsidiary.

The San Francisco floor is unique also in that it sits atop an earthquake fault. On April 24, 1984, when the severest earthquake in fifty-eight years rocked the area, traders' booths shook, papers fell to the floor, some traders crouched down, and others bolted for the door. In the midst of the panic seventy-four-year-old William Farrell, one of the oldest members, calmly continued writing an order for 20,000 shares so as to complete it before the exchange's regular closing time ten minutes later. The exchange's president, James Gallagher, whose office is located across the street, raced down seven flights of stairs (elevators cannot be used during quakes) and into the exchange's control room to check if everything was all right. He need not have bothered. None of the equipment had stopped working, and by the time he arrived, cheering had broken out over the end of the quake. (I happened to be at the exchange that day, and found that the quake demonstrated Gallagher's good-humored nature. In the midst of checking equipment, he paused to say, "This will be good for your book.")

The PSE maintains that the rivalry between traders in the two cities benefits investors because it narrows the spread between the bidding and selling prices and is often the breeding ground for new trends in the securities industry. The exchange led U.S. exchanges in computerization and was the most outspoken in favor of the 1975 establishment of the electronic Intermarket Trading System (ITS) linking the U.S. exchanges and NASDAQ. The entry of banks into discount brokerage began in California, too. San Francisco-based Charles Schwab & Company, the nation's largest discounter with 1 million customers, is now owned by the BankAmerica Corporation, also headquartered in San Francisco. Schwab is among the three-largest suppliers of business to the PSE.

Most recently, the PSE was a pioneer in permitting full-service brokerage houses to own specialists; hitherto, U.S. exchanges prohibited cross-ownership for fear that a firm's specialists would unethically inform its traders about competitors' orders. The NYSE has had difficulty in implementing a policy similar to that of the PSE because institutional traders, who contribute the bulk of the Big Board's business, protest such tipoffs would occur. In addition, current NYSE specialists do not relish an invasion of their turf by more specialists. Since individuals generate most of the PSE's business and since the exchange has restricted the number of specialists accepted to one-third the number of applicants, the PSE has avoided these problems. The exchange's rewards from this initiative are big: In August 1985, it recorded its highest ever percentage in trades on stocks initially listed on the NYSE that are also traded at the PSE, and many of the NYSE's biggest members, including its leading specialist firm, are now also PSE specialists.

Only a handful of American states have stock markets. That California does is an outgrowth of the discovery in the last century first of gold and then of silver in the western United States. In 1848 San

Francisco's population was just 800. The 1849 gold rush swelled the population to 15,000 as explorers, adventurers, criminals, and prostitutes flocked west to make their fortunes. San Francisco became the financial center of the new state of California, established the next year.

An exclusive market developed in silver mine shares. Brokers privately visited wealthy San Franciscans, and they haggled over a price for the shares. Dissatisfaction quickly arose over this closed circle and led to the creation in San Francisco of California's first stock market, the Stock and Exchange Board, in 1862. It had a rocky start because banks refused to lend to anyone speculating in stocks. So deep was suspicion of the exchange that its forty members were derided as a group by being called the forty thieves and individually, Ali Baba. But as the value of mining stocks soared, the lure of prosperity outweighed any doubts of potential investors about the exchange. During its heydey investors, including clerks, waiters, printing shop mechanics, and grocers, crowded outside the exchange's building, awaiting the day's results. A policeman had to clear a path for exchange members to enter.

It was a period when great luxury and violence coexisted in San Francisco. High society, dressed in silks and satins, attended concerts and balls. Criminals did a flourishing business in vice, gambling, and drugs on the city's Barbary Coast. The rowdiness carried over to the stock market. In one incident a stockbroker named A. J. King slashed the lip of another broker, Charles Sutro, over a missing parcel and then proceeded to knife Adolph Sutro, Charles's cousin, from ear to mouth.

During the 1870s San Francisco installed water and gas, lighting, and telephones and developed its first cable car; this led investors to switch from mining stocks to those of public utilities and railroads. All the activity prompted the creation in 1882 of the forerunner of the present PSE, the San Francisco Stock and Bond Exchange. Started by nineteen local brokers, the exchange first met in the basement of an insurance company, just a few blocks from the current site at 301 Pine Street.

Only one of the founding brokers' firms has survived: Sutro & Company, begun by Prussian emigrants Adolph Sutro, later a mayor of San Francisco, and his cousins Gustav and Charles. The firm is

California's largest independently owned regional broker and has considerable clout outside the state. Whoever is Sutro's president or chairman frequently serves on the board of the New York Stock Exchange. Sometimes both do. No member of the family is at the firm today, but the Sutro name is all over San Francisco, thanks to Adolph. He had made a fortune during eighteen years of silver mining in Nevada, where he built a town near Virginia City bearing his name. In the 1880s he moved to San Francisco and bought up half the city.

Adolph erected a mansion on eighteen acres overlooking San Francisco; he named the estate Sutro Heights. He also built Sutro Baths—four saltwater pools and one freshwater—for the city. In 1894 Adolph was elected mayor of San Francisco on a slate to erase political corruption. He had little success and lost his bid for reelection.

In 1957 Sutro & Company merged with the only other remaining founding member—Berl and Company, a "carriage trade" firm. Warren Berl, now chairman emeritus of Sutro, was the connection between the two firms; his father-in-law was a senior partner at Sutro. "I am the only living person who has been a partner with a father and a father-in-law and survived," he says jokingly.

The exchange's San Francisco address is at the foot of the perpendicular streets leading up to Nob Hill, now home to exclusive hotels and formerly the premier residential district. The building is fronted by ten Tuscan-style columns. At each end are carvings of a man, a woman, and several children. In 1980 about fifty members of the San Francisco chapter of the National Organization for Women tried to chain themselves to the columns as part of their protest in favor of the Equal Rights Amendment. The women said they regarded the exchange as a symbol of an anti-ERA attitude by business. They were foiled by the building's security guards, who had armed themselves with giant wire cutters as a precaution.

The exchange replaced a United States subtreasury building that was vacated when the establishment of the Federal Reserve System made the massive basement vaults unnecessary. The PSE demolished everything except the vaults and parts of the outer walls. At the completion of the renovated building in 1930 members celebrated by setting off firecrackers and marching from their previous ramshackle plywood quarters accompanied by a German glockenspiel band.

The San Francisco headquarters of the Pacific exchange sits on top of an earthquake fault.

Their celebration was doubly joyous because at one point there was concern the exchange might not be able to pay the $2.7 million construction cost. In 1928, when it acquired the site, the exchange was battered by a massive drop in the value of the shares of a key stock, the San Francisco-based Bank of Italy (now known as BankAmerica). The bank was popular with average investors because founder A. P. Giannini made a point of sitting out in the open to be accessible to everyone. This personalization cemented public faith in Giannini and his bank, and people who otherwise did not buy stocks invested in Bank of Italy stock.

In those days brokerage houses had to settle transactions immediately, but their customers had thirty days to pay. When the bank's price began to tailspin, San Francisco brokers were stuck with worthless contracts. Unfortunately Giannini, a genius at public relations, was ill with pleurisy and neuritis in Rome and unable to stop the run on the stock.

On the wildest sell-off day, Monday, June 11—termed Blue Monday—the stock's price plummeted by $64. Newspapers reported that in brokerage offices "old men cried, women fainted, and brokers were frantic." The run on the bank's stock spread to all PSE stocks, and many dropped up to 30 percent in value. Giannini poured $60 million of his bank's money into supporting the stock, but the bank still lost $20 million. No sooner had the PSE recovered from this hammering than the 1929 nationwide stock market collapse occurred.

Sixty years later the market is sounder, but the San Francisco building is showing signs of age. The lighting is dim, and the temperature hot since the high ceilings made it impossible to install air conditioning. Members walk right onto the floor from the entrance of the building; as the exchange grew in membership, space dwindled. To provide for an options division, opened in 1976, an adjoining wall was knocked down. Options trading now spills over into the adjacent building. The exchange once owned this building, which still houses the Stock Exchange Club, an exclusive private luncheon preserve opened in 1929 shortly before the crash. Current members are mostly businessmen rather than brokers. With its Art Deco furniture and plug-in switchboard, the club is very evocative of the 1920s.

The options division swiftly outgrew its makeshift quarters. Exchange officials found a suitable new site around the corner from the PSE's main floor, in one of the few buildings to survive the city's calamitous 1906 earthquake. But under San Francisco's building code, structures must be seismically strengthened after changes in occupancy or in the weight of the existing floor. Since this would have doubled the cost of the facilities, the PSE sought an exemption, saying that the new options floor would hang from existing columns and be above an existing floor slab. The exchange further argued that it would be senseless to upgrade from its third-floor level to the basement since the floors above could still collapse in an earthquake. The city accepted the PSE's reasoning, no reinforcing was installed, and there was no damage in the 1984 incident.

From 1931 to 1985 the Los Angeles floor was on Spring Street, known as the Wall Street of the West. The thirteen-floor building was the maximum height allowed in 1931. The trading floor was the country's second-largest, after the New York Stock Exchange's. Later the area deteriorated and the building also declined. The air conditioning, with vents located precisely above where trading activity did not occur, rarely worked. The elegant elevators, run by operators rather than automatic push buttons, often stalled. Parts were no longer available for the old Western Union ticker tape machines. The new

From 1931 to 1985 the Los Angeles floor of the Pacific exchange was on Spring Street, known in its heyday as the Wall Street of the West.

site, with a trading floor twice the size of the original, is at a freeway exit a mile from Spring Street. The exchange leases, rather than owns, the building.

Having two trading floors has been a financial and administrative headache. The board of directors' monthly meetings alternate between the two cities. Chairman Charles Rickershauser, Jr., is based in Los Angeles but has a secretary in each city. He spends two days a week in San Francisco, and despite the extra cost, his San Francisco secretary flies to the Los Angeles board meetings because she is responsible for taking minutes. President James Gallagher is stationed in San Francisco.

Sixteen telephone lines link the two floors with color-coded buttons. The public-address system instructs traders to pick up a particular color (the red line, for example), a faster and less confusing system than calling out extension line numbers. Western Union hot lines between the floors provide teletype information. Each city's computer order-routing system serves as a backup for the other.

Rivalry between the two cities impeded the 1957 merger. Originally San Francisco was dominant in both population and financial power. But Los Angeles's current population of 3 million is almost five times that of San Francisco, and whereas once the city was little more than a center for selling beef, now it, too, is a major financial and industrial hub.

Consolidation was first broached in 1949 by the chairman of the San Francisco exchange. Negotiation on all the side issues, including a name, went smoothly, but the talks ran aground over what would always be the crucial stumbling block: which of the two cities would get the trading floor. The Los Angeles group rejected a San Francisco offer to make the L.A. exchange part owner of San Francisco's building in return for the latter's having the sole trading floor. "They felt they would be run out of town on a rail by a chamber of commerce type of committee," recalls Richard Gross, a San Francisco member of the negotiating committee and a governor of the San Francisco exchange at the time.

Another San Francisco exchange chairman revived the merger idea in 1956. Under the agreement that was reached, each locale retained its floor, board of governors, president, and chairman. Economic necessity had made the two enemies reluctant bedfellows. "Separately the two exchanges were not big enough to compete with the New York or American exchanges, and it was felt that adding one and one together would make two and a half," says Warren Berl, one of the negotiators. All was serene until 1960, when it was decided to have just one president. The San Francisco president, learning that the Los Angeles president would be chosen, leaked the news to the local papers—hoping that the ensuing uproar would save his job. He got half of what he wanted. There *was* an outcry about San Francisco's selling out to Los Angeles, but the final outcome was that he lost his position. Los Angeles's winning argument was that at the time it did more business—60 percent of the total. Today each city accounts for 50 percent.

Keeping both floors was murder on the exchange's finances. By 1973 a $2.1 million deficit prompted the exchange to propose a merger with the New York Stock Exchange. Despite the NYSE's dominant position, it saw some benefits in that it would then be operating on both coasts. In turn, PSE traders, through special associate NYSE membership, could capitalize on New York's premier position as an exchange to attract more business. But finding the NYSE's terms too tough and its own outlook brighter, the PSE broke off the talks.

The financial reprieve was brief. After the exchange had suffered heavy losses in 1975 and 1976, the PSE's chairman and president, both Los Angelenos, suggested in 1976 that stocks be traded in Los Angeles and the newly opened options division remain in San Francisco. (Los Angeles did not, and still does not, have an options section.) The chairman and president based their recommendation on calculations that indicated eliminating one floor would save $500,000 annually.

The 1976 vote fell a few percentage points short of victory. Another try in 1978 was rejected by four votes. The Los Angeles traders were scared they would lose their best stocks to the San Franciscans who would transfer to Los Angeles under the plan. The options division, which comprised 30 percent of total membership, opposed centralizing all stock trading in Los Angeles because options trading is tied to the movement of stock prices. The concern of the options traders was not solely economic. Many had relocated from the Chicago Board Options Exchange to the younger San Francisco options facility, where they expected to be on the ground floor of a 1980s-style gold rush. They felt ignored by what they viewed as a "club-like" board of governors.

The leader of the revolt was twenty-nine-year-old Douglas Engmann, a former management consultant, who with his twenty-eight-year-old brother, Michael, founded their own firm, Engmann Options, in 1976. They were among the original seventy-six members of the PSE's options division. Douglas patterned his campaign on political elections in which he had been an organizer. "I formed an association of like-minded members from which money was raised to send mailings to all members to encourage them to give us their proxies for the vote. The other side simply relied on the exchange, which supported their cause." Engmann's success was capped by his appointment to the PSE's board of governors.

The dispute triggered a chain reaction in the exchange's executive suite. Four-year President G. Robert Ackerman abruptly resigned three days before the vote in the face of indications that his side would lose. His replacement was the exchange's San Francisco-based executive vice president, Charles Henry. Henry had supervised the installation of the PSE's innovative computerized order processing system in 1969. Later, in 1976, he volunteered to head the PSE's new options division. Henry became the PSE's first full-time president; his predecessors' main job had been the presidencies of securities firms.

"I like the challenge of doing something from scratch," the soft-spoken Indiana native says. "I traipsed back and forth across the country to interest people in memberships and raised over one million dollars, which was adequate to fund the division. I even spoke to founders of the CBOE and persuaded some to buy memberships." Henry was so successful that in August 1979 the CBOE hired him away as its president.

His successor was Rickershauser. He first held the title of president, but within a few months he was promoted to chairman and chief executive officer. A lawyer, who had served as special adviser to the Securities and Exchange Commission and as California commissioner of corporations, Rickershauser had been outside counsel to the PSE. He has put an indelible stamp on the PSE, acting decisively—some might say ruthlessly—to improve operations, including sweeping out longtime staff. His restructuring has shifted the PSE's focus of power to San Francisco, although Rickershauser lives and works in Los Angeles. His obsession to make the PSE a survivor leaves him little time to fraternize. The common joke among staff and members is that "it is easier to see the pope than Chuck," but there is high praise for his accomplishments.

"He has done an outstanding job of cutting costs, while increasing the visibility of the exchange," says John McClure, senior vice president and chief financial officer at Bateman Eichler, Hill Richards, Inc., of Los Angeles. (Bateman Eichler, now owned by the Kemper

Group of insurance and financial service companies, is the second-largest regional securities firm in the U.S.)

Because the two floors are by now a permanent fixture, Ricker-shauser had to look elsewhere to slash expenses. He grouped the marketing operations, hitherto separate for the two cities, in San Francisco, halving the number of staff. The money saved was applied to aggressively recruiting new listings, heightening public awareness of the PSE by exhibits at financial trade shows, and developing books for schoolchildren about the exchange.

Rickershauser has had it tougher making profitable the exchange's clearance and depository system, which checks the accuracy of the buy and sell sides of a trade and handles the paperwork in transferring stock ownership. He first transferred the data processing to outside firms, eliminating the greater expense of doing the work internally. Next, he consolidated the operational functions in Los Angeles—and, to placate San Francisco, moved the research from Los Angeles to San Francisco.

In 1979 Rickershauser combined the chief executive officer positions of the clearing and depository operations. For president, he hired William Crabbe, a thirty-seven-year veteran of Merrill Lynch with a background in dealing with clearing and depository companies of exchanges. Despite these efforts, there were losses, so Rickershauser consolidated all functions in San Francisco to pare costs. To lure large institutional business to the PSE, Rickershauser opened clearing and depository branches in Seattle, Portland, Denver, and New York. Customers could thus deal with the local center rather than via mail with San Francisco.

In 1981 Rickershauser reached over to the New York Futures Exchange (NYFE), a subsidiary of the New York Stock Exchange, to tap James Gallagher, vice president of market operations, for the PSE presidency. Gallagher, who holds master's degrees in English and business, originally planned to teach English literature. He stumbled into the brokerage business as a part-time employee to pay his tuition and stayed because teaching jobs were hard to find.

Gallagher had gained Rickershauser's attention by readying NYFE's floor for operations on schedule in 1980 despite onerous circumstances. "The members wanted changes right up to the opening,"

Gallagher recalls. "They threatened not to trade unless a certain machine was installed, so at midnight preceding the ceremonies, we had cable engineers welding the machine with tarpaulin protecting the floor."

Gallagher's affability is an antidote to the hard-driving Rickershauser. On Gallagher's desk is a glass jar filled with candy resembling peas and carrots, purchased to enable a staff member who prefers junk food to vegetables to claim he eats vegetables. In another goodwill gesture Gallagher revived Los Angeles and San Francisco members joint get-togethers, which had ceased during the dispute over separate floors.

Rickershauser subsequently employed a new chief financial officer, a senior vice president of data processing and planning, and a vice president of options. Then he focused on increasing memberships and membership fees. The exchange was smarting from the humiliation of a seat's being sold for a mere twenty-five cents on April 11, 1978. On the same day a NYSE seat went for just seventy-five cents. The low prices reflected the depressed state of the market nationwide. The PSE reacted by establishing a minimum $100 price, promising it would intervene if the price dropped below that amount. It did so several times in 1978 and 1979.

Since membership fees are a major source of income to an exchange, one way of getting more money is to create additional memberships. In 1981 the number of PSE seats was expanded from 440 to 484 at a cost of $10,000 each. Two years later membership was enlarged by 32 seats, which sold at $30,000 each, an offer made exclusively to existing members, each of whom received the opportunity to buy a seat and immediately sell it for the prevailing price of $53,000. The following year 9 seats remained unsold, reflecting a steep drop in their value.

The exchange's options division at first seemed a further burden on the already financially stretched exchange, but it turned out to be a godsend. The exchange decided not to siphon off options as a separate entity (as the Chicago Board of Trade had done with the Chicago Board Options Exchange), an astute decision since more than half the PSE's members are options traders. By 1984 options contracts numbered more than 11 million, compared with 500,000 the first year. Using the measure that one options contract is equivalent to 100 shares of a stock, options volume on the PSE has become heavier than that of stocks. The surge has required an increase in options staff from 10 in 1976 to 120 by 1984.

"Institutional portfolio managers realize it is important not to put all their eggs in one basket, and we also believe there is strength in diversity," explains Charles Rogers, PSE senior vice president, options. "In 1984, when options volume at the PSE was above projections and equity volume below, the options offset the slower equity business."

It was the first PSE president after the 1976 flare-up, Ross Cobb, chairman of Sutro & Company, who suggested options trading because "a regional exchange needs a broad revenue base." Although the CBOE and the American and Philadelphia exchanges already were in options, Cobb regarded the CBOE as "the only one with a significant foothold since the others were just getting off the ground." The PSE has never considered having twin options floors in imitation of its equity floors in San Francisco and Los Angeles; management is averse to further costly duplication and doubts if it is possible to coordinate the more freewheeling style of options trading. Options feature competing traders in each option; at most U.S. stock exchanges stocks are assigned exclusively to specialists.

The PSE modeled its options trading methods and record-keeping systems on those of the CBOE, but with its own twists. In fact, the CBOE adopted the PSE's procedure for recording orders from the public. The CBOE's system for assigning traders, rather than its own staff, to oversee the order book had sparked allegations of biased record keeping, so the PSE assigned this task to its own officials. The CBOE switched to a similar system in 1979 after winning a court case filed by traders ousted from this job.

The PSE was the first U.S. options exchange with a quasi-computerized matching system for same-day settlement. At the CBOE the buyer and the seller both report the transaction to their firms' data-processing centers. The information then goes to the exchange, where it is sorted the next day before the market opens. The scheduling did not appeal to PSE officials because of the need to complete the work before trading starts at 7:00 A.M. (10:00 A.M., New York

reluctance to turn up before 7:00 A.M.; the earliest
any U.S. exchange, forced the exchange to resort to the
programming.

ions division proceeded swimmingly until a 1981 insider
tra   scandal in stock and options of the Santa Fe International
Corporation, both of which were listed on the PSE. The trades occurred just prior to the announcement by the Kuwait Petroleum
Company that it planned to take over Santa Fe, and the Securities
and Exchange Commission alleged that a Kuwaiti investor and several Swiss banks were involved. Two PSE options traders went bankrupt, and others lost millions of dollars when forced to buy the Santa
Fe stock at a much higher price than anticipated as the time came
for their options to be exercised.

Located in a state known as a high-technology hotbed, the PSE
has done best with a high-technology options index. The success was
such that the PSE wanted to turn the index into a competitor of other
options exchanges' broad-based indexes, inasmuch as its trends often
matched those of the Dow Jones industrial index representing the
market as a whole. Government authorities refused permission, stating that the mirror pattern might not continue since the index rep-
resented only one industry.

California has a reputation for introducing fads, be it hot tubs or
primal scream therapy, so it is not surprising that the state gave birth
to the discount brokerage business. Discount brokers came into existence in 1975, when the SEC ordered that negotiated commissions
replace fixed rates. Discounters charge up to 70 percent below normal rates since they do not bear the costs of full-service houses for
investment advice, tax shelter, real estate, underwriting, and merger
and acquisitions departments. All they do is sell and buy stocks.

The discount brokerage business in California began as a young
man's game. Charles Schwab founded his firm when he was thirty-
four. Stephen McLin, senior vice-president at BankAmerica, was also
thirty-four when he hatched the idea in 1982 for the bank to buy
Schwab. Robert Smith, who suggested his bank, Security Pacific,
move into discount brokerage, saw his career soar as Security Pacific

---

* Insider trading, in which those with access to information unavailable to the public about
a company's financial and business conditions use that information to reap personal profit,
is illegal under U.S. securities exchange law.

Brokers rapidly became the bank's largest subsidiary. In 1984 the forty-seven-year-old Smith stepped up from executive vice president to vice-chairman. James Quandt, the president of Security Pacific Brokers, was the magical thirty-four when he became president in 1983.

After graduating from Stanford University in 1962, Schwab joined a small investment advice newsletter publisher. He later bought the business, but it never did well. A decade later, as the newsletter floundered in debts, Schwab's childhood friend Hugo Quackenbush (now senior vice president of Schwab), came to the rescue. Quackenbush, who was with an investment counseling firm, foresaw the opportunities for a discount brokerage business aimed at individuals if brokers' commission rates were deregulated. He reasoned that the door was wide open because most brokers were considering giving volume discounts only to large institutional clients and suggested that Schwab change the nature of his business into a discount house.

Schwab took the advice and leaped ahead of competitors by employing newspaper advertisements, just as he had done to promote his newsletters. For $1.50 he purchased a picture of himself taken by the *San Francisco Examiner* and used it in ads he placed on the back page of the *Wall Street Journal*, the first time that spot was used for advertisements. Borrowing from the McDonald's billboards that regularly announce new sales levels of hamburgers, each week Schwab substituted the current number of his customers for the previous week's total. He also blanketed the country with branches, like the hamburger chain.

The rapid expansion made Schwab dominant in the discount business but strained its finances because it needed expensive new computer systems to cope with the volume. Security Pacific offered to lend Schwab money, provided it would teach the bank about the brokerage business, but "we told them where to fly," Quackenbush says. Subsequently BankAmerica acquired Schwab.

The bid might not have happened if Stephen McLin had not been getting married in the winter of 1981 and decided to cash some stocks to finance a Hawaii honeymoon. "It seemed silly to pay my broker a big commission on something for which I did not need advice, so I called Schwab and the commission quoted was half my broker's rate," McLin recalls. Mulling this over, McLin recalled that his former employer, the First National Bank of Chicago, had an employee stock desk through which staff could place orders to buy and sell stock. Quick mental price comparison of what it would have cost to sell his honeymoon shares at his broker, Schwab, or the bank revealed the bank was the cheapest with a fee one-sixth of Schwab's.

Shortly after his honeymoon McLin was appointed to jury duty. In between listening to legal arguments, he mused more about the different fee structures. "During jury break I rushed to a pay phone and called the bank's chairman, Leland Prussia, with the idea to buy Schwab. I also told my secretary to call the planning person at Schwab's and invite him to lunch." To cloak the discussions in secrecy, McLin code-named them Project Charles after Charles Schwab.

The merger went swimmingly at the outset. The bank poured in millions of dollars which Schwab used for doubling its customer accounts and improving its bottom line. One year after its takeover Schwab ranked thirty-eighth among U.S. brokers in terms of capital, a jump from number fifty-six, and twenty-fourth in number of employees, up from number forty-one. Symbolic of the strings that bind it to the bank, Schwab planned to move into a new building in the shadow of the bank's headquarters. But the glow vanished in 1985 as BankAmerica posted big losses due to problems in other areas. Management at Schwab, which was profitable, regretted that their company no longer was independently traded—so they could participate in its profits—and expressed the desire that BankAmerica would let go of their firm.

Rival Security Pacific mapped a multiple-choice entry into discount brokerage. It started by using an intermediary, Fidelity Brokerage Services of Boston. When the number of brokerage accounts turned out to be four times its expectations, Security Pacific decided to buy a brokerage firm, just as BankAmerica had. Considering too high Fidelity's asking price of more than $50 million (the same range that BankAmerica had paid), Security Pacific instead acquired small discounters in the Southwest, Southeast, and Northeast. Within two months there were 45,000 accounts, and by the end of the first year, in 1984, there were 250,000. Security Pacific also sells a "how to set up a discount business" program to affluent regional banks. Purchasers must use Security Pacific's Financial Clearing Corporation for clearing their trades.

Despite its feistiness, the PSE remains a regional exchange dwarfed by the NYSE. The Intermarket Trading System, which enables traders to choose the best price for a stock listed on the NYSE and Amex as well as one or more regional exchanges, has not strengthened the regional exchanges to the degree hoped for by its chief proponent, Edward Wedbush, 1975 PSE president and founder and chief executive of Wedbush, Noble, Cooke, Inc., of Los Angeles. Wedbush says that instead the NYSE has done best by "being very careful that the structure of the system maintained the status quo, rather than altering it in favor of the regional exchanges."

At first the PSE placed second after the NYSE in volume, with about 20 to 25 percent of ITS business. It has lost ground to an increasingly pushy Midwest Exchange. The PSE does a greater percentage of trades outside New York for NYSE stocks, but in volume it is neck and neck with the Midwest, with each recording 15 to 20 percent of total volume. The NYSE averages between 45 and 60 percent. The PSE does surpass other regional exchanges in small orders since it does not levy a floor brokerage fee on 100-share orders. In addition, there is no fee for transactions in which an odd lot is combined with a round lot.

Although the PSE is a neighbor to Silicon Valley, the heartland of California's high-technology industry, California securities firms avoid it when they place emerging local high-technology companies on the market. Such companies often shoot to multimillion-dollar proportions. For example, when Ungermann-Bass, Inc., a producer of equipment that electronically hooks together computers located far apart, went public in 1983, it was valued at $300 million, compared with $48 million in 1981. Founder Ralph Ungermann, who owned 1.5 million shares, overnight became worth $27 million on paper.

Most high-tech firms prefer a NASDAQ listing to the PSE or even the NYSE. William Timken, executive vice president of Hambrecht and Quist, Inc., a San Francisco securities firm specializing in taking high-technology firms public, explains: "There is a certain prestige in a NYSE listing, and some high-tech companies do switch from the over-the-counter market to the NYSE. But the PSE is a regional exchange, and other than for some very local companies, there would not be enough exposure if a company were exclusively listed on the PSE." Such California high-technology stars as Apple Computer, Inc. (personal and small business computers), the Intel Corporation (semiconductors), and the MCI Communications Corporation (tele-communications equipment) have bypassed both the PSE and the NYSE in favor of NASDAQ.

High-technology stocks have dipped recently, but in their heyday they made specialty houses like Hambrecht and Quist, founded in 1968, and another San Francisco outfit, Robertson, Colman & Stephens, established in 1969, very rich. In the 1970s Hambrecht and Quist had 50 employees. In 1980, as global interest in California high-tech stocks boomed, it decided, Timken says, "to become an international firm rather than remain in a corner." Four years later the firm had 375 employees in five U.S. locations as well as an office in London, a major source of investment money directed toward high technology. Timken estimates that about 25 percent of Hambrecht and Quist's business now originates in Europe.

Robertson, Colman & Stephens has enjoyed similar success. It expanded from 35 people in 1978 to 110 in 1984 and was still hiring during the general downturn for the securities business in late 1984. High-tech is a relatively young field, making it difficult to find analysts who can interpret what is happening, let alone understand the jargon. "Nobody can know everything about biotechnology, local switching networks, disc drives, mainframe computers, artificial intelligence, robotics, and computer-integrated manufacturing," says Sanford Robertson, president of Robertson, Colman & Stephens. "All that is possible is to get a good sense of those markets." Knowledgeable analysts drive hard bargains over salaries, asking for more than $1 million a year. "In return, they work eighty-hour weeks," Robertson claims.

Because it is located in a time zone three hours earlier than that of the East Coast, the PSE almost became the West Coast terminus of a form of national exchange, under a proposal by NYSE Chairman John Phelan. He suggested in January 1985 that the Big Board acquire the PSE as part of his vision of eventual global trading in securities with multinational investor interest. No name was suggested, but possibilities were the New York/Pacific Exchange or the New York Stock Exchange West. Such a union was meant to be a rival to the nationwide NASDAQ network, the increasing success of which is a threat to the NYSE.

If members of both exchanges and the SEC had approved the

takeover, the PSE, already largely dependent on dually traded stocks listed originally on the NYSE, would have traded all current and future NYSE stocks. The PSE now lists 835 companies, 670 of which are native to the NYSE. Since the NYSE has a total of 1,543 listings, the PSE in effect would have almost doubled its listings.

In addition, the options business of the two exchanges would have been merged. The PSE, which has no broad-based index covering the whole market, would have gained access to the NYSE's composite index option, and in turn, New York could have benefited from the PSE's much bigger overall options volume. A joint venture in financial futures was also contemplated. New York entered futures in 1980 but does far less volume than the Chicago futures markets. A PSE proposal to the Chicago Board of Trade for a joint futures venture was spurned twice in 1982. The PSE persisted in its desire to trade futures. Immediately after the collapse of the merger talks with the NYSE, the PSE became the first U.S. exchange to hook up with the International Futures Exchange (Intex), a fledgling automated futures exchange whose central computer is in Bermuda.

The PSE would have become part of a holding company under the umbrella of which the NYSE and the New York Futures Exchange would also have functioned as separate bodies. The PSE would have been a very junior partner. The value of current memberships would have determined the assignment of shares in the holding company, and PSE memberships in 1984 were selling for just one-fifth the price of those at the NYSE.

The PSE would have kept its administrative staff and its own board, chairman, and president, just as the NYFE does. The PSE would also have retained its two stock trading floors and its options facilities. The NYSE would have paid $20 million toward PSE facilities, products, marketing, development, and promotion.

The NYSE's initial eleven-page proposal dwelt at length on the significance of extended hours for U.S. markets to remain predominant in securities trading but contained no specifics on what the extension would involve. If the PSE stayed open after New York closed, trading in Big Board stocks would have continued without East Coast brokers' having to bear the cost of remaining open longer. In a different scenario, London and Tokyo could have been largely frozen out of the international trading scene through adjustment of the PSE's trading hours. New York, five hours behind London, has slightly nicked London's time advantage by its half-hour earlier opening, effective in the fall of 1985. New York's day now begins at 2:30 P.M. London time. The PSE, seventeen hours behind Tokyo, could have opened and closed later than its present 7:00 A.M. to 1:30 P.M. day. If it had begun at 10:00 A.M. and terminated at 4:30 P.M. Pacific time, its last half hour would have corresponded with Tokyo's first half hour. U.S. investors could then have still done business on the PSE rather than wire Tokyo.

The PSE now stays open until 4:30 P.M. New York time, a half hour longer than the NYSE, to pick up last-minute business from across the country. At one time the PSE's hours extended two hours beyond the NYSE's. It cut back because the increased cost outweighed the revenue. Prior to the NYSE's takeover bid, some PSE members had pressed for their market to remain open for an extra hour rather than just a half hour.

"The NYSE has a big name, money, and talented people; it's the IBM of stock exchanges, and so we have to take a close look at what they propose," PSE President James Gallagher reflected after the NYSE had made the discussions public. There are warm personal ties between Gallagher and Phelan, forged when Gallagher was at NYFE at the time Phelan was its chairman. Gallagher has a picture of New York's skyline in his office and prominently displays a school bell rung at NYFE's launching. Their friendship aroused speculation that Phelan might pick Gallagher to fill the NYSE presidency, vacant since 1984, when Phelan became chairman. However, Gallagher said neither side suggested this, and the president of the American Stock Exchange was appointed.

If the NYSE had wanted simply to facilitate after-hours trading of NYSE stocks, a joint-venture partnership would have sufficed. But the Big Board did not want to be placed in the position of having the much smaller PSE on an equal footing as a partner; the NYSE's preference is always to be in total control.

However, Phelan's proposal proved premature and an embarrassment to him. Usually, NYSE executives do not float such a major innovation without the knowledge that their members are in full support. In this case, PSE members were more receptive to Phelan's proposal than those at the NYSE. The PSE contingent figured loss of identity and control were less important than the probability of increased volume. Most New York members believed their expenses would outweigh any incremental increases in business. Their principal clients, institutional investors—the majority of which are based in New York, Boston, and Chicago—were opposed, too. They did not want the added expense of staying open longer.

If the issue had reached the SEC, it would have had to consider two countervailing arguments: One is that such a deal would have strengthened PSE traders against those on other floors, including those in New York; the competition might have narrowed the spreads between bid and asked prices, benefiting investors. The second is that competitiveness would not have been augmented since NYSE traders were chary of passing on business to the PSE. Also, a merger would have clashed with the congressional mandate to the SEC to enhance competition through the Intermarket Trading System. The debate would have also hinged on how broadly the term *marketplace* would have been defined. When one applies it to the trading of all securities in the U.S. on exchanges, NASDAQ, and related options markets, the NYSE's share is not overwhelming. But in listed securities alone the NYSE is dominant.

The PSE's attitude was something of an irony. Its rival components fought bitterly against ceding even a speck of identity to the other. Yet this exchange, which has learned to weather the onslaught of severe earthquakes, came perilously close to being engulfed by the New York Stock Exchange 3,000 miles away. Only the greed of NYSE members, unwilling to share their business, saved the PSE's distinctiveness and independence.

5

Toronto

What Wall Street is to the U.S.'s investment community, Bay Street in downtown Toronto is to Canada's. The windy intersection of Bay and King streets midway between Lake Ontario and the City Hall is the money capital of Canada. The skyscrapers on the corners house the head offices of four of Canada's five biggest banks (the fifth is a few blocks south), earning the crossroads the nickname of the MINT. The term is an acronym for Bank of Montreal, Canadian Imperial Bank of Commerce, Bank of Nova Scotia, and Toronto-Dominion Bank. The towers, up to seventy-two stories high, also serve as the headquarters for many of Canada's securities firms and for the country's largest industrial corporations. Toronto is the head office for half of Canada's 500 biggest companies. By contrast, New York has only one-tenth of the 500 biggest U.S. firms.

King and Bay are also home to the Toronto Stock Exchange (TSE), the largest of Canada's five exchanges, with a 75 percent market share. The TSE displays many features of the stock exchange of tomorrow. Its technology for automated off-floor trading of inactive stocks is regarded as the world's most advanced. Both the Tokyo and the Paris exchanges have used the system as a model. Paris is paying to try out the system at night in a trial run, and TSE executives are hopeful that other exchanges will do likewise. If they do, the result would be a trading system common to many countries, which TSE officials hope could lead to an electronic alliance of smaller exchanges around the world that would compete with the prospective New York/London/Tokyo axis. The exchange was one of the first to employ touch screen programming, through which traders obtain updated share price information with simple touches of the display screen, and boasts that it provides the swiftest telephone connection between a trading floor and brokerage offices.

So far the TSE's chief rival in selling computerized technology overseas is NASDAQ. The TSE argues that its system handles greater volume because its auction-oriented trading method, similar to that of the New York Stock Exchange, lends itself to aggregating many orders in one trade. NASDAQ's dealer-to-dealer organization permits only one trade at a time.

The TSE believes that isolation is harmful in the emerging global securities village and that electronic links between exchanges can be mutually profitable. In this spirit, in the fall of 1985 it became the first exchange to initiate a two-way trading link with an exchange in another country—the American Stock Exchange (Amex). A similar hookup with the Midwest exchange in Chicago was scheduled to begin at the end of 1985. Actually, the first international link was started with Boston in 1984 by the TSE's rival, the Montreal Exchange, but orders in that arrangement so far only go south because Boston lacks the necessary technology. The TSE-Amex partnership was a logical outgrowth of their already close ties: Two-thirds of the foreign firms listed on Amex are Canadian—mostly oil companies—and they account for slightly more than 25 percent of Amex business. Nevertheless Amex was the TSE's second choice. The TSE had first approached the NYSE but was rebuffed because the NYSE does relatively little business, compared with overall volume, in the two dozen interlisted Canadian stocks.

TSE President Pearce Bunting, an avid proponent of electronization of exchanges and of global linkages, is pursuing opportunities that combine both. The TSE's Computer-Assisted Trading System (CATS) is unique among world exchanges in its ability to receive or-

ders electronically from abroad and direct them straight to the trading floor, the exchange's automated small-order execution system, or
the traders' booths around the floor. All that is necessary is that a
terminal in another country be connected to the same telecommunications switching network as the TSE. Already several TSE member
firms with offices in London are engaged in a trial run, using the
network to send orders for Canadian stocks to Toronto.

Not only is Toronto's technology in the vanguard, but it is also representative of global trends toward dissolving the barriers separating
financial sectors, such as banks and securities firms, and opening the
door to increased foreign ownership. In urging deregulation of what
Canadians term the four pillars—the securities industry, insurance
firms, banks, and trust companies (the Canadian version of U.S. savings and loan associations)—Canadian government officials are ahead
of those in the U.S., where the issue remains unresolved despite years
of debate. Canadian authorities maintain that deregulation will give

*The Toronto Stock Exchange, near the windy corner of Bay and King streets,
stands at the hub of the money capital of Canada.*

consumers a greater choice in their financial purchases and that expanded foreign ownership will infuse much-needed capital into the
investment industry.

But the securities industry, as the smallest of the four pillars, feels
the most vulnerable. It is concerned that financial trade and power
could wind up in the hands of a few huge conglomerates and dimin-
ish or wipe out smaller brokers. Even though the combined capitalization of the country's ninety-eight securities firms has doubled since
1979, the total is still less than the assets of the smallest of Canada's
Big Five banks. The Canadians see no incongruity in their desire to
bar outsiders, especially Americans, from owning Canadian businesses at the same time as they are invading the U.S. in order to
expand their revenues. Within weeks of much of the industry's decrying the government's plans to permit more foreign ownership, a
dissenter to the outcry, Nesbitt Thomson, Inc., one of Canada's top
ten dealers, became the first Canadian firm to buy an American investment house—medium-size Fahnestock & Company of New York.

The crumbling of the pillars is destroying the clublike nature of
Canada's investment community. Many senior executives attended
the same private schools and married into one another's families. Their
offices ooze old money: the oriental rugs, the china cabinets filled
with Wedgwood, the spiral staircases connecting the two or more floors
most firms occupy, the walls lined with huge abstract or landscape
paintings, the Eskimo carvings or modern sculpture, and the vast reception areas where the only noise is the ticking of a grandfather clock.
Glass windows provide spectacular panoramas of Toronto's water-
front. For lunch, the "club" walks a block north of King and Bay to
the exclusive Winston's where tables are reserved on a yearly basis,
their route taking them through the chic underground shopping
concourses interconnecting the King and Bay towers.

In the midst of this homogeneity, there is a notable exception: Joseph Pope, the crusty, opinionated founder and president of Pope &
Company, the sole remaining unincorporated proprietorship in the
Investment Dealers Association of Canada. In his mid-sixties, Pope
delights in going counter to every prevailing theory in the investment world. With his Victorian, no-nonsense approach, Pope &
Company is unique in not entertaining clients at lunch, eschewing

financial news wires, and forbidding customers from buying stocks on margin. "By definition, it means the customer is overextended," Pope says.

Pope avoids the herd at King and Bay and boasts that his office, located a few blocks west, is "the only one in Canada with a sidewalk front door." The district was once known as "legislation, education, salvation, and damnation" after the government offices, private boys' school, church, and tavern located opposite one another. Pope & Company's annual reports are filled with multisyllabic words, picked from the fourteen dictionaries in Pope's office, and are written in the style of a nineteenth-century novel. While other Toronto brokers relax by golfing or raising horses, Pope has a more unusual sideline: He is the president and major shareholder of the Park Lawn Cemetery Company Ltd. of Toronto. Pope & Company acquired the cemetery in 1977, when it purchased a small Toronto investment house that specialized in unlisted industrial shares, including those of the cemetery.

Forming the TSE in 1852, eighteen years after Toronto's incorporation and fifteen years before the Confederation of Canada, was an act of faith that Canada would become industrialized at a time when farming, forestry, and fishing were the primary occupations. The commercial enterprises that did exist were too small to seek public listing.

Business on the exchange was limp, and by 1867 the daily half-hour sessions had been reduced to weekly ones. Between 1869 and 1871, following the failure of three major banks, the TSE suspended operations. Later the rival Standard Stock and Mining Exchange, started in the late 1880s, surpassed the volume on the TSE. In 1934, suffering from the depression, the two exchanges decided to merge despite their differences. TSE traders did not regard those at the Standard as social equals since they did not belong to the Toronto Club, the city's snootiest private men's club. Standard members were more boisterous than Toronto members. Once, when pigeons flew in through the Standard's ceiling, a trader bought a rifle at the neighboring gunshop and killed the birds.

The merger necessitated larger quarters, and the combined exchange bought property on Bay Street from Henry Pellatt Jr., builder of Toronto's Casa Loma, a $3 million,* ninety-eight room chateau. Opened in 1937, the new TSE featured the Art Deco style so beloved by North American exchanges. By the 1970s it was one of the few buildings in the city that still had elevator operators rather than automatic push buttons.

Canadians suffer from an inferiority complex, believing their history boring compared with that of Europe and of the U.S. This may be why the TSE makes a point of spotlighting its worst scandal, the 1964 collapse of Windfall Oil & Mines Ltd., in its promotional film for visitors. In the middle of the movie there is a picture of a tiny, vivacious middle-aged brunette, Viola MacMillan. President for twenty-one years of the Canadian Prospectors and Developers Association, she controlled Windfall with her husband, George. On the strength of rumors of a major mineral strike by Windfall, the company's shares climbed from 31 cents to $5.50 in just fifteen days. The stock collapsed later when it was discovered Windfall's property was merely a cow pasture. Sentenced to a nine-month prison term, Mrs. MacMillan was paroled after two months and fined $10,000 for stock manipulation.

The episode did not end there. A director of the Ontario Securities Commission (OSC) was forced to resign when it was found that he and his wife, both friends of the MacMillans, had traded in Windfall shares at the very time he was urging the commission not to call for the TSE to suspend trading in the company. An investigative commission appointed by the province of Ontario lambasted the TSE for acting like "a private gaming club." The TSE and OSC tightened their rules, and the OCS's regulations became a yardstick for Canada's other securities regulators.

That the TSE is at its present site stems from a quirk of fate. The builder, Olympia & York Developments Ltd. of Toronto, one of the world's biggest privately held developers and owner of many of the buildings around Wall Street, originally had signed an insurance company as the main tenant. Following a disagreement, the insurer withdrew, leaving Olympia & York scrambling for a replacement. Fortunately for the developer and the exchange, the TSE was then looking for a new, bigger site. Because Olympia & York was desper-

---

*All dollar figures cited in this chapter are in Canadian dollars. From January to the end of July 1985, the Canadian dollar averaged 73 cents U.S.

ate to rent the space, it is leasing the trading floor area to the exchange, which took it in 1982, at a token $1 a year. It also named the skyscraper the Exchange Tower.

The rent is cheap, but the furnishings cost the exchange $26 million. It spent the money on bird's-eye maple for the telephone booths, brass entrance doors, mahogany trading posts, and the latest in computer and telecommunications technology. TSE floor staff call the floor high-tech heaven since about $1 million worth of computer equipment is stuffed into each of the five trading posts. The computers provide more auxiliary information on prices at other markets and more last trade information than is available at any other major exchange.

Toronto's trading methods are largely identical to those at U.S. exchanges. One dissimilarity is that instead of the U.S. specialist, the TSE has the registered professional trader, nicknamed the pro. As with the specialist, a number of stocks (eight at the TSE) are exclusively assigned to a pro, but unlike the U.S. specialist, he does not have a limit order book for brokers to leave limit orders (those with specified top prices) if they cannot be filled immediately. Instead, TSE traders must fill such orders on their own, although the pro acts as a traffic cop in bringing them together. He is therefore not eligible for the handling fee a specialist receives. The pro is exempted from paying commission on any transactions he makes for his own account in the stocks traded at the trading post at which he is stationed.

Toronto trades equities, options, and futures in one place. Such side-by-side trading was prohibited until 1985 in the U.S. for fear it would trigger market abuses. Toronto is confident its surveillance system can prevent misconduct, although the weak futures and options trading has not fully tested its ability.

The touch screen technology enables traders to request detailed trading data on each stock while the press of a button on their telephone instantly connects traders and their offices. Bell Canada, which developed the system, is trying to sell it to the New York Stock Exchange. Planning for future growth, Bell installed 6,000 telephone lines at the TSE, but only one-third are currently in use. Also singular are a sectored air-conditioning system capable of channeling cool air to areas where there are large congregations of traders, a nonglare acoustical ceiling, and carpeting on the trading floor.

President Pearce Bunting's prediction of a future of electronic trading contradicts his claim that the cavernous floor, triple the size of its predecessor and much bigger than the present volume of activity dictates, was necessary to allow for expanded trading. The exchange introduced the use of pocket pagers to relay coded messages to traders since the area's size prevented shouted instructions. Traders still complain the distant placement of the trading posts makes it impossible for them to know intuitively from the decibel level if there is a rush to buy or sell. In addition, smaller firms have had to hire bigger staffs, an expense they begrudge, because the space between trading posts is far too great for one person to get back and forth. Even the carpeting, meant to provide comfort and muffle sound, has annoyed some traders both because their shoes get caught in the material and because it is not sufficiently thick to keep the steel floor underneath from producing calluses. Many have followed the example of Harry Abbey, a fifty-five-year member, who switched to soft-soled gardening shoes from leather ones.

The luxurious trading floor, much of it unused, and the high cost of rent for the five staff-occupied floors instead of the three that members expected badly hurt the exchange's finances. The exchange barely scraped into the black in 1983 and 1984. Some angry members demanded Bunting's resignation, but the storm died down after he had cut back on floor space and staff, on orders from the newly elected chairman, Robin Younger, chief operating officer of Canada's largest securities firm, Dominion Securities Pitfield Ltd. Bunting did keep the exchange's public reference economics library, unique among exchanges in its extensiveness, but the layoffs elsewhere triggered a union drive by retained employees, scared about their job security.

A systems and high-technology buff, with an extensive home library of management books, Bunting initiated the TSE's first ever management-by-objectives program, involving organizational restructuring, specific goal setting, and frequent reevaluation. His technological bent fitted the TSE's penchant for innovation, which had featured, for example, its pioneering in the 1930s the use of teleregisters for signaling price changes at trading posts. It was Bunting who urged the creation of a computer-run system in inactive stocks. When a Bell Canada study declared the system would cost as much as $28 million, two TSE staff members volunteered to develop it, and the price tag ended up under $5 million. Covering 820 relatively inactive stocks out of the 1,350 listed on the exchange, the system is monitored by 3 people; 100 TSE staff members are required on the floor to handle operations for the remaining stocks.

Normally, whenever the U.S. investment industry revamps itself, Canada is the first country to follow. In this spirit the Canadian investment community was the first to copy the American move to negotiated commissions, discount brokers, and banks with discount brokerage divisions. Canadian securities dealers could live with these changes because their impact was slight. The discount business, introduced in 1983, accounts for less than 3 percent of total Canadian investment activity. Only one of the country's Big Five banks, the Toronto-Dominion (the smallest of the five), quickly established a discount division called Green Line Investor Service. It has made little headway since Canadian investors, more conservative than their American counterparts, prefer the full-line securities houses that also offer investment advice. On most days the Green Line does only twenty-five trades.

Because the traditional securities houses remained strong, they willingly coexisted with these changes. What most oppose, though, is further deregulation permitting banks to issue securities as well and to purchase up to 30 percent of an investment firm. Current legislation restricts Canadian banks from owning more than 10 percent of other financial institutions. Most of Canada's securities firms argue that they lack the strength to compete against the country's much larger banks.

Although the government does not prohibit the banks from entering fully into brokerage services outside Canada, no bank took advantage of this loophole until late 1985. The establishment in London of a brokerage subsidiary by the Royal Bank of Canada, the country's largest bank, is regarded as a sign that the banks believe the constraints against them in Canada will soon disappear. The other major Canadian banks are expected to quickly follow the Royal's lead.

Canada has a national banking system with only 9 major banks, compared with the U.S. regional system of 14,000. The Big Five banks could swamp the securities firms in number of branches, for they have more than 7,000 and the dealers a total of 450. Being able to offer banking and insurance services would be of little value to the Canadian dealers since they lack the financial resources to handle more than their own line of business.

The clubby securities industry dreads outside competition at a time when a maverick within its own ranks is making life tougher. Until 1984 bought deals—in which one securities firm or a small group of firms buys all of an underwriting issue rather than the conventional syndication among many houses—were rare in Canada. Then, in May of that year, a mid-size firm, Gordon Capital Ltd., used a bought deal to snatch away a $228 million underwriting for the Royal Bank, which traditionally had dealt with five establishment securities houses. Such deals are now common and have severed the generations-old loyalties between clients and their longtime securities dealers. Profits are also pinched because the size of the transaction enables clients to demand lower commission rates from their investment dealers. Because decisions to do bought deals must be lightning swift so as not to lose them to competitors, the investment houses yield to their clients' terms. The commissions on bought deals average 1 percent, compared with the usual 3 percent. Along with a 12 percent decline in trading value from the record set in 1983, higher expenses, and the new negotiated rates, bought deals depressed TSE members' combined profit in 1984 to $34 million, compared with $110 million in 1983. Half wound up with losses. Higher volume in 1985 improved the industry's bottom line, but bought deals kept the recovery below what it otherwise would have been.

Canada's regulatory tangle may buy the investment community time. Eliminating the four pillars raises a thorny constitutional problem because not all are under the same jurisdiction. The banks are covered by federal law, the trust and insurance companies by federal and provincial rules, and the investment industry by provincial legislation. Provincial laws often vary from province to province, compounding the confusion. Regulators, though, are considering uniform rules on matters of nationwide concern as a prelude, perhaps, to a federal securities and exchange commission in Canada. Currently the Ontario Securities Commission is treated as a guidepost by similar authorities in other provinces, but not all its regulations are copied. The provincial commissions lack statutory authority, and their recommendations to alter or dump ordinances must be accepted by the governments, which then have to submit changes to provincial legislature votes.

Although barriers against Canadian membership on the New York Stock Exchange were lifted in the late 1960s, the Canadian financial community, concerned about protecting itself from foreign competition, did not reciprocate. Since 1971 single foreign ownership of Canadian stockbrokers has been limited to 10 percent, and total foreign ownership to 25 percent. Firms already controlled by nonresidents were allowed to remain under a grandfather clause, but only three of the twenty-six stayed. They are Merrill Lynch Canada, Inc., Bache Securities (a subsidiary of Prudential-Bache Securities, Inc. of the U.S.), and the Dominick Corporation (a subsidiary of Dominick & Dominick, Inc., of New York).

Several U.S. companies already own the 10 percent maximum allowable to a single foreign owner. They include Citibank, which has its stake in Canada's tenth-largest broker, Walwyn Stodgell Cochran Murray Ltd. of Toronto, and Shearson Lehman Brothers, Inc., which owns 10 percent of McLeod Young Weir Ltd. of Toronto, also a top ten firm. McLeod Chairman Austin Taylor is enthusiastic about the arrangement. "We wanted to enter the commodities business but knew little about it and had insufficient capital to pay for the costly infrastructure necessary to execute such business. The Shearson connection enables us to participate without this expense because we can utilize Shearson's research in U.S. securities, which has helped double our activity in this area."

The combined capital of Merrill Lynch, Bache, and Dominick equals only 10 percent of the Canadian industry total. But foreign ownership could swell if the Ontario legislature were to approve an Ontario Securities Commission proposal to widen the proportion all foreign firms together can own to 30 percent. No single firm could control more than 1.5 percent.

Gordon Capital's bought deals indirectly triggered the OSC's activity. In order to finance more such deals, the firm wanted to secure an influx of outside money and approached a large Belgian financial company, the Lambert Brussels Corporation, to be a 40 percent partner. Because the proposed holding would have exceeded the 10 percent that a foreigner can have in a Canadian broker, the OSC, itching to study the matter anyway, used the situation as a springboard to start its examination.

On its own, the suggested extension would alarm the industry, but because of the already strong inroads by outsiders into Canada's relatively small market, it seems even worse. Foreign firms have snipped away at the Canadian share of domestic underwriting, slicing it from a blanket 100 percent in 1973 to 71 percent. Merrill Lynch Canada has become one of Canada's ten largest investment houses. It upstaged its Canadian competitors by becoming the first broker in Toronto to have a tower bear the firm's name. Nesbitt Thomson, Inc., the large Canadian broker, which moved into the building before Merrill, had not thought of asking for the building to be named after it. Only one Canadian firm, Dominion Securities Pitfield Ltd. of Toronto, the product of two mergers since 1981, has more than $100 million in capital, and a mere nine firms have more than $25 million. The capitalization of Merrill Lynch, the largest U.S. broker, is nearly two and a half times that of Canada's entire investment community.

Stock exchange listing was opened to Canadian brokers in 1983. Only four of Canada's top ten investment dealers have turned to the market to increase their capitalization. Just a minority interest was offered. Merrill Lynch is 100 percent publicly owned. Canadian firms were right to be cautious since investment in their shares has been shallow. Unfortunate timing is one reason. Usually Canadian economic trends follow those in the U.S., but this pattern was broken in 1984, when the TSE had a lackluster year compared with records set at the NYSE. The TSE slump resulted from concern over whether growth in the U.S. would slow down and trigger decreased American demand for Canadian exports.

Another reason for the lackluster performance of brokerage house shares is that the percentage of Canadian adults who invest in the stock market is half that in the U.S. It is also hard to attract foreign investors. When they consider investing in the North American market, foreigners automatically gravitate toward the larger NYSE. "Certain markets like New York always draw capital, and institutional investors can justify the expense of hiring one person solely to follow the New York market; but Canada is lumped in with other countries," says Eric LePeu, manager of the Paris office of Loewen Ondaatje McCutcheon Ltd. of Toronto. "Therefore, we have to be more aggressive than U.S. brokers, because foreign investors who want to buy a popular stock like IBM don't need brokerage advice, whereas we must educate potential investors about Canadian companies."

Inasmuch as Canada's population is only one-tenth that of the U.S., Canadian brokers have a history of looking outside the country for other opportunitites. Wood Gundy, Inc., of Toronto, which has the biggest commitment to foreign markets among Canadian brokers, is the first investment firm in a Western country to have gone to the People's Republic of China. In 1984 Gundy formed a joint venture, based in Shanghai, China's financial center, with Ralph Franklin Calatchi, an international investment banker and economist fluent in Mandarin, to scout out investment opportunities, including the possible syndication of bond issues. In 1916, just nine years after its founding in Canada, Gundy opened a New York office, and it was the first Canadian broker to enter the U.S. real estate syndication business. In 1984 it began offering investors limited partnerships in Florida office and apartment buildings.

While Canadian firms such as Gundy stretch outward, the economic nationalism of the Pierre Trudeau government further scared off both foreign and domestic investors. Between 1980 and 1983, at the height of anxiety over Trudeau's measures, investments held by Canadians in U.S. stocks rose a whopping $5 billion (U.S. dollars), according to the balance of payments division of the U.S. Department of Commerce. Trudeau retired in 1984. Pearce Bunting hopes the TSE's links with the American and Midwest exchanges will repatriate much of the outflow of Canadian money as well as regain foreign investors who sold off $2 billion worth of Canadian investments from 1981 through 1984. The foreigners, soothed by the warm welcome of the present government of Brian Mulroney towards outside investment, are slowly reinvesting in Canadian stocks. U.S. exchanges now handle more than half the value of trading in Canadian-based interlisted stocks. The southward drain in Canadian business is substantially due to Canada's lack of a national intermarket trading system in which orders are transacted at the exchange offering the best price in interlisted stocks. The smaller Canadian exchanges favor a Canadian version, but the TSE opposes it for fear it would draw business away from Toronto.

Investors are also wary because less research analysis on the market is available in Canada than in the U.S. Research departments are relatively new to Canada. It was not until 1957 that Wood Gundy introduced formal research to the Canadian marketplace. "Previously researchers were called statistical clerks and stayed only two or three years in that job," Robert Morgan, the company's first research director, recalls. "There had been no demand in Canada for analysis because investment firms concentrated on underwriting and distributing new issues."

Canada has few stock market gurus comparable to the U.S.'s Joseph Granville, who has single-handedly swayed prices on Wall Street. There are only four authors of newsletters on the Canadian market, this following an Ontario Securities Commission crackdown on such tip sheets in the late 1960s to protect investors against touters of pie-in-the-sky mining stocks. When Canada's best-known forecaster, Ian McAvity, left a Toronto broker a decade ago to start his technical chart analysis *Deliberations,* the OSC no longer had any suitable application forms around for him to file. McAvity deals with major world markets, not just Toronto, and two-thirds of his subscribers live outside Canada.

Besides the Toronto exchange, Canada has exchanges in the three western cities of Winnipeg, Calgary, and Vancouver as well as one in Montreal. A fledgling version of the very successful NASDAQ, termed the Canadian Over-the-Counter Automated Trading System (COATS), started in late 1985. Vancouver specializes in inexpensive "penny" mining stocks of little-known junior companies, some of which Toronto exiled after the Windfall Mines affair. The speculative nature of the Vancouver exchange has attracted strong international interest; U.S. investors account for one-third of the volume, Britishers for 10 percent, and continental Europeans for another 10 percent. But the exchange's laxer rules have gained it the hard-to-shake image of a Wild West casino. Even overseas representatives of the Canadian banks, in giving talks on the Canadian market, warn about the risks of Vancouver, emphasizing the point by showing Canadian newspaper stories about the exchange's problems.

Despite its national-sounding name, COATS is beginning as a provincial operation in Ontario with indefinite plans to go countrywide. No longer will the telephone be needed to determine the best price or next-day reporting of bid and asked prices; COATS will electronically supply up-to-the-minute information as NASDAQ does. Also like NASDAQ, COATS will have multiple market makers in stocks. Only 100 of Canada's 2,300 OTC stocks trade actively because financial institutions take little interest in the market. But if COATS parallels NASDAQ, its electronic system will make it a rival to the traditional stock exchanges.

Where the system differs from NASDAQ is in its administration. The U.S. electronic over-the-counter market is run by the National Association of Securities Dealers (NASD), which is registered with the SEC and has responsibility for maintaining business ethics among its broker and dealer members. In Canada, because there is no federal securities regulation, the Ontario Securities Commission supervises the unlisted market in Ontario. It has the power to designate an agent to disseminate over-the-counter information, a task handled by the Investment Dealers Association (IDA) of Canada until 1984.

When the IDA relinquished the job, the OSC decided an electronic system was necessary because the existing rudimentary method was not keeping the public informed. As was the case before the NASD went electronic, bid and asked prices in Canada's over-the-counter market were not available until they appeared in the following day's newspapers.

The OSC polled a combination of five companies and exchanges about their interest in assuming responsibility for dispensing the information. Just two—the TSE and a small Toronto securities firm—applied, and the OSC chose the TSE. Its role will be confined to supplying a computer and software programming to COATS, for which it will be paid. NASDAQ, on the other hand, does this work itself. John Leybourne, OSC deputy director of enforcement, says the commission does not foresee COATS's breaking away to become a separate NASDAQ type of entity.

The chief rival of the TSE is the freshly emboldened Montreal Exchange.* During the four-year tenure (1981–85) of its aggressive young president, Pierre Lortie, the exchange's share of the $36 billion value of stocks traded in Canada rose to 19.5 percent from 10.3 percent. It listed fifty more companies and the exchange now does

*The exchange has dropped the word "stock" from its name to reflect its expansion into options and futures.

28 percent of options volume in Canada, compared with 13 percent in 1981.

Pragmatically accepting the reality that the TSE is well ahead in Canadian volume of business, the Montreal Exchange has set its sights higher: to become a major international player. It is gleefully slaloming around the bigger North American exchanges in the fiercely competitive quest for international listings through a novel procedure among world exchanges. Introduced in late 1985, the method waives Canadian listing requirements for firms that met stipulations for listing in their home countries. By contrast, foreign companies seeking listing on a U.S. market must comply with SEC disclosure rules and American accounting standards as well as issue fresh prospectuses, a process that discourages many firms.

No cumbersome paperwork is involved in the Montreal system. Canadian investors buy a foreign stock listed on the exchange without the stock's actually being delivered; instead, the foreign depository system retains the certificate, and the transaction is flipped via computer into Montreal's depository records. Exchange officials also tout the system as a handy entry to overseas markets for U.S. investors without their having to purchase American Depository Receipts. Instead, since Canadian and U.S. depositories already are electronically linked, a three-way flip by investors from the U.S. to Canada to Europe is possible.

Furthermore, Robin Schweitzer, vice-president, development, says there is a nifty offshoot: The exchange is inviting foreign banks both to list and to become the specialists in their stocks, thereby increasing the exchange's trading population. (The Quebec Securities Commission allows the Canadian subsidiaries of foreign banks to be traders.) The exchange initially is canvassing continental Europe, capitalizing on the fluent French of its staff and the fears of the Paris, Zurich, and Frankfurt exchanges of being eclipsed by the reconstituted London exchange. Preliminary discussions are also under way with Japan.

The listing drive comes on the heels of Montreal's becoming part of the first global network in the trading of options. The other participants in the system, called the International Options Clearing Corporation, are the Vancouver, Amsterdam, and Sydney exchanges. The group trades options in gold, British pounds, and German marks.

The sleek Exchange Tower is the home of the Montreal Exchange.

Several major U.S. options traders have been drawn to Montreal by the larger-than-usual size of the contracts and the international linkage. Under Lortie, Montreal also was the first North American exchange to introduce the trading of foreign currency options as well as an option on the stock of the newly recovered Chrysler Corporation.

The revival of the Montreal Exchange shocked the TSE, which had grown complacent from lack of competition. When the prematurely gray Lortie, a graduate in both engineering physics and business administration and former executive assistant to the Quebec minister of finance, had become president at the age of thirty-four (coincidentally the same age at which many people associated with the Pacific Stock Exchange became senior executives) the exchange was dying. Its share of total trading in Canada was hovering just above what was regarded as the bare minimum necessary for its continuation.

Following the 1976 election of the separatist Parti Québecois, many frightened businesses pulled out their executive offices, while others removed their entire operations from Montreal and went 300 miles west to Toronto. This reflected the historic tendency in Canada for the country's financial center to shift westward as settlement has moved from east to west. "The election of the Parti Québecois supertelescoped into five years a trend that otherwise might have taken twenty years," says Richard Hallisey of the Toronto investment firm of First Marathon Securities Ltd.

Montreal brokerage houses of both English-Canadian and French-Canadian origin were part of the exodus. The biggest English Canadian firm, Nesbitt Thomson, still labels Montreal as its corporate headquarters, but it has only 200 employees there, fewer than the 350 at its eight-year-old Toronto office. "As Toronto became the financial center, it was imperative for us to move in order to be at the heart of the action," says Nesbitt's president, Brian Steck. Since the change Nesbitt's capitalization base has increased tenfold, and its staff more than doubled.

French-Canadian brokers benefited by becoming part of the flow of business to Toronto. Levesque, Beaubien, Inc., the largest French-Canadian broker and the eleventh-biggest in Canada, opened a Toronto office in 1974. The office has grown from a dozen employees to 125. For the first eight years the firm had to settle for the crumbs untouched by the big Toronto firms in major deals, even though it hired a Torontonian with connections as the local manager.

To enlarge Montreal's volume, Lortie cherry-picked from the strategies of U.S. stock exchanges. From the New York exchange he borrowed the idea of assigning specific stocks to specialists and placed them on a quota, booting out poor performers. He credited the concept for "80 percent" of the exchange's market gains because traders found the spread dropped by 25 percent between bid and asked prices on interlisted stocks on the Montreal and Toronto exchanges. Montreal had never had a marketing department; Lortie established one and sent its staff on promotional tours and seminars, just as the U.S. exchanges do.

In a parting shot a week before he left to become chairman of a large Quebec-based food firm, Lortie ran a full-page newspaper advertisement charging the TSE with giving investors a raw deal. The reference alluded to the TSE's plan to stop trades of the public from having priority over those of professional floor traders. Institutional investors had complained that traders' on-the-spot access to changes in market sentiment would give them an unfair advantage over their clients. Lortie's ad was aimed at attracting discontented institutions to Montreal, which had no plans to stop giving preference to the public. The TSE countered that the change would narrow spreads between bid and asked prices.

Lortie already had battled the TSE head-on by undercutting Toronto's transaction fees for large trades. He developed a computer system that specializes in handling small orders, the same strategy U.S. regional exchanges had successfully employed against the NYSE. "These days, the ability to increase market share depends as much as forty percent on technology," Lortie told me. "When I joined the exchange in 1974, there were ten lawyers and one engineer; today it is a technical game, and about 10 percent of our staff are engineers." His initiatives placed the TSE in an unaccustomed defensive position. As business began drifting to Montreal, the TSE was forced to copy what Lortie had done.

A past campaigner for the provincial Liberal party, Lortie also convinced the socialist-leaning Parti Québecois to enact programs helpful to the exchange. This was easy because the Parti Québecois was alarmed at the flight of business in the wake of its election. It introduced incentives encouraging firms to go public. In addition, it funnels through the exchange all stock investments by the huge Caisse de Dépôt et Placement du Québec, a government agency that invests Quebeckers' pension funds. The Caisse controls Canada's largest capital pool and is the only provincial pension fund that buys shares.

Montreal's surge in options trading at the expense of Toronto might not have happened if TSE executives had kept their tempers in check during negotiations over the financing of a jointly owned clearing facility for options trading. When Montreal refused to pay what the Toronto exchange considered a reasonable sum, the Toronto exchange issued an ultimatum: Only one exchange should run the facility. "In retrospect, it probably was not the best way to solve the problem," TSE President Bunting concedes.

Angry investment dealers insisted they would not support two clearing systems. They suggested the financial quarrel could be settled if each exchange traded different options, selected through a lottery, instead of the same ones. The idea of holding a lottery was copied from what U.S. exchanges do in the allocation of options. A three-year trial arrangement, subject to renewal or modifications at the end of 1985, was established. TSE executives say the lottery has drained off 10 percent of former business. Much of that loss comes from the switch of the Gulf Canada Ltd. option to Montreal, where it accounts for 25 percent of options volume.

Lortie caught the TSE by surprise, but Toronto did not remain a sleeping giant for long. In 1984 it launched the Toronto Futures Exchange (TFE), the first new exchange established in Canada since 1948 and in Ontario since 1897. In the U.S. futures exchanges can be subsidiaries of stock exchanges, but the Ontario Securities Commission ruled that the Toronto stock and futures exchanges should be distinct in an effort to increase the liquidity necessary to make the TFE succeed. (In any case, the TSE had fared poorly with an in-house futures division it had run for four years, inspiring futures advocates to request a separate exchange for some time.) As an independent exchange the TFE can admit banks and foreign investment firms, which the stock exchange still bars.

The TSE benefits financially as the landlord of the futures exchange since the TFE is housed in a section of the TSE floor. That location was chosen both because the space was vacant and because Toronto was mindful of the huge expense the NYSE had incurred in 1980 by building separate facilities for its futures subsidiary. The ties between the two Toronto exchanges are close. The opening ceremonies for the futures market were held on the TSE floor to the fanfare of trumpets blown by musicians dressed in beefeater costumes. The TSE contributed $800,000 interest-free toward development costs, giving the TFE five years to repay. The futures exchange's first president, Huntly McKay, is also vice president of markets and market development at the TSE. His TFE staff of three used to work for the TSE.

Poor timing got the futures exchange off to a slow start. The Ontario legislature, embroiled in controversy over a trust company scandal in the province, delayed considering the matter of a futures exchange for two and half years. Adding to the discouragement, the Canadian subsidiary of a large U.S. commodities broker which had been a leading drumbeater for the exchange at the government hearings declined to join; instead, it continued sending orders to the Chicago futures markets. Along with these obstacles, securing banks as members was hard, even though TFE officials believed the exchange's U.S. dollar contract, allowing hedging against price fluctuations between the U.S. and Canadian dollars, was exactly what the banks would like. That was not the case. All but one of Canada's Big Five banks stayed on the sidelines, directing their futures business to Chicago.

The exception was the Bank of Montreal, which demanded harsh concessions. Not only did it want a representative on the exchange's board, but it also insisted on his participating in the ceremonial first trade opening the TFE. The bank regarded both actions as a symbolic blow against the brokerage industry's insistence on the four pillars division of financial powers. The TFE bowed to the bank's stipulations on the advice of Mark Powers, a U.S. consultant on the futures industry. Powers believed it was essential to include the banks if currency contracts were to succeed and suggested a big step in this direction would be to have a bank executive on the TFE's board. The executive, James Williams, vice president of domestic investments, says the Bank of Montreal became involved "to regain its former position of leadership in bond underwriting and trading." The TFE has a contract for long-term Canadian government bonds. Because the original price of TFE seats was only $6,500, it was not a major expense for the bank.

Through the futures exchange the TSE has taken an indirect swipe at the Montreal Exchange's options business. The TSE, under the terms of its options agreement with Montreal, is not allowed to trade options on commodities. But since the TFE is separate from the TSE, it is perfectly free to do this, and McKay has gleefully introduced several such contracts. It is mostly an empty victory. On a typical day there is only a handful of traders, and they are busier chatting than trading. So far Canadian investors, in line with their traditional preference for government bonds and long-term bank certificates over the stock market, are giving futures the deep freeze.

Because Toronto is the financial center of Canada, it is likely that the TSE will remain the leading Canadian exchange—at least for some years. But this does not mean it can contentedly coast along. President Pearce Bunting is not blind to the realities of today's fiercely competitive global market. He pragmatically accepts that "securities gravitate to one place in one time zone" and that in the time zone in which Toronto is located, the central place is New York, 500 miles to the southeast. His hope is that the exchange's computer systems will make it possible for "secondary financial centers like Toronto not to be eliminated" since they can participate in multinational electronic arrangements. Whether he is right will be anxiously watched by the many other world exchanges facing a similar time zone dilemma.

6

Paris

The Paris Bourse is the only major stock exchange whose building was designed by an emperor. Because he was dissatisfied with the architect's plans, Napoleon sketched the palacelike structure with a few bold strokes of black ink shortly after becoming emperor in 1804.

Today the bourse is again an exception among exchanges. It is singular in having a whopping 98 percent share of the market in its country. The maximum share elsewhere is the New York Stock Exchange's 85 percent in the U.S. The bourse is also the sole exchange in a Socialist nation.

François Mitterrand's Socialist government, elected in 1981, at first debilitated the exchange by nationalizing one-third of the market and slapping a premium on the purchase and sale of foreign stocks. As the government's popularity waned, partly because of its economic measures, the Socialists became a friend to the exchange. They retained nationalization but introduced tax incentives to encourage stock market investment. The government backed the establishment in 1983 of a second tier for junior stocks and the switch in 1986 to trading methods similar to those in the United States. It has also encouraged a gradual deregulation of commission rates. The aim is to make Paris more competitive in the rapid internationalization of stock trading.

It has far to go. In just four trading days the New York Stock Exchange racks up more volume than the Paris Bourse does in a year. "The market value of companies on the bourse accounts for only seven percent of the gross national product," says Philippe Cosserat, secretary-general of France's stock exchanges. "That shapes up badly against sixty percent in the U.S., close to fifty percent in Japan and the United Kingdom, and almost fifteen percent in such other European countries as Germany, Scandinavia, and Belgium." A mere 6 percent of the French population invests directly (that is, not through pension or other institutional funds) in the stock market, compared with 20 percent in the United States.

The exchange dates back to 1141, when King Louis VII established a meeting place in Paris for money changers on a wooden— later a stone—bridge called Le Grand Pont, over the Seine River. The bridge remained the money changers' office until the 1700s, when fire and floods struck it. For the next century the exchange was rootless and drifted. It began this period near the prison at the Palais de Justice in a narrow, dark side street. Then, briefly, it was stationed in the courtyard of the Mazarin Palace, originally the home of Jules Cardinal Mazarin, regent for the young Louis XIV, and after Mazarin's death the headquarters of the French East India Company Bank. The next stop was a square now known as the Place Vendôme, located near the Louvre. A prominent official living in a mansion overlooking the square found the traders' hubbub disturbing and asked the regent to get rid of them. The regent was unsympathetic. "Where do you want me to send these people?" was his reply according to historical records. The Prince of Carignan, who was present at this encounter, had a solution, which, not so incidentally, also solved his financial problems. A gambler, in desperate need of money, the prince offered to sell to the exchange as a meeting place a hotel he owned. The exchange accepted his offer, and he used the money to settle his debts.

The hotel was demolished thirty years later. The exchange first returned to the courtyard of the Mazarin Palace. Then, for a few months during the French Revolution, it moved into the ground floor of the Louvre Palace, occupying former royal apartments. Then it was on to the Church of Notre Dame des Victoires and, after that, a warehouse for opera scenery. The floor planks in this building were so poorly joined that the uncomfortable, unhappy brokers beseeched Napoleon for their own building. Construction took from 1808 to 1827, with the work interrupted by Napoleon's battles and exile, as well as by the death of the architect whom Napoleon, despite his rejection of the man's suggested design, had entrusted with the project.

The handsome butterscotch-colored building stands in the middle of a big square situated one métro (subway) stop from the Paris Opera House. From the time an eleven-pound bomb was defused on the trading floor with only minutes to spare in October 1980, guards have been posted at the black grille gates to the entrance and nobody is admitted without a pass. Since 1977 the bourse has charged the public a nominal seven-franc admission and restricted outsiders to a visitors' gallery. Before, demonstrators for various causes would walk onto the floor, present their views to television camera crews that they had called to the scene, and hand out leaflets to traders. The only major exchange to charge admission, the bourse gives visitors their money's worth in a one-and-a-half-hour explanatory program, and 60,000 people tour the bourse annually. (The New York Stock Exchange may implement a fee of up to $2; the Bourse's charge of 7 francs equals about 80¢ U.S.)

For lack of space, the bourse's administrative officials are scattered through several nearby buildings. The offices are austere. But the executive dining room, across the street from the bourse and in the same building as the exchange's computer, is elegantly furnished with Restoration chairs (from the period after the restoration of the Bourbons to power in 1814 under Louis XVIII, following the fall of Napoleon) and a black lacquer dining table. The executives dine on gourmet meals prepared by the bourse's chef and finish with cigars lit by a waiter using a red candle in a glass candlestick. For a while the gracious atmosphere was marred by a slight gastronomic problem: Most of the executives prefer Bordeaux wines, but the bourse's president, who had a Beaujolais vineyard, favored Beaujolais. His successor, the current president, does not care what wine is served. The bourse is unique among exchanges in that it has its own wine cellar, located in the basement.

Just as historically the government dictated where the bourse would meet, it has determined from the bourse's earliest days who can be the *agents de change*—the securities dealers through whom all buy and sell orders must pass and the French version of the U.S. specialists. In the bourse's infancy *agent de change* commissions were purchased from the king. The *agents de change* had the powers of a public notary and were obligated to make certain that quotations were legally correct. Today they are still sworn government officials, appointed by the Ministry of Finance, but their role is primarily a trading, rather than a legal one. Unlike U.S. specialists, *agents de change* have not been allowed to trade for their own account (this restriction will end in 1986), but they may do portfolio management. *Agents de change* must have five years' working experience in the industry and pass an examination. Their applications then go to the Compagnie des Agents de Change (National Brokers' Association) for a vote and subsequently to the Ministry of Finance. The vote has been held on a national basis since 1966, when the *compagnies* of the six regional exchanges were abolished in favor of the nationwide *compagnie* because Paris has all but 2 percent of total French trading. The regional exchanges are in Lyons, Marseilles, Bordeaux, Nancy, Nantes, and Lille. Successful candidates are welcomed with flair. The bourse holds a black tie and tails ceremony on its premises for new *agents de change*. They are escorted around to existing members to shake hands, and the bourse's wine cellar provides the champagne to celebrate the event.

Becoming an *agent de change* does not depend solely on ability. Resignations or deaths of other *agents de change* are perhaps even more important since centuries-old government rules restrict their number. As of now, the total for all of France is 125, of whom seventy-eight belong to the Paris Bourse. Twenty-four of the Paris *agents de change* also hold memberships in one or more regional exchanges. The 125 *agents de change* are grouped at sixty-one *charges* (brokerage firms) of which forty-five are in Paris. Unlike North American exchanges, the bourse does not sell memberships in the form of seats. Instead, shares are bought in the Compagnie des Agents de Change from an outgoing member. It cannot be just any dropout—the purchase must be from somebody leaving the candidate's firm. That is why members in the bourse's annual report are listed according to the year a person became a member rather than alphabetically.

Only the government has the authority to increase the number of *agents de change*—something it rarely does. It may take years for an opening to occur, and until recently owners' sons were traditionally first in line. (There is only one female *agent de change* in France; she is in her family-owned firm in Lyons.) There is now, though, a growing tendency among young men to elect not to go into their fathers' businesses. The upshot is that 60 percent of today's members are not heirs. The rules sometimes force those that are to work for competitors. The bourse's syndic (chairman), Xavier Dupont, typifies this trend. The lack of an *agent de change* vacancy at his father's brokerage firm in Lille spurred Dupont to join a Paris firm. In principle an *agent de change* at one French exchange cannot deal at another. Unofficially, however, this prohibition ended in 1967, when mergers were allowed for the first time in the brokerage industry, all of which is privately owned, because of the hunger for more capital.

The 1966 formation of the national *compagnie* made the Paris Bourse's syndic commander in chief of France's exchanges, assigning him the power to appoint the regional syndics, termed *syndics délégués*. In effect, the regionals are now just satellite exchanges. Dupont says the regional exchanges' parochialism saves them from complete oblivion. "Their listed companies are small but have good results, so there is no reason to kill off these exchanges. Besides, the local *agents de change* are mainly portfolio managers and, as such, bring most of their orders to Paris."

The Paris syndic and a board of seven governors make up the *compagnie*'s executive body, called the Chambre Syndicale des Agents de Change. It elects the syndic annually by 51 percent of the votes until the fifth year, when 75 percent is stipulated. It then reverts to 51 percent. The eight-year term of the immediate past chairman, Yves Flornoy, set a record, but members' dissatisfaction over its length may prevent such a long term from recurring.

Technically the *compagnie* and the syndic are independent. In practice they are under *la tutelle* (supervision) of the Ministry of Finance, which appoints the bourse's secretary-general. The syndic personally benefits from the government connection. Traditionally he receives the chevalier of the Legion of Honor from the government after a few years in the job. The syndic has autonomy over everyday operations, yet if the bourse wants to do anything from as minor as changing or introducing a rule to as momentous as establishing a new product or market, it must obtain government sanction.

The government usually automatically authorizes proposals that bourse officials cannily pitch as in the country's interest. Such was the case, for example, with a proposal for the trading of futures in government bonds, a popular product in North America and the U.K. and newly introduced into Japan. "The pressure of international development was so important that it was easy to get approval," Dupont says, and the futures market in bonds began in the fall of 1985. Trading in share options will start in late 1986.

Improved salaries and benefits have prevented a recurrence of the rash of strikes by administrative workers that forced the bourse to close several times in the 1970s. The last strike was in 1979 and lasted for a month. Its cause was the bourse's fluctuating compensation system. Above their regular salaries, employees receive bonuses based on the average of salaries brokerage firms pay their workers. A big firm of 130 employees (fewer than the number of senior executives at a large U.S. securities firm) might pay bonuses equivalent to a year's wages in a good year. But in the bad years of the 1970s the bonuses apportioned to exchange staff were low, and the employees struck in protest. Current labor harmony rests largely on a generous time-off policy. Under French law workers get four weeks' holiday after one year; the bourse allows five weeks. In addition, bourse employees receive *les journées complimentaires*—fourteen half days a year to use for medical appointments or other personal matters.

Trading at the bourse is split between the *marché au comptant* (cash or spot market) in which settlement is immediate, as in the U.S., and the *marché règlement mensuel*, a forward market in which settlement is in the future on a regular monthly basis. In this market the most common settlement day is seven working days before the completion of the trading month, which ends in the third week of a calendar month. The second choice for settlement is on the day after the transaction on a "contango" basis—buyers sell their shares at a fixed price and arrange to repurchase them at the same price at the end of the next trading month. Sellers do the reverse; they buy at a fixed price and agree to resell the shares the following month.

Forward market securities can also be traded conditionally, a system that resembles the U.S. method of buying options to purchase or sell stocks in the future. On the French forward market, if a *prime* (premium) is purchased, settlement can be canceled over a three-month period, in which case the *prime* is forfeited. Alternatively, traders can buy *options de vente* (put options) or *options d'achat* (call options), providing the right to sell or buy a specified number of shares at a fixed price during a nine-month period. A nonrefundable premium is part of the purchase price of an option, as in the United States.

Until 1983 trading in the bourse's 260 most active French and foreign stocks was done on either the *marché au comptant* or the forward market, then known as the *marché à terme* and now as the *marché règlement*. Currently the active stocks can be traded only on the forward market. It is estimated that these stocks account for 80 percent of the bourse's volume. Trading in less active stocks was always done on a cash basis, and the second *marché* is also *au comptant*.

Trading on the cash and forward markets begins at the ringing of a large church bell attached to a side column. In the cash market trading takes place *par casiers* (by pigeonholes). There is one *casier* for each security. A fixed block of *casiers* is assigned to an individual brokerage firm, which is responsible for collecting all orders in that block. A clerk representing each firm stands at an appointed place on the floor where at the beginning of each session he receives the total number of orders from every brokerage house, including his own. He summarizes the buy and sell bids to arrive at a midway price.

Forward market trading is performed *à la criée* (by open outcry). Trading cannot be done in a stock until an official of the exchange, colloquially called a *coteur* (from the verb *coter*—to quote prices) who acts as an auctioneer, yells out its name. Standing above the floor on a wooden catwalk, the *coteur* opens the trading in a stock at its closing price the previous day. The traders cry out their bid and offer prices, and the *coteur* writes a median price on a chalkboard, (this is called underlining the price). As new orders are brought onto the floor, the process is repeated until the closing price for the day is reached. Because those who make up the floor population know one another well, oral confirmation of orders is deemed sufficient, unlike the case in the U.S., where buyer and seller sign and countersign the order slip, which is then time-stamped.

The stocks are split into six groups according to their volume of activity in such a way that each group has a certain number of strong sellers, to avoid dead zones in floor activity. But one of the groups, while no different in function, is apart in its style and has more prestige. Called *la corbeille* (ring), it is a circular forged iron balustrade, about ten feet in diameter, with a handrail covered in red velvet. The traders stand outside it and lean on the handrail as they negotiate deals. As a status symbol *la corbeille* has an unwritten conservative dress code—black (not brown) shoes, a gray or blue suit, a tie, and preferably a vest.

La corbeille is a quiet, sedate oasis in the middle of the surrounding tumult. Inasmuch as only senior partners may trade at *la corbeille*, all are able to stand right at the handrail, easily see one another, and conduct business in quiet tones. There is no *coteur*; instead, the participants run it themselves. Organizing its trading rotates every ten sessions. The snobbishness of *la corbeille* led French President Charles de Gaulle to say, "Politics is not made at *la corbeille*." The compagnie's secretary-general, Philippe Cosserat, dryly describes *la corbeille* as "a beautiful museum piece." Since *la corbeille* regards itself as the elite of the brokerage community, the natural corollary is that it feels it deserves the cream of the stocks. The bourse's forty-five most blue-chip stocks are its prerogative, a contradiction to the stated goal of spreading good—and bad—activity around the floor.

Until late 1985 trading ran between 12:30 and 2:30 P.M., a custom started in Napoleon's reign. That period was originally chosen to avoid conflict with the breakfast hour, but today it clashes with the custom of the big lunch. In France a gracious, relaxing lunch is part of the social structure. Companies have *billets de restaurant* (tickets for certain restaurants) on hand for junior executives to entertain clients; senior executives have freedom of choice. The big lunch extends from noon until 2:30 P.M. or even as late as 3:00 P.M., with one or two clients or potential customers as the usual number of guests. The host pays careful attention to whether meat or fish is preferred, and

At the bourse, la corbeille *(foreground) is a quiet oasis surrounded by tumult.*

makes an effort to avoid taking a guest to the same place more than once.

The custom is the despair of the head offices of foreign brokers located in Paris because their Paris divisions usually turn in some of the firms' biggest expense accounts. But the moaning does not stop there. The big lunch usually is followed with invitations to play golf or go shooting on the weekends at the broker's country home, all of which also goes on the expense tab. Needless to say, the big lunch is staunchly defended by French and foreign brokers as invaluable in building up personal contacts at institutional investors and banks, at which, the brokers maintain, individual managers rather than committees make investment decisions. The brokers also say the familiarity makes clients less reluctant to give their private home telephone numbers to brokers, who may want to call their clients in the evening.

During 1986 the bourse will shed its centuries-old unique and picturesque customs, made obsolete by today's electronic revolution and surging global competition in securities trading, for American methods. A computerized system will display orders on video screens, trading will be continuous in all stocks, and trading hours will stretch to six from two in order to match the length of U.S. sessions. As a prelude a ninety-minute morning session, from ten until eleven-thirty, was added in late 1985 to supplement the two hours in the afternoon. For the first time *agents de change* will be able to trade for their own accounts rather than just be a conduit between investors and the trading floor.

But instead of exclusively assigning a stock as in the NYSE specialist style, the bourse will employ a multiple market maker system in which many traders will provide competing price quotations in a stock. It believes this will create more competition and tighter spreads between bid and asked prices. The bourse tried this procedure with its second-tier market and found it created good liquidity. For continuous trading to succeed on the main market, liquidity is essential. "The changeover should reduce the floor population to five hundred from three thousand, and instead of fifty people shouting about one stock, only five to ten likely will be," predicts Alain Ferri, an *agent de change* and vice-chairman of the exchange.

Widely credited as the guiding force behind the changes, Ferri has a reputation for progressiveness, although his ideas sometimes strike out. One of his biggest disappointments is that "everybody laughed" when he proposed options on stock indexes a decade ago. Such options, which were not introduced until 1982 in the U.S., have become the darling of investors. Ferri was one of the first French *agents de change* to recognize the importance of not remaining insular. In 1983 his firm (A. Ferri, B. Ferri, C. Germe S.A.) joined with three other Parisian firms and three regional ones to form France's first internationally oriented partnership, Inter-Finance. As part of its drive to sell French stocks to U.S. investors, it bought 4 percent of the medium-size New York firm of Moseley, Hallgarten, Estabrook & Weeden, which lets Inter-Finance use its facilities.

The bourse's computer system will be similar to that of the Toronto and the Tokyo exchanges. Like Tokyo, Paris is using Toronto as a model. The bourse deviated from the other two exchanges in deciding to put its biggest volume stocks on the computer first. Toronto has only inactive stocks on its system; Tokyo started with inactive ones and then advanced to the active list. "We did the *règlement mensuel* initially because there is little buying from outside France in the *marché au comptant*, and a continuous market, to be successful, needs to be interesting to foreign investors," Ferri says. Some members supported making all trading on a cash settlement basis, as in the U.S. But Ferri favored retaining forward settlement, arguing that it allows the purchase or sale of shares without resorting to the margin system prevalent in the U.S., under which clients can become overextended. "Why change just for the sake of change?" Ferri asks rhetorically in defense of forward trading.

In 1984 the bourse began a trial run, using Toronto's system, for which it pays a fee. Under the arrangement the French trade French stocks listed on the bourse, but Toronto's computers execute the trades in the middle of the night. Notwithstanding this early testing, the bourse elected to delay its changeover to 1986, partly so members could install necessary back office equipment, but, more important, because of the need to raise the funds for the transformation. To pay the bills, the bourse hiked the normal 6.5 percent per commission fee that members contribute to it to 10 percent.

Although it is adopting many U.S. practices, the bourse has steered clear of full-scale negotiated rates. Nonetheless, in 1985 it took a major step in this direction under pressure from the Socialists, who want investors to get a better deal through more competition in the marketplace. For share transactions of under 2 million francs,* the discount was raised to 35 percent from 27.5 percent and will eventually be 40 percent. On transactions between 2 million and 60 million

---

* From January to the end of July 1985, the average rate of exchange was 10 francs to the U.S. dollar.

francs, rates are now open to negotiation. Commissions were eliminated on deals of more than 60 million francs.

Pressure for discount rates is relatively new in France because institutional investment is not yet a major force, as it is in the U.S. Large block institutional trading, a mainstay of the NYSE, is only ten years old at the bourse. The reason institutional investment is low is that pensions are not a big factor in France. Company pension plans are not a common practice. In France pensions are paid from money collected in a particular year; in the U.S. and U.K. they are paid from money accumulated from previous years. Government restrictions fence in insurance companies, normally the other big source of institutional investment. They can invest only a small amount of their funds in stocks, especially if they are foreign ones, although there is greater leeway for foreign stocks listed on the bourse than outside France.

So far France lacks the partnerships that are developing in London between banks and securities firms. But because 80 percent of their business comes from banks, the new commission structure makes the already undercapitalized securities firms vulnerable to takeovers by banks, for their commission income could shrink by as much as 25 percent. The existing closeness between bankers and brokers is seen in the way banks have booths adjacent to the trading floor, alongside those of the brokers. Before each session the representatives of the banks at the bourse put their banks' orders in labeled envelopes for their regular brokers, who pick them up fifteen minutes before trading starts.

The bourse does not, nor does it plan to, admit foreign members, unlike the U.S., even though the number of North American, British, and Japanese securities firms in Paris is swelling in anticipation of the exchange's 1986 transformation. The French brokerage houses do not want to end their membership monopoly because they are dwarfed in numbers by the outsiders and do not relish head-to-head competition in trading activity.

The bourse's journey to its altered state has consumed eight years. Other exchanges have taken long periods, too, but France is charmingly apologetic for its slow progress. Officials give a Gallic shrug and a half-amused, half-"That's the way it is" sheepish smile when questioned about the snaillike pace. "Here we are in France," says Yves Flornoy, who initiated the modernization as chairman of the bourse from 1976 until 1984. "We always have to think about changes for a long while."

Adds Alain Ferri: "In France to make something new is quite hard." And Yves Mallet, chief inspector for the eighteen-year-old Commission des Opérations de Bourse (the French counterpart of the U.S. Securities and Exchange Commission), told the 1984 conference of the International Association of Securities Commissions, "Ours is not the most innovative of markets." That change is difficult in France is epitomized by the strong-willed de Gaulle's once exasperatedly complaining after he had failed to get a necessary consensus: "How can you govern a country that has three hundred and sixty different cheeses?"

What finally spurred the bourse into action was the revolution across the English Channel at the London exchange. The French feared the freshly aggressive Londoners would lure away the business they took for granted from French banks. Their concern deepened when several of the nation's biggest banks, including the Banque Paribas, Société Générale, and Crédit Commercial de France, bought into British securities firms in preparation for London's 1986 Big Bang.

Flornoy, an avid opera buff and past amateur orchestra conductor and choirmaster who formed his first choir when he was just seventeen, fought this endemic resistance to change, with élan and aggressiveness. Gaining familiarity with the many plot twists of operas was perhaps a useful preparation for the storms Flornoy encountered—and engendered—as he sought to reform the main market and introduce a second tier for junior stocks. His ambitious plans were stymied by the bourse's placid contentment with the status quo and by the political shift in France from right to left.

More than a century earlier, in the 1860s, Paris, which previously had had only a cash market, unofficially imported forward trading techniques from London. Such transactions were done clandestinely "under the columns" at the side of the trading floor. Many of these traders were unscrupulous, and angry cheated French investors filed many court cases. The result was an 1884 law decreeing that *agents de change* were not obliged to execute contracts on a forward basis for clients if those contracts seemed unsafe. Since then the forward and cash systems have been fixtures at the bourse, especially since their existence has benefited astute investors.

"Lots of very clever people were arbitraging* between the *à terme* [forward] and *au comptant* [cash] *marchés,*" Flornoy explains. "They were very happy with the results, but their clients did not understand why the price of the same stock was more expensive on one market than the other. The only exchange rules governing this double market was that the gap between the price on the cash market and that on the forward market could not exceed two percent. The bourse could not afford to have two simultaneous markets in the same stocks if it wanted continuous trading. Instead, those markets had to be unified. The problem was whether the united market would be a cash or forward market. It took three years to decide which it would be."

During those three years the bourse's officials wove back and forth between opting for the cash or the forward system, depending on what they thought the political scene in France augured for the exchange. "When we started our deliberations in 1978, federal elections were called, and it appeared that the left wing, which had pledged to suppress the forward market, would win," Flornoy continues. "So we decided we would have a cash system, as in New York. But the left wing lost the election, and the view at the bourse swung back to favoring a forward market. By 1981 we were ready to start, but the left wing won those elections. The Ministry of Finance said that after it nationalized much of the market, it would see if there was enough remaining business to warrant unification into a forward trading system. It finally gave its approval a year later, and ten months after that the *règlement mensuel* was begun."

With the first hurdle out of the way the bourse officials thought continuous trading could be started quickly. They were wrong again. They had to overcome another stumbling block: what the French call the dematerialization of stocks and bonds. This means eliminating the actual delivery of stock and bond certificates to clients. Physical stock transfer tends to create a paperwork jam for the issuers of the

---

*Arbitrage involves simultaneously buying a security on one exchange and selling it on another at a price that yields a profit to the arbitrageur.

certificates and can result in the whole financial trading system clogging.

France began the dematerialization process in 1945 through the establishment of Sicovam (Société Interprofessionelle pour la Compensation de Valeur Mobilière), which is coowned by the banks and brokers. Close to 95 percent of all securities transactions are done through Sicovam via the *au porteur* method, which is similar to the North American bearer security—a stock or bond which does not have the owner's name recorded on the books of the issuing company or on the certificate itself. The holdouts possess *nominatives*, the equivalent of the American registered security that is recorded in the owner's name on the books of the issuing company. Ownership of a bearer certificate can be transferred without the signed endorsement of the owner, but a registered security can be transferred only after being endorsed by the registered owner. Because the *nominative* system is time-consuming and costly, the *securities dealers* pressured the bourse to ram through 100 percent use of Sicovam.

Little headway was made because the holders of *nominatives* stubbornly refused to switch to the *au porteur* method. The standoff might have continued indefinitely if the bourse's unexpected ally, the Socialist government, had not passed legislation on another matter that had the end result of also getting rid of *nominatives*. When the government passed a new property tax law in 1982, it stipulated that dematerialization should apply to real estate ownership forms. It reasoned that putting the records on computer tapes would help prevent tax avoidance by uncooperative citizens. Once it was cracking down on property owners, the government used the opportunity to make dematerialization complete in the stock market. Subsequent difficulties in expanding Sicovam were not overcome until late in 1985.

The time it took to reform the main market had a precedent; similar procrastination marked the establishment of the second market for junior stocks which is now the pride and joy of the bourse. The bourse first considered setting up this market in 1974—after the 1973 oil price crisis, which, as the London exchange also found, deterred companies from going public. In 1978 the bourse had a big price rally; still, no companies sought listing. By 1981 the bourse was again unappealing in the aftermath of the Socialists' far-reaching nationalization program.

The new government was not the only deterrent: companies were reluctant to bare their financial figures, a procedure made more revealing in recent years by tougher shareholder disclosure rules. Companies that might have listed were nervous their competitors would gain unfair advantage through access to publicly filed information. In addition, many French companies remain family-controlled, and their owners fretted about their vulnerability to takeovers via the stock market if they were listed on the bourse.

Similar to London's Unlisted Securities Market, the bourse's second market proffers less exacting listing rules to calm apprehension. Less disclosure is required than on the first tier, and only 10 percent of a company need be publicly offered, compared with a minimum of 25 percent on the first market. More than eighty companies are now on the second market. A typical company has annual revenue of 150 million francs and 500 to 1,000 employees. Yet there is room for improvement. Bourse officials estimate that another 400 companies are eligible for listing and that the second market has replaced only about 5 percent of the business lost through nationalization of stocks on the main market.

While the Socialists had a devastating impact on the exchange, the relationship between the government and the bourse has a history of edginess regardless of which party is in power. "It is not a matter of socialism or nonsocialism," Flornoy says. "Valéry Giscard d'Estaing never attached as much importance to the market as he did to what he, as president, and his minister of finance did regarding the economy. There has always been the fear in France, since the end of the last century, that too great an evidence of capitalism would give the left wing the opportunity to win elections."

The sweeping 1981 nationalization ripped away the bourse's across-the-board representation of the French economy, the normal role of an exchange. The government took over thirty-nine banks and the leading producers of electricity, industrial glass, aluminum, chemicals, electronics, and household appliances. Later the nationalization spread to encompass two steel companies and the top manufacturers of armaments and military aircraft. It is estimated that if these stocks were still listed, the market capitalization of bourse companies would double.

Former shareholders were compensated with government bonds,

and French brokers and economists say the government was overly generous in its payment of up to three times the value of some shares. The replacement bonds provide up to 15 percent annual interest, compared with dividend yields on the shares as low as 2 percent. Some calculate that it will cost the government 13 billion francs a year to retire these bonds, which are being amortized over a fifteen-year period.

Even if, as many French political observers expect, the procapitalist opposition wins in the 1986 National Assembly elections, the nationalization program is not expected to unravel easily despite the opposition's vow to denationalize everything taken over by the Socialists. It would be difficult to arouse potential stockholder interest since most of the companies, ailing or undercapitalized before nationalization, have not improved noticeably. Some state-owned companies, starved for capital, have sold nonvoting shares through the bourse, but such shares have limited appeal because investors lack a voice in management.

On the other hand, if the election results are as predicted, they could affect overall investor confidence. It would be the first time since the Fifth Republic was formed in 1958 that the president of France, elected every seven years and thus not up for reelection until 1988, would belong to a different party from the dominant forces in the National Assembly. If this happens and the president and Assembly clash, there could be a demoralizing spillover effect on trading at the bourse.

The bourse's trading nose-dived following the nationalizations but then rebounded. Pierre Uri, an economist and key Socialist party consultant on nationalization who also was an adviser in the 1950s in France's participation in the formation of the European Economic Community, has a novel theory about what spurred the revival. His piquant explanation? The impact of a TV show on which he appeared shortly after the nationalization measures had been introduced and an article he wrote in an influential financial journal.

"I was on a debate program that is watched by about forty million people—a huge audience, considering that France's population is fifty-four million. The topic actually was whether small shareholders are cheated by management. But when I found the right moment, I made a fiery speech on the advantages of the Socialist plan to compensate stockholders and against what I described as the scare tactics of the opposition. The next day trading was very strong on the bourse." Uri's article, in *Analyse Financière*, had a certain disarming logic. "I wrote that since nationalization had reduced the list of companies on the bourse, business in the remaining stocks would shoot up." Uri's optimistic forecast came true, but the resurrection really had its roots in a global surge in financial trading that struck Paris more than a year after New York.

France has long had tough foreign exchange controls to stop the exodus of money into foreign bank accounts, especially in Switzerland. Under the Socialists the curtailment has intensified through the application of a dollar premium on the purchase and sale of foreign stocks. The premium applies to stocks issued in all foreign currencies, although the prime target is investment in U.S. stocks, the chief area of foreign investment by the French (hence the name dollar premium).

If both the U.S. market and the U.S. dollar are strong, the premium can yield a double profit for investors. If both are slumping, a double loss is in store. If one is up while the other is down, they can balance each other out. The premium fluctuates according to the amount of foreign currency available and is tacked on top of the normal conversion rate. It has ranged from 8 percent to 34 percent but usually averages between 10 and 15 percent. The Mitterrand government borrowed the idea from what Harold Wilson's Labour government in the U.K. had done. In the case of the U.K., though, the premium rose much more, up to 100 percent over the official exchange rate.

When the premium was introduced, government officers raided U.S. brokerage offices in Paris and searched company files to determine whether any transactions had contravened the rules. They found no incriminating records. The U.S. ambassador to France complained about the tactics to the French government. Then the furor died down quickly because similar raids on French financial institutions convinced the Americans they were not being singled out. Indeed, the chairman of Banque Paribas resigned over government charges of violating the currency export laws. (He was acquitted in a 1984 trial.)

The crackdown has not dampened French foreign investment at all. French brokers compute that as nationalization constricted the choice in French stocks, French investors now have on average 30 percent of their portfolios in foreign, mostly U.S., stocks. American brokers say Paris is one of their four biggest overseas sources of investment in U.S. stocks, along with London, Geneva, and Hong Kong. Not all that money is French in origin. Much comes from residents of the Middle East, especially from Lebanon and Syria (Saudi Arabian money goes to London). These two countries' historic ties lie more with France, just as Saudi Arabia's links to England are greater. The Lebanese and Syrians can buy and sell as many securities as they wish without being subject to French taxation so long as the actual settlement of the transactions does not take place in France.

After first gutting much of the market through nationalization, the Socialists are now encouraging investment in the marketplace. By levying taxes that decreased the traditional appeal of gold and real estate, the government redirected investors to the bourse. The number of French households investing in the market has since doubled. The Mitterrand government retained the Giscard administration's incentives for encouraging the French to turn to pooled investment funds, similar to North American mutual funds. The Socialists have also acted to increase investor confidence by stiffening shareholder protection laws. The new rules require more frequent company reports; consolidated statements by publicly quoted companies, encompassing subsidiary as well as parent financial results; and more information about the shareholdings of the board of directors in a company. Nonetheless, disclosure is still not as extensive as in the U.S.

Despite these concerted efforts, total investment continues to be much smaller proportionately than in the U.S. Medium-size French investors believe they can do as well at their banks since interest on special savings accounts of up to 60,000 francs is tax-exempt. In turn, the government channels the money into subsidized, low-cost corporate loans to encourage industrial growth. The low-key salesmanship of the securities dealers is another factor. "The typical French broker has a small sales force and concentrates on portfolio management for private clients," says Jacques Perquel of Gorgeu Perquel Krucker et Cie., one of the oldest *agents de change* firms at the bourse.

The 1986 changes at the bourse will further strain the already thin resources of the Commission des Opérations de Bourse (known as the COB), the French version of the SEC. The COB was established in 1967, and its officials are government appointees. The president of France selects the COB's chairman, with the Ministry of Finance choosing the secretary-general and the members of the board. Four board members are from outside government—a representative from industry, the bourse's chairman, a bank president, and a member of the Supreme Court—and serve four terms with two spots up for reappointment every second year. There is also one government representative who has two backup alternates. Although he has no outright veto power, he can request fresh deliberations. In addition, the government supplies the COB's budget.

The commission deliberately chose a location on the left bank of the Seine to avoid being near either the Ministry of Finance or the brokerage community on the right bank. Despite their close ties, the officials have not always been in agreement. The first COB president had a strained relationship with the finance minister at the time. Giscard d'Estaing was often at loggerheads with the COB's chairman, and the Socialists and the immediate past chairman of the commission also differed on occasion. The COB's present chairman is Yves Le Portz, former chairman of the European Investment Bank, which gives companies financial assistance.

The COB's dependence on the Ministry of Finance for its budget has put it in a frustrating position as the scope of its activities has broadened. The cold breath of government austerity programs has prevented the COB from ever enlarging its staff. It still has the same small number of employees—90—as when it was founded. By contrast, the SEC in the U.S. has 2,000. The personnel constraints are of major concern to the commission because the introduction of continuous trading at the bourse will stretch its supervisory resources to the limit. COB officials are trying to decide what administrative and technical rules will be necessary and how to implement them. One possibility is the establishment of a stockbrokers' board that would have direct responsibility for overseeing the market but would send reports to the COB. "The commission can help in the evolution and push for improved competitiveness, but it cannot do so by itself; it must have the consensus of the financial community," says Gérard de La Martinière, secretary-general of the commission.

Supervising a reorganized bourse is only one concern of the understaffed COB. It must also oversee a hodgepodge of investments, ranging from shares in forests to those in herds of cattle or horses, pleasure boats, and diamonds. Such items annually attract about 90 million French francs in investment. The COB never wanted this added responsibility and has made no secret of its unhappiness, particularly over its lack of legal powers to back up its jurisdiction. The strain will worsen when futures, now in the wings, and expansion of trading in options, still to be approved by the government, make their debuts at the bourse. Unlike the situation in the U.S., where the SEC and the Commodity Futures Trading Commission, split up regulation of these products, the COB would have sole jurisdiction.

One solution to the workload that COB officials are considering is a computerized data information bank on companies and markets. It is also toying with ideas for easing its money troubles. The first step was a summer 1985 government statute permitting the commission to charge companies an annual fee for its endorsement of information on new issues. The fee, payable by March 31, is based on net assets as of the end of the previous calendar year. New listings of stocks on the bourse are exempt.

The COB has also come into the limelight by clamping down on insider trading. Until 1983 the commission lacked disciplinary powers over brokers and could only request unofficially that the brokerage community take self-disciplinary action. The tepid authority was further weakened because the brokers never had to tell the COB whether they had acted or what had been done. Such flouting of the commission ceased in 1983 following the revelation of five insider trading incidents. The cases provoked a public outcry and created a severe public relations image problem for the bourse. As a result, when the COB pressed the bourse's syndic, Xavier Dupont, and the government to give it greater investigative strength, including the power to waive the right of secrecy claims by brokers, it got what it wanted.

Both the first and second markets come under the COB's authority, but the bourse's *hors cote* (over-the-counter) market does not, unless insider trading has occurred. The lack of specific rules and the thin trading on the *hors cote* are an embarrassment to bourse officials, who do their best to pretend that these limitations do not exist. The *hors cote* is primarily a market for the sale of shares in unlisted securities between people working at the same company, usually a small enterprise. Once employment at the company reaches 200 people, it falls under the COB's supervision. Despite the lowly regard for the *hors cote*, there are no plans to abolish it; bourse and COB officials believe it provides the "freedom" for the shareholders involved to sell their shares.

By the end of 1986 the bourse, the most robust exchange domestically, hopes to be more attractive to international investors, but it has an uphill fight against London. Still, an exchange that survived the French Revolution and the Napoleonic Wars in its early days and a Socialist government in this decade should not be underestimated.

7

Zurich

The Zurich Stock Exchange (Zürcher Börse), like the six smaller Swiss stock exchanges, is an appendage of the Swiss banking system. There are no brokers in Switzerland. Instead, the banks are the sole members of the exchange. They bring companies to the market, organize the trading, and take care of most operational functions.

The monopoly arises from Switzerland's universal banking system. The banks perform the traditional functions of American and British consumer banks—deposit taking, lending, foreign exchange—as well as own shares of industries and engage in the securities business. The only missing element is the sale of insurance, but even there, the banks are not out in the cold because they own shares in leading insurance firms. The *Börse* has no specialists as in the U.S., no jobbers as in the U.K., no *Makler* (specialists) as in Germany; since the banks are the only members, there is no need for intermediaries. A century ago there were floor brokers who executed orders at the *Börse* for the public; they were dispensed with as the Swiss grew to like the convenience of one-stop shopping for mortgages and stocks at their banks.

Banking, after all, is what makes Switzerland tick. Although the entire 6 million population of Switzerland is less than that of New York City, the country wields financial power disproportionate to its size. For the past decade it has been the second-largest net exporter of capital in the industrialized world. A century ago Switzerland was one of the poorest nations, without natural resources such as oil, gas, or coal; today finance has transformed it into one of the most prosperous.

Switzerland has close to 500 banks, 120 of which are foreign-controlled. The assets and liabilities of Swiss banks and financial companies are double the national income, a high ratio unique to Switzerland. The Swiss have always regarded themselves as bankers to the world and are estimated to manage up to 1 trillion Swiss francs* in investments for domestic and foreign clients.

For centuries savings from abroad have flowed into and loans have flowed out of this tiny, beautiful country. In the sixteenth and seventeenth centuries the emperor of Austria, king of France, Bank of England, and diamond cutters of Amsterdam all were in debt to the cantons of Switzerland. In 1934 the Swiss government put the concept of banking secrecy under penal law to protect the thousands of Germans who had transferred their assets to Switzerland as Hitler rose to power, and did not report the existence of these accounts to German authorities. In the covering legislation, the government made divulgence of information about bank customers a criminal offense. Swiss banks have cultivated foreign business by offering multilingual service in English, French, German, Italian, and Spanish. Critics charge some of the foreign money is of dubious origin, but nobody actually knows how much money foreign investors have salted away in Swiss bank accounts. Estimates range as high as $350 billion.

Foreign investors also entrust the Swiss banks with managing most or all of their stock portfolios. The total value of securities holdings administered by Swiss banks has been placed between 260 and 300 billion Swiss francs. Swiss stocks are judged to account for up to 130 billion francs of this amount, and foreign stocks the rest. About half the securities are held by foreigners, most of whom are from other

---

* From January to the end of July 1985, the average rate of exchange was 2.6 Swiss francs to the U.S. dollar.

European countries although some are from the Middle East oil-producing nations.

There is no legal obligation for stock transactions to be executed at the *Börse* or for all Swiss banks to belong to it. The banks are required only to report their total trading volumes to the local canton (the Swiss equivalent of a U.S. state), which has jurisdiction over the exchange, rather than breakdowns of the proportion done on and off the trading floor. It is this figure that the exchange uses in compiling its annual report. Thus global comparisons of the volume of stock exchange trading, in which the Swiss exchanges place high, cannot be accepted as 100 percent accurate.

Since trading can be done away from the floor and member banks run the *Börse*, it might seem that Switzerland has no need of an exchange. Richard Meier, general manager of the *Börse*, has a ready counterargument. If there were no exchange, bank loans would be insufficient to fund today's magnitude of corporate expansion. He further maintains that an exchange produces greater efficiency and liquidity. "In the Eurobond market, in which the size of issues is large but their number and the quantity of traders [are] small, it would be inefficient to have everyone in a central trading place. Thus the telephone is best suited for that market. In the United States, where large-size stock transactions for institutional clients constitute the bulk of the volume, trading is possible either through NASDAQ's electronic system or [through] off-floor telephone negotiations that are then formally consummated on the floor, as at the New York Stock Exchange. But in Switzerland there are many small and medium trades as well as large ones, and the sheer volume makes it more sensible to have a floor. It would be too cumbersome, especially as people have just two ears, to do the large number of trades by telephone." Some off-floor trading is in store, though. Zurich is planning a computer-assisted trading system in inactive stocks, similar to that of the Toronto Stock Exchange.

The Swiss bank-controlled system keeps the *Börse*'s operational and administrative costs to a bare minimum. The Zurich exchange has an administrative staff of just six people. At year-end 1984 the NYSE had four executive vice presidents, fourteen senior vice presidents, twenty-four vice presidents, and fourteen assistant vice presidents;

they deal with public relations, marketing, market research, new products, market operations, government regulations, and regulatory services. In Zurich Meier handles all these functions. An economist, with experience in business administration and the application of computer programming to stock exchanges, he joined the *Börse* in 1971 and became its first full-time manager in 1980. Geneva, the number two exchange, doing half the volume of Zurich, and Basel, number three, with about one-third of Geneva's volume, also have full-time managers. Bern and Lausanne have part-time managers, and the two smallest exchanges at St. Gallen and Neuchâtel have none.

The simplicity of the Swiss system has its good points—lower costs and less bureaucracy than at exchanges in other countries—but it also causes problems. Indeed, some bankers candidly admit to its chief problem—elitism. Says Karl Baumgartner, senior vice president of the Union Bank of Switzerland, the country's largest bank: "Even in a capitalistic country like Switzerland the stock exchange is only meant to be for rich people, and that is completely wrong." Switzerland has the highest per capita ratio of gross domestic product among industrialized nations (about $15,000, compared with $13,000 in the U.S.), yet only one out of every twelve Swiss, compared with one out of four adults in the United States, invests in the stock market.

To find the reasons for so few Swiss stock market investors, one must begin with a look at the high price of Swiss stocks. While the minimum par value is $50, the average price is much heftier, ranging from $200 to $500. By comparison, the average price of a share in the U.S. is around $35. Psychologically the U.S. system encourages more investment; shareholders believe their stake is larger when they have ten shares worth $50 each than just one share worth $500.

The banks are not interested in small investors because they consider them a drag on earnings. To cover their costs of handling a stock portfolio account, the banks calculate it must contain at least 65,000 Swiss francs—the point at which the commission on the account would be sufficient to pay off the expense of maintaining it. This snubbing of the average person reflects the orientation of the big banks in Switzerland (and Germany) to commercial clients and wealthy individuals. Consumers bank primarily at the post office and pay most bills through it. The post office assumed a second role of banker when the banks saw no profit in operating branches in the tiny villages that dot the mountains and valleys of Switzerland. While the post office can use existing staff, even a small branch bank would have to hire several people.

Low dividends and the lack of both discount commissions and additional investment choices, such as financial futures and options, also discourage Swiss investors. Research analysis is underdeveloped and suspect because the banks hesitate to criticize the performance of big corporate customers. There is no independent service to rate the quality of corporate bonds; the banks do the assessment. Laws against insider trading were not introduced until 1985, and there still is no national securities and exchange commission.

Just ten stocks account for 56 percent of total market capitalization in Switzerland. They include the big three banks—the Union Bank of Switzerland, the Swiss Bank Corporation, and Crédit Suisse—Nestlé (food products); and three chemical and pharmaceutical manufacturers—Hoffman–La Roche, Ciba-Geigy, and Sandoz. Also on the list are Zurich Insurance, Swiss Reinsurance, and Oerlikon-Bührle (Bally Shoes, military products, industrial machinery). These stocks represent the highest concentration of power among the world's markets, except for Belgium (57 percent). By contrast, the top ten U.S. companies on the NYSE, in terms of market capitalization, account for 16 percent of the total; the top ten U.K. firms, 26 percent; and the top ten Japanese on the Tokyo exchange, 17 percent, according to a study by Lombard, Odier et Cie of Geneva, a major private bank and investment dealer.

The Zürcher Börse, established in 1877, is regarded as the chief market for banking, insurance, and food shares. Geneva places special emphasis on Italian and British bearer certificates. Basel's hallmark is the pharmaceutical and chemical sector, reflecting these firms' nearby location. Ninety percent of all securities listed in Switzerland are traded on these three exchanges. "Switzerland could be considered as one financial market with several floors, just as the Pacific Stock Exchange has floors in San Francisco and Los Angeles," Meier says. "The exchanges are competitive, but the majority have the same banks as members and trade the same merchandise." The St. Gallen, Lausanne, and Neuchâtel exchanges stay alive through arbitrage with the three bigger exchanges.

There are no plans to centralize all Swiss trading in Zurich, although along with Basel and Geneva it is developing joint electronic information, settlement, and trading systems as a basis for plugging into the looming era of 24-hour trading. Meier says complete consolidation in Zurich would be "unthinkable" since the Swiss social and political structure thrives on achieving harmony by encouraging a wide spectrum of views. Although home to four language groups—German, French, Italian, and Latin-derived Romansch—Switzerland has not suffered any divisive conflict such as has occurred in Canada between just two major language groups, English and French.

The four-party Swiss government embraces diametrically opposed views, ranging from socialist to archconservative, but remains stitched together by checks and balances in Switzerland's political system. Chief among these is the power given to the voters to create or overrule laws by referendum. That is why Swiss bankers shuddered in 1984 when the socialists pushed for a referendum to end bank secrecy laws. It was defeated because most Swiss have socked away some money in accounts that they do not divulge to tax authorities.

Symbolic of its dependence on the banks, the Zurich exchange has the Big Three Swiss banks as neighbors. The exchange, Crédit Suisse, and Swiss Bank all are near the Paradeplatz, a circular intersection in downtown Zurich. The Paradeplatz is bordered on one side by the Bahnhofstrasse, one of the world's most famous and expensive shopping streets. In between couturier women's dress shops, stores selling jewel-encrusted watches, and pastry *confiseries* are more member banks of the *Börse,* including the Union Bank.

Other exchanges are wrestling over their structures, new products, commission rates, and memberships. Zurich's biggest annoyance was a just-settled twenty-year struggle to get a new building in place of its cramped, fifty-five-year-old quarters. The difficulty arose from the Swiss penchant for referenda, peculiar zoning regulations, and a maze of cantonal procedures. "Switzerland is the only country with a regulation requiring the erection of poles giving the height of a proposed building, and there can be lawsuits even over these poles," says Nicolas Bär, current president of the exchange. Urbane, with a liking for modern art and furniture that contrasts with the somber taste of most Swiss banks, Bär is chairman of Bank Julius Bär & Company, a large private bank.

Under a 1912 law the canton of Zurich must issue the exchange's

The current cramped quarters of the exchange in Zurich will be replaced by a new building in 1991.

official quotation sheet and provide it with a building in return for the right to collect a tax based on volume at the exchange. In 1982 the canton received 20 million francs, and in 1983, 28 million. According to Bär, this annual tax compounded over the years has paid "many times over" for the present building, with the government using the surplus for other purposes within Zurich.

The exchange would have been delighted to build its own new quarters years ago but could not circumvent four obstacles. First, it could not wrest away the issuing of the quotation sheet from the government. The canton declined to cede this duty to the exchange because in addition to the taxes it collects, it earns about 2 million francs annually from selling the list on a subscription basis to investors. The second obstacle was that any building costing more than 20 million francs must be approved in a public referendum and the proposed new exchange would amount to around 24 million francs. Thirdly, the exchange did not want to agree to a zoning rule calling for all new buildings to contain apartments. Lastly, its choice of site, where the city's old barracks are located, was objectionable to historic-preservation buffs. The site was finally approved by the cantonal Parliament in December 1984, and public approval was given in a June 1985 referendum. The goal is to open the new building by 1991 at the latest.

The exchange could have sidestepped all this trouble if it had spread into available space adjacent to the present building; no vote would have been necessary. It rejected this compromise because there was not enough room for it to install its planned computer trading system for less active stocks. Also, the members, who realize they will lose ground competitively if options and futures trading are not started soon, want a bigger site.

"We are already very late. I hope when we start, it will not be too late and that this business will not have been lost to New York, Chicago, or London," Bär says. The exchange launched a study of options and futures in 1982 but was reluctant to proceed since there is no overwhelming Swiss demand for either product. Bär is certain that waiting until the new building opens would be a fatal delay. His provisional solution is to start options and futures trading in 1986 or 1987 on the second floor of the present exchange building. His suggestion could create another hornet's nest for the exchange since that particular floor happens to be the central meeting hall in Zurich for the various political parties. They are not at all happy about the prospect of having to relocate.

Zurich's chief rival exchanges in Geneva and Basel had it much easier when about the same time they, too, decided to build new quarters. Unlike Basel and Zurich, the Geneva *Bourse* is independent and is not subject to cantonal approval. Its building was completed recently. Geneva's old quarters, built in 1913, had room for only sixteen of its twenty-nine members on the floor. The new building is seven times larger, and the exchange's chief executive, Kurt Schneuwly, optimistically expects membership to quadruple. That will enable entrance fees to be lowered to where the cost would be comparable to that which a smaller nonmember bank now pays a member bank to do transactions for it. Schneuwly also proudly points out that the building features a more in-depth video display computerized information system than Zurich has in its current building—a contention Zurich does not dispute.

Basel, like Zurich, was subject to a referendum, but the exchange cleverly managed to get the vote scheduled to coincide with the height of the Swiss skiing holidays. The ploy worked. A squeaker vote approved the new building.

The Zurich exchange has only twenty-four members, dubbed the "A" banks. Of these, four are foreign-controlled—one each by a German, an Italian, a Dutch, and a British bank. There is an incestuous relationship among the members about which Swiss authorities have done nothing. Nearly one-third are linked to the Big Three banks. The Union Bank, in effect, has three memberships—its own plus two others through major shareholdings in Bank Julius Bär and Bank Cantrade. Crédit Suisse controls Bank Hofmann, and the Swiss Bank Corporation, the Swiss Deposit and Credit Bank.

The president of the exchange traditionally works for a private bank, as is also the case with the president of the national bankers' association. "This helps reduce the small banks' jealousy of the big banks," Bär says. "Also, it is felt private bankers will be more neutral in stepping or not stepping on toes, depending on which is necessary, because they have a much smaller proportion of new issues business than the Big Three." The Big Three still are supreme because each always has a representative on the exchange's six-member executive committee. The other three committee members are from the private banks.

The exchange also has 150 "B" license associates: smaller Swiss banks and foreign brokers and banks that place their orders through the "A" team. It is not easy to become a "B" associate since such a license is a pawn in an international economic chess game of "If we give you this, what will you give us in return?" Like other nations involved in this contest, what the Swiss want is reciprocity—membership for Swiss banks on the leading exchange in the country of the applicant. Failing that, they would like permission to move from representative to branch office status so they can personally engage in securities dealing rather than just show the flag for the parent company.

To obtain a "B" license at the Zurich exchange, candidates must be sponsored by three banks, the local manager must live in the canton of Zurich, and a guarantee of stability must be provided in the form of share capital worth 500,000 francs. The money can be either deposited with a bank or guaranteed in writing. To a big broker, this is very little money, and its primary purpose is to keep out quick-money artists.

The Swiss trading system borrows heavily from the French *corbeille* (ring), *criée*, and spot and forward techniques. The exchange has three wooden *corbeilles* (a fourth will be added in the near future). The traders, all male, stand around the ring, each at the place allotted his bank. In front of each trader, attached to the far side of the wide counter encircling *la corbeille*, is a video display terminal showing price quotations on the other Swiss exchanges. Behind each trader is a lectern type of stand to which assistants bring new orders and receive executed ones; they report these to the large traders' room on the perimeter of the floor. Up to fifty-five people congregate in the room: traders waiting for the session to start, institutional salesmen in constant touch with clients by telephone, clerks tearing off other orders transmitted by head offices from teletype machines and confirming their execution the same way, and arbitrageurs dealing back and forth between Swiss exchanges to make a profit by buying a stock at a low price on one exchange and selling it at a high price on another exchange.

At the center of the ring are two exchange clerks and one government employee. The stock exchange clerk calls out the securities for trading and records all final quotations; the stock price reporter transmits trading information to a computer center; the cantonal stock exchange commissioner monitors all operations to ensure conformity with security trading laws. The responsibility for overseeing the trading rotates among the vice presidents in charge of the securities divisions at the Big Three banks and three representatives from the private banks. Trading in stocks is done in two stages, starting with transportation stocks, banks, finance, and insurance companies. When this section is completed, the bank representative in charge asks if all business is done. If so, trading then proceeds in industrial stocks. As in Paris, trading is performed *à la criée*. The stock exchange clerk calls out the name of the security, and the traders shout price quotations back and forth until a deal is struck. *Geld* (the German word for "money") is the expression used in offers to buy, *Brief* (German for "paper") is used in offers to sell, and *bezahlt* (German for "paid") is used in stating the agreed-upon selling price. This procedure takes place once a day for bonds and twice for stocks. Usually only three or four traders participate in all shares; the rest remain silent.

In Switzerland official trading cannot begin until a stock is issued in printed form. The banks run an unlisted market for these stocks at the exchange for forty-five minutes before official trading starts. The banks use the telephone to conduct over-the-counter trading for companies that never plan to list. Ring One at the *Börse* is for trading in Swiss bonds from 9:20 until 11:00 A.M., followed by foreign stocks until the end of the session. Ring Two is first for premarket trading in foreign bonds and then for Swiss stocks; Ring Three, first for unlisted trading and then for foreign bonds. Trading in Swiss bonds continues in whichever of the other rings becomes vacant first. Premarket trading is not subject to government supervision, and no official quotation sheet is kept.

Unlike the Paris Bourse, the Swiss exchanges have no intention of dumping *la criée*. While Paris is convinced such a system is outmoded, Switzerland is equally positive it is part of the wave of the future. As evidence, the exchanges point to the success of the open outcry system at the options and futures exchanges in the U.S. "It doesn't matter whether it is a securities or commodities market, open outcry is the most viable system because everybody is present at the same time in bidding on a certain item," says Kurt Schneuwly of the Geneva Stock Exchange. "Besides, why do something else when it has worked for years? The continued use of open outcry at fish and vegetable markets, a centuries-old technique, shows that it works as well today as in the past."

Trading in Zurich officially runs from 10:00 A.M. until 1:00 P.M. but in practice stops sooner or runs longer, depending on volume. Closing varies from as early as noon until as late as 3:00 P.M. At 4:00 P.M. Zurich time (10:00 A.M. New York time) the banks begin dealing with New York. The open-ended closing hour became contentious in 1984, when, according to Bär, the cantonal stock exchange commissioner abruptly said one day at 2:00 P.M.: "That's enough for today. Good-bye." Suddenly the exchange saw the wisdom of fixing longer hours. Bär is pressing for at least a five-hour trading session (most other countries' exchanges are open for six hours).

Whereas Paris trades active stocks on a forward market and inactive ones on a cash one, Zurich likes to portray itself as letting all stocks trade either way. In reality, though, only 30 percent of the business is on a forward basis. Bonds, which outstrip stocks in volume, are traded on a cash basis, as are insurance companies and banks, which account for half the volume of share trading. Under a gentleman's agreement years ago, the banks were excluded because they feared depressed prices could cause depositors to panic, touching off a run on the banks' money. Today the banks have more confidence in their customers, and forward trading on insurance companies and banks is expected to start within the next few years.

Switzerland welcomes foreign investment in the stocks of Swiss companies but wants to retain control over the firms. Only Swiss citizens can buy registered shares with voting rights. Nonresidents may buy only nonvoting shares; these yield lower dividends than registered shares. Many companies have created a third category of shares called participation certificates; they have no voting rights but pay the same rate of dividends as bearer shares. All interest and dividends from Swiss bank deposits, bonds, and shares are subject to a 35 percent Swiss withholding tax. Residents of countries that have double taxation agreements with Switzerland can claim refunds. Denmark gets a complete rebate, and France 30 percent, but the standard amount for most countries, including the U.S., U.K., Japan, Germany, and Canada, is 20 percent.

Just as the banks take charge of the trading floor, they run a computerized depository for member and nonmember banks. The system, termed SEGA (Schweizerische Effekten-Giro AG), is a nonprofit organization owned by 175 Swiss banks. Established in 1970, it does away with the need for securities actually to be delivered. Another 235 banks also participate. SEGA currently has offices in Zurich, several blocks from the financial district, and in Basel. Members of the exchanges in Bern, Lausanne, and Geneva drop off their settlement advice notices at the local exchange, which forwards them to Zurich. This practice is stopping in 1986; members will mail notices directly to Zurich. Afterward the Basel office will be closed, and everything centralized in Zurich.

SEGA processes about 10,000 transactions daily. SEGA executives estimate this amount is only 60 percent of what it could handle. The problem is that insurance companies and some banks have snubbed it. The insurance companies have steered clear because of restrictions applying to their industry and the banks because they charge more than SEGA and do not want to lose this revenue.

Dissemination of price and other relevant financial information is transmitted via Telekurs, a joint venture of 350 Swiss banks. Its purpose is to reduce costs of common operations through consolidation. Unlike SEGA, it is a profit-making operation. It is also much bigger, with 640 employees (up by 200 since 1982), compared with 68 at SEGA. Telekurs is located at the opposite end of Zurich from SEGA. The stock exchange is about midway between the two.

Telekurs makes money through many other functions than its work for the exchange. It also performs the processing and settlement of payment transactions by the banks, their cash dispensers, Eurocheque and Eurocard. Europeans traveling in Europe may fill out Eurocheques (instead of traveler's checks) in any denomination, and Eurocard is the European version of Master Card. All paperwork arising from Eurocard transactions goes to Eurocard; this frees the banks from the need for big credit card divisions.

The Zurich exchange first ignored advances in mechanization; it later became a leader. It saw no necessity to install a ticker tape service on prices and volume until 1930, more than sixty years after the New York Stock Exchange. But in 1961 Zurich introduced what was the most advanced television price transmission system of its kind. It became part of Telekurs when the latter was established in 1962. Today Telekurs provides the latest market prices on 78,000 securities traded on eighty stock exchanges around the world as well as on transactions on eighteen commodity exchanges. While much of this information is also available from news wire services, in selling its service Telekurs has an unbeatable advantage in Switzerland. As its executives put it, the Swiss banks "prefer" to give data to Telekurs first since they own it.

The relationship between the Zurich and Geneva exchanges has similarities to the one between the New York and American exchanges. Just as the smaller American exchange often introduces marketing ideas or products that the bigger NYSE then copies, so, too, is Geneva frequently more creative and aggressive than Zurich. Yet, like Amex, it still remains far behind in volume of business. Reflecting the NYSE, Zurich enjoys the luxury of being entrenched as the leader and so contentedly—critics might say complacently—waits until Geneva has suffered the pangs of trial and error. Then, drawing on that experience, it introduces the same thing.

This pattern dates back to the origin of the two exchanges. Geneva was the first Swiss city to form an exchange—in 1850, twenty-seven years before Zurich. Geneva was also the first to suggest mutual cost sharing of electronic information, trading, and settlement systems between its exchange and those in Zurich and Basel. Settlement now takes twenty-four hours; it can contain errors since there are no immediate checks on accuracy. Whether to include the four smaller Swiss exchanges in the systems has not been decided.

This technological cooperation could be the forerunner of similar joint action in options trading. Since many doubt that there would be sufficient options business for all the exchanges, a national options market would likely be set up, with the exchanges linked by a computer. If so, it would be a first in options trading. If the exchanges cannot reach an agreement, each will establish an options market on its own trading floor.

If they concur on an arrangement, it will be a departure from their customary clashes on trading matters. This is most evident in the way Geneva and Basel have been operating nine-month forward trading since October 1984, while Zurich has been sticking to a maximum of three months. The Basel head office of the Swiss Bank Corporation proposed lengthening the period of time, but the bank's Zurich division had doubts about the potential.

"Why would somebody be interested in buying and selling over such an extended time period?" Robert Bischoff, the bank's vice president in charge of its Zurich exchange operations, asks rhetorically. "Three months is a relatively foreseeable future, but a lot of problems, such as bankruptcy, mergers, and rights* issues, can arise in nine months, causing many technical difficulties."

Zurich Börse President Nicholas Bär at first dismissed Geneva's and Basel's initiative as "no success," but he is now swinging opinion to favor copying the two rival exchanges. "I believe that since the other exchanges are doing it, with the result that the banks are having to redesign their programming for clients, Zurich might as well do the

---

*A right is the temporary privilege granted to a shareholder to acquire additional shares directly from the company at a stated price.

Standing around the corbeille, *traders at the Geneva exchange check video display terminals for stocks listed on other Swiss exchanges.*

same. The board at our exchange is slowly coming 'round to my way of thinking."

Not only does Geneva regard itself as a more fertile territory for new ideas than Zurich, but it also claims a more hospitable climate for foreign brokers. Unlike Zurich, the Geneva exchange does not require a deposit to demonstrate financial worthiness, nor does it require any sponsorship to open a branch. Schneuwly points out that because Switzerland is so small, it takes only a few hours at a low fare for Geneva brokers to go by train to Zurich to see clients. The distance between the two cities is little, but the language differences are big. Securities dealers say that residents of Zurich, which is near Germany and principally German-speaking, are more willing to converse in French than people in Geneva, at the French border and primarily French-speaking, are amenable to conversing in German. "Traditionally, French-speaking people are less willing to learn foreign languages than German-speaking people," says Charles Heusser, vice president of the Geneva office of Dominion Securities Pitfield Ltd., Canada's largest securities dealer. He is fluently trilingual in English, French, and German. "German is mandatory at Geneva schools, but there is not much enthusiasm, whereas in Zurich they like to learn French, which is also compulsory at school."

Foreign brokers say Zurich dwarfs Geneva in international underwriting, and its cocktail circuit yields more corporate finance contacts. On the other hand, they describe Geneva as having the upper hand in portfolio management because Switzerland's biggest private banks, which specialize in portfolio management for the ultrarich, are located in Geneva. The Geneva bankers are ambivalent about the invasion by North American securities dealers. They are proud of this international recognition of Geneva as a financial center but displeased about the increased competition for business and staff. Several U.S. outfits, including Citicorp, Chemical Bank, and Merrill Lynch, have purchased small Swiss private banks not so much as a back-door entrance to exchange membership as for direct participation in the syndication of Swiss underwritings.

Retention of personnel is of equal concern to the private bankers. "Geneva is two-thirds surrounded by foreign territory—France and Italy—and is attached to Switzerland by only a spit of land. Therefore, Swiss work permits are essential for employees from these countries," says Thierry Lombard of Lombard, Odier et Cie, the large Geneva private bank. Obtaining permits is difficult because to maintain its remarkably low level of unemployment, Switzerland admits few foreign workers. "Whenever a foreign bank opens in Geneva," Lombard continues, "it can only obtain a few permits and so hires headhunters to steal workers from the existing pool. Zurich is better off because it has a greater reservoir of people."

In Zurich the Big Three banks do close to 70 percent of stock exchange business. In terms of assets they number among the world's fifty largest. But in Geneva two private banks—Lombard, Odier, founded in 1798, and Pictet et Cie, founded in 1805—rank second and third (or third and second, depending on which firm is speaking) in volume of business at the Geneva exchange. "Although private banks are licensed as universal bankers, they have voluntarily restricted themselves to portfolio management, whereas the big banks derive two-thirds of their profits from commercial banking," Lombard says. "Our bank initiated portfolio management in Switzerland almost two hundred years ago."

Pictet et Cie also claims history is in its favor. A member of the Pictet family played a prominent role in Switzerland's adopting its policy of neutrality, and four streets in Geneva are named Pictet. The firm developed computer programming that provides clients from Argentina to the Middle East with the current status of their portfolios in fifty different currencies.

There is a mythology about the Swiss private banks. Only twenty-three, half the number of twenty years ago, remain in existence. (Under Swiss law private banks retain their status only as long as a member of the founding family still works at the bank.) Their near-legendary status revolves around their wealthy clientele and the personalized attention they receive. "A private banker is not only an investment adviser but also a friend and sometimes a substitute for a priest," says the president of one small Zurich private bank.

A private Swiss bank shuns accounts of under $250,000 and is not really happy with those of under $1 million. There are the very discreet private banks that resemble fine residences and that are located away from the financial district, their only signs of identification are business card size nameplates at the entrance. There are also the very public private banks like Julius Bär, with its name emblazoned across its building at the center of the Bahnhofstrasse. Inside, the banks' furnishings range from antique to ultramodern. Usually there are two uniformed guards at the reception desk.

One client never sees another at a Swiss private bank. Customers are quickly whisked into salonlike private meeting rooms. Outside there is no indication that millionaries and billionaires are inside because there are no limousines or huge retinues of bodyguards. Clients walk to their banks or arrive by taxi, carefully disguising their wealth by wearing tatty, old raincoats or other dingy attire. The reason for the stealth is simple: The clients do not want anyone, especially government tax bird dogs from their own countries, to know they are there. France and Italy are particularly vigilant since they do not want their citizens to circumvent their exchange controls. Both countries have been known to station spies in hotel lobbies to nab culprits or to rent rooms across the street from the private banks and use binoculars or telescopes to watch arriving clients.

A small private bank has assets of about 200 million francs, and a large one has around 2 billion. The Union Bank's assets exceed 110 billion francs. In terms of staff devoted to portfolio management, the private and public banks are more equal. The Swiss Bank Corporation has 3,000 employees, about 100 of which are involved in the securities business. Staffs at small private banks range from 30 to 300 people, but their whole universe is securities.

The private banks survive by carving out their own niches. They provide the personal touch that the big banks extend to the very few. "Private banks appeal to institutional clients because when a client calls with an order, the private bank executes it immediately, but at the big banks it might not be done until later in the day or the next day," says Alexander Vannod, president of the exclusive Private Bank and Trust Company of Zurich (Privat und Verwaltungsgesellschaft). "For individuals, the private bank maintains the personal contact that a big bank cannot. At a big bank the person a client is dealing with can change every six weeks. People with a million dollars feel they are important—and they are—but a big bank has many million-dollar customers and declares only one-hundred-million-dollar clients may meet the general manager. The smaller customer at a big bank might only meet younger employees who do not have adquate experience."

The private banks prevent heavy staff turnover by paying much higher salaries than the big banks. J. Vontobel & Company, which is still family-run and -controlled, has gone a step farther. In 1984, on the occasion of the bank's sixtieth anniversary, the chairman, Hans Vontobel, the firm's courtly elder statesman, gave shares as a gift to all 320 employees, the first time such a gesture had been made in Switzerland. Other private banks sell a limited number of shares to employees and restrict their resale.

The private banks claim—and foreign brokers back them up—that their research analysis is more incisive about listed companies than that of the big banks. Because the big banks control the financial destiny of both corporations that borrow from them and investors who buy stocks through them, there are inevitable conflicts of interest.

The banks are drawn toward their corporate clients by the interlocking directorships of the large Swiss companies and their bankers.

In the U.S. research reports consuming dozens of pages are a boon to the paper-manufacturing industry; in Switzerland they consist of two or three pages. Readers of these reports must read between the lines since they are getting a retouched portrait. The reports are sent to the banks' clients, who vet any harsh remarks contained in them. The banks do keep "honest" by not writing anything glaringly positive; conversely, only those familiar with their sanitizing methods would know that "a good long-term investment" translates into "a bad buy at the moment."

In the past few years, as commercial banking has become less profitable, the big banks have beefed up their research departments. But as a vice-president of Crédit Suisse admits, the private banks remain "more courageous." While Vontobel put its analysts on the same pay scale as portfolio managers more than ten years ago, the big banks did not until recently. Private banks remain at an advantage since their analysts generally have greater experience and more sources at companies. This is imperative because Swiss firms are extremely closemouthed and because the balance sheets of Swiss companies are uninformative as a result of accounting disclosure rules that are less stringent than in the U.S. Anyone may obtain the tax records of any Swiss citizen by merely sending a request and three francs to the local town hall. Although individual privacy may be invaded this way, it is not as easy to lift the veil on the financial status of publicly owned Swiss corporations. Their true profit picture is impossible to ascertain because of what are referred to as "quiet," "still," "hidden," or "secret" reserves. Whatever the term, the end result is the same: an overestimate of liabilities which makes profits look slimmer than they actually are. Often hidden reserves are as large as the shareholders' equity figure published by the company. It is perfectly legal for companies to have hidden reserves.

"There has been no protection for minority shareholders," says Anne-Marie Ledermann, banking and insurance columnist for *Finanz und Wirtschaft,* the largest-circulation financial newspaper in Switzerland. "Swiss banking law is built on the principle of protecting depositors and not the shareholders. Business corporation law does not protect minority shareholders because they cannot get hold of the records of the majority shareholders. A recent example is the case of a financially troubled small father-and-son company listed on the exchange, which changed its auditors almost monthly as each auditor refused to handle its accounts. There was nothing the government could do." Having no other recourse, the shareholders turned for help to the supreme authority in Switzerland—the banks—and they brought the company to heel by stopping all its credits.

Even if investors were to know all the dirt about companies, they would still face the difficulty of obtaining portfolios that fit their own tastes. Just as Japanese securities dealers are accused of pushing a "stock of the week," the Swiss banks, which derive half their profits from investment counseling, do much the same thing.

Until a few years ago the employee at a bank's investment desk in the foyer provided custom-tailored advice for each client. But in the cause of cost efficiency the banks now have central committees that draw up masterlists of recommended securities and send them quarterly to the branch investment desks. The branch investment counselor can pick only from such a list when advising clients. Bank fund managers receive similar lists with asterisks beside those stocks approved for purchase at any time, depending on the managers' judgment. To buy others, fund managers must receive approval from the bank's executive committee. Caution takes precedence; the banks worry that if investors who follow their advice lose money, other clients might take their business elsewhere.

The branch manager merely has to take a personality profile of clients based on income, age, and aversion to risk. The profiles are compared with a standardized portfolio for each personality type developed by the bank, thus allowing no leeway for the desk representative to give individualized advice. The system is adequate for those interested in investing in the market but not in monitoring every development. Risk-minded investors resent the sterotypes. As for the banks' recommendations of foreign stocks, those on the master lists are not swallowed whole since they include many foreign stocks listed on the Swiss exchange just because they are on the exchange. It is not uncommon for a stock that has been dropped from analysts' recommendations in its home country to be on a list in Switzerland.

Caveat emptor (let the buyer beware) describes other dilemmas facing Swiss investors. They are caught in a Scylla and Charybdis situation between paying a lot of money and getting only one share that gives them no voting power or paying less for shares the value of which is regarded as overly diluted. This, for example, is the case with the bank stocks. In 1973 the Swiss Bank Corporation did a five-for-one stock split, decreasing the value of its bearer shares from 500 to 100 Swiss francs, in response to public pressure for more affordable bank stocks. Since Union Bank and Crédit Suisse left theirs at 500 francs, Swiss Bank has five times as many bearer shares outstanding. Nor did the stock split win it many long-term investors. In recent years public nervousness over the worldwide trouble of banks with bad debts in third world countries prompted a heavy sell-off of Swiss Bank's shares even though it was not heavily exposed in third world loans.

People invest in the stock market hoping for big profits or, if they are not risk takers, for high dividends. There is little chance of realizing either prospect in Switzerland. The high par value of shares curtails volume and hence price movement. Because the hidden reserves policy artificially reduces profits, dividend payments are low, yielding a nominal 1 to 3 percent. By comparison, dividends in the U.S. average 6 percent. The innately conservative Swiss shareholders do not object, as their U.S. counterparts would, so long as the dividends do not decrease. Grumbling is also kept to a minimum by the common practice of exclusively offering new share issues to existing shareholders at a discount to the current price. They make a gain by reselling the following day at the prevailing price. In the U.S. such secondary offerings are available to everyone at a price that is the average of the last week's trading.

Switzerland lacks a national securities and exchange commission and a national securities act. Businesses must comply only with a federal commercial code (Schweizerische Obligationenrecht). The code merely requires public companies to publish annual reports and hold annual meetings. Otherwise, the securities laws are drawn up by the local cantons and vary from place to place.

U.S. irritation over the absence of Swiss legislation against insider trading was assuaged in 1985, when the Swiss government, bowing to years of U.S. pressure, introduced a law making such behavior a criminal offense. SEC authorities had complained that they were frustrated in prosecutions against investors allegedly using Swiss banks to do insider deals on U.S. stock exchanges since the banks were not obliged to release pertinent information. For their part, the Swiss resented U.S. efforts to impose the American way on Swiss codes especially since the incidence of U.S. insider trading is rising despite the American rules. Under the new law, the U.S. will be able to extradite from Switzerland a U.S. citizen charged in a U.S. court with insider trading.

The questions surrounding much that happens on the Swiss stock market have contributed substantially to bonds attracting more business than shares. Bonds' low rates of interest do not deter investors since Switzerland's minimal inflation makes the real rate of interest (after the amount of inflation is deducted) much higher than is immediately apparent. Because Switzerland's inflation level is considerably lower than that in the U.S., Swiss bonds outperform U.S. ones.

The caution that pervades—some might say, smothers—individual investment in Switzerland also permeates the institutional investment scene. Switzerland has a huge, growing pool of domestic pension fund assets, a prime source of institutional investment money. This money is now equivalent to nearly half of Switzerland's gross national product and is expected to quintuple over the next ten years. Yet the funds' performance is far outdistanced by North American ones as the result of polar views on the role of pension funds.

"U.S. pension managers are out to make more money, and even if they are only investing two to five percent of the fund in European securities, they divide the account between the best two or three out of five presentations," says Christian Wagner, a trilingual American on the research staff of the Zurich office of Merrill Lynch for more than a decade. "Swiss institutional fund managers are not under the same performance pressure and therefore are more conservative and long-term-oriented. Their philosophy leans to preserve, rather than make, money. The tendency is for a hundred-million-dollar portfolio to still be worth a hundred million dollars a year later and the client to be more apt to talk about health and the weather than to ask why the portfolio is not worth a hundred and one million. But the first thing U.S. institutional clients ask is why the portfolio is not worth a hundred and one million dollars, and then they may talk about the weather."

Swiss institutional clients may seem timid in comparison to their bolder, brasher U.S. counterparts, but they are fighters in their own way. Well aware of the benefits U.S. investors have derived from negotiated commissions, they have forced the Swiss banks to give volume discounts on large transactions in lieu of the fixed commission rate system. Individual clients, who generally invest about one-third of their portfolios in foreign stocks, applied similar pressure. Furious over the banks' practice of buying stocks on their behalf in the U.S. at a 70 percent discount over the old U.S. rates but not passing this saving on to them, these clients threatened to take their business directly to U.S. brokers. Like magic, these customers suddenly received the discount. A gentleman's agreement made in the 1930s between Swiss banks and U.S. brokers allows U.S. firms to solicit for institutional clients but not for retail (individual) ones. However, if individuals go to U.S. brokers of their own free will, the Americans are not obliged to turn them away, nor do they.

The Swiss have taken adventurous steps in developing institutional investment business, but the initiative has come from the private, not the commercial, banks. In 1982, for instance, Bank Julius Bär created a division to seek business from U.S. and U.K. pension funds and insurance companies. The following year Lombard, Odier became the European partner in a $700 million worldwide high-technology mutual fund called SCI/TECH. Its partners are the biggest U.S. broker, Merrill Lynch, and the largest Japanese securities dealer, Nomura. SCI/TECH's portfolio consists of shares in high-tech companies in the U.S., Japan, and Europe.

Because the Swiss lack certain North American stock market characteristics—universal discount commissions, financial futures, high dividends, and substantial shareholder disclosure—they are concerned about being a lonely island in the financial world. "The Swiss are not as enthusiastic about change and new ideas as Americans," says Robert Bischoff of the Swiss Bank Corporation. "There is such a variety of people in Switzerland, with Germanic and Latin Swiss thinking differently and speaking different languages, that it is difficult to bring everyone together under one hat."

Yet Zurich is not behind the times in some ways. It is a prototype for the U.S. and the U.K. in its universal banking system, toward which these two countries are veering. Whether they will evolve into exchanges controlled and run by the bankers, as in Zurich, is a question that American and British investors and securities houses may have to face, just as the Swiss are debating which foreign customs are suited for their country.

8

Frankfurt

Amid the hurly-burly of self-examination and revision rattling through major stock exchanges around the world, the Frankfurt Stock Exchange (Frankfurter Wertpapierbörse) is an unruffled exception. It has not been hasty—or eager—to accept or promote change. Only now is it planning longer trading hours to match the duration of sessions elsewhere in the world and a second-tier market for junior stocks. After much lapsed time there is a drive for privately owned German firms to seek public listing, but the credit for this activity goes to a nonmember firm rather than to the exchange or its members.

The *Börse* is accustomed to rolling along quietly like the Main River, which flows serenely through the center of Frankfurt. Even the 1984 involvement of the *Börse*'s unpaid chairman in one of Germany's worst financial scandals since World War II was brushed off like a speck of lint. The *Börse* simply yanked him off its board, replaced him with his predecessor, and business proceeded in its undisturbed fashion.

The same kind of calmness is evident in Frankfurt's ready acceptance of foreign members. Many other exchanges seeking international business either exclude foreign firms or are feuding over their admissions. Frankfurt includes them without any fuss or bother. Of the *Börse*'s ninety-four members, twenty-six are foreign banks or brokers.

The foreign firms say they could get business just as well without belonging. But they elected to join since admission to the stock exchange brings with it membership in the affiliated (and adjacent) Frankfurt Foreign Currency Exchange as well as the opportunity to trade gold and options on stocks. Also, they find the entrance requirements simple and cheap. There is no seat price, as there is in the U.S. Instead, the fee is based on annual volume of business; on average, foreigners say this ranges from 3,000 to 150,000 marks.*

The *Börse*'s lack of turbulence over the competitive presence of foreign members reflects its equanimity about home front challenges. While exchanges in other countries engage in bruising rivalry to slice off a smidgeon of the market share of other domestic exchanges, Frankfurt is unabashedly content with only a 50 percent market share in Germany. Although critics might charge this contentment borders on dangerous complacency, Frankfurters maintain they have realistically accepted the economic and political facts of life in federalist West Germany.

Frankfurt is only one of several significant economic locales in Germany, each of which has its own exchange. All told, Germany, with 61 million people, has eight stock exchanges—one more than the U.S., which has a population four times as great. Düsseldorf is the number two exchange, with a 33 percent market share, and the remainder is divided among Munich, West Berlin, Hamburg, Hanover, and Stuttgart. Until 1945, when it was split into East and West sectors, Berlin was Germany's central stock exchange. Of the eight, only Frankfurt and Düsseldorf do substantial international business. Regional pride prevents unification, but Frankfurter Börse officials have proposed consolidation of some functions out of concern that the German exchanges, which already had lost business to London, will lose even more once London adopts greater automation in 1986. Starting this year, a central computer center based in Frankfurt will process all transactions, and there will be one annual report for all the exchanges, so as to end costly duplication and increase efficiency.

---

*From January to the end of July 1985, the average rate of exchange was 2.2 marks to the U.S. dollar.

Frankfurt's desire for trading supremacy has its roots in political and economic history. Frankfurt is where Charlemagne, the first great ruler to arise among the barbarian kingdoms that developed on the ruins of the Roman Empire, held his first congress in A.D. 792. The *Börse* is within a few minutes' walking distance of the Paulskirche (St. Paul's Church), one of Germany's most historic buildings. And Frankfurt was the site of the landmark creation in 1848 of the German national assembly that tried unsuccessfully to create a federated superstate that would supersede the power of the sovereign states throughout the area. The church is now used for meetings and exhibitions.

Although Bonn is West Germany's political capital, Frankfurt is its banking hub. The Deutsche Bundesbank (Central Bank) has its head office in Frankfurt. There are 358 banks, 219 of them foreign, cheek to jowl around Frankfurt's downtown shopping district, the Zeil, which a few yards from the *Börse* cuts a swath through the city. Frankfurt was also where the famous Rothschild, Bethmann, and Metzler banking families set up shop. The trio were the first bankers to suggest that large share and bond issues should be sold piecemeal to several people instead of the often slow process of convincing one wealthy person. Together with other German private banks, they played a substantial role in financing construction of the railroads in the U.S. during the nineteenth century.

The *Börse* traces its roots to the mid-fourteenth century, when Frankfurt became a self-governing city-state and world center for trade fairs. When the merchants attending these fairs congregated to settle contracts, disputes often arose as the result of conflicting valuations they placed on one another's currency. In 1585, after many years of argument, some petitioned the Frankfurt City Council to enforce a common agreement on the value of nine different coins.

The *Börse* regards that year as its official birthdate. In 1985 it celebrated its 400th anniversary, even though the first official price list of the exchange was not printed until 1727 and the first dividend-yielding shares were not issued until 1820. So important did the *Börse* regard its 400th anniversary celebrations that it postponed much-needed renovation of its building.

Even today trade and commerce are bound together at the *Börse*. Its building is owned by the local chamber of commerce, which has a small promotional office on the ground floor (its executive offices are elsewhere). The chamber also pays the wages of the *Börse*'s forty-five-member administrative staff, for which it is reimbursed by the exchange, which also compensates it for the operational and maintenance expenses of the building. In addition, the chamber serves as the legal representative for the *Börse* in litigation. Until 1807 the *Börse* and chamber shared a board of directors; since then the *Börse* has been self-governing. Of Germany's other seven exchanges, only Berlin has a similar chamber of commerce connection. The Frankfurt *Börse* and chamber occasionally discuss severing, but the talks never reach the serious stage for a very practical reason: They share a common membership.

As in Switzerland, the banks in Germany are universal, selling securities as well as performing traditional banking functions of deposits and loans. They are the backbone of both the chamber of commerce and the *Börse*. Because the banks are "universal," Germany, like Switzerland, has no domestic securities dealers. The banks and the exchange maintain that universal banking benefits corporate share issues since the banks generally have more capital to back their underwritings than have most securities firms. The banks further say their multiple functions allow them to make good losses in one sphere with profits from others.

Compared with the commotion at the U.S. and Japanese stock exchanges, the pace of trading at the *Börse* seems slow and unexciting. Official trading hours run between 11:30 A.M. and 1:30 P.M. Until 1985, when Düsseldorf's exchange proposed extending its trading to five hours, Frankfurt was adamant about not lengthening its session. "We easily handle volume of one million marks in two hours," General Manager Herbert Schlict said shortly before Düsseldorf made its announcement. Because the activity spans the lunch hour, traders sip coffee or soft drinks and snack on cucumbers, herring, or sour gherkins to sate their hunger.

In contrast with Switzerland, which has no intermediaries on its trading floor, Germany has the *Kursmakler*, to whom certain stocks are assigned, as with the specialist in the U.S. Like the French *agents de change*, *Kursmakler* are government appointees, but while the federal government delegates the position in France, the minister of economy in the local state government does so in Germany. In bank

This quiet, tree-lined street is an appropriate setting for the Frankfurt Stock Exchange, which is not as eager for innovation as other major exchanges.

teller fashion the thirty *Kursmakler* stand inside the floor's sole trading post, a long, rectangular enclosure, and their customers line up in front of them. At one end of the room are three tables for newspaper financial reporters to observe the action. *Kursmakler* receive a handling fee, called a *courtage* (commission), 40 percent of which they put in a pool for *Makler* who have had a poor day.

Before 1968 the banks could decide where they wished to conduct deals, but in that year the Bundesbank and the commercial banks reached a gentleman's agreement that trades in officially quoted shares would be performed at the exchange unless customers requested the transactions be handled away from the floor. Orders for bonds can be done independently of the exchange and are several times greater in volume than those channeled through the trading floor.

Those stocks in which there is normally little interest are traded only once a day for twenty to twenty-five minutes. Until 11:55 A.M. trading is at the previous day's closing price. At noon the *Kursmakler* calculate a midway price between buy *(Geld)* and sell *(Brief)* orders received that morning, and at 12:15 P.M. trading recommences at the new price, called the standard price. Popular stocks, in which orders must be placed for a minimum of fifty shares, are traded consecutively. Because of the volume of the stocks, the *Kursmakler* can figure an opening standard price before commencement of the day's trading. Throughout the session the *Kursmakler* dispatch notes of price changes via pneumatic tubes to exchange clerks in a glass booth overlooking the floor. The clerks push buttons on an electronic panel to update the prices on display boards above the floor.

In 1970 Frankfurt started an options market on its most active stocks. In 1983 it reduced the number of expiration dates from two, three, or six months to a three-month schedule, and since then volume has doubled. Frankfurt does 90 percent of the options trading in Germany. There is no rule against trading options and stocks in the same place, so the options business is squashed into one end of the exchange floor.

The *Börse* is severely short of space. Bond and gold trading are in a separate room to allow space for some traders' booths on the main floor. Smaller operations do not get booths or even direct telephone lines to their offices. They are relegated to a public pay telephone, and their incoming calls are announced over a public-address system.

Because the building is a designated historic site, the *Börse* cannot move. The ingenious solution, now under way, is to construct three floors for administration offices in the fifty-six-foot-high cupola above the trading floor ceiling. Bond trading will then move into the vacated administration wing on the second floor. The work should be completed by 1988.

The affiliated Frankfurt Foreign Currency Exchange is located in a small room a few feet from the main trading floor. Trading begins at 1:00 P.M. and is carried on in seventeen currencies. The U.S. dollar, which accounts for nearly half the transactions, is traded first. The currency exchange acts as the nerve center for other currency exchanges in Berlin, Düsseldorf, Hamburg, and Munich. They are connected by a conference line telephone, and the official exchange rate is fixed in Frankfurt.

Apart from the official market, there are two semiofficial ones, run entirely by the banks and *freie* (free) *Makler*. One is the *geregelter Freiverkehr* (over-the-counter) market, on which trading is conducted during the main market's hours and the listings of which must be approved by the exchange. It is similar to London's Unlisted Securities Market, and the *Börse* plans to convert it into an official second tier. The other is the *Telefonverkehr* (telephone market) for stocks traded by telephone. Listed stocks can be traded on either of these markets as well as on the official market. The revamped *geregelter Freiverkehr* will have lower listing costs and less documentation than the top tier but more legal protection for its investors than now exists.

Immediately after Schlict, formerly manager of economic research at a major Frankfurt bank, became the *Börse*'s general manager in 1970, he established the Börsen-Daten-Zentrale (BDZ Exchange Data Center) for automated processing of transactions. Frankfurt was the first German exchange to establish such a system. The big banks also rely on computers to perform back-office tasks. Orders arrive over one computer, and another prepares invoices.

The banks boast that universal banking boosts investment in the market because the public can convert its savings deposits into securities investments in a one-step expedition. However, reality does not match the claim. Only 8 percent of German households invest in the market, down from 12 percent twenty years ago.

Even though Frankfurt is a leading financial center and Germany has the largest gross national product (GNP) in Western Europe, the stock market plays a modest role in the economy. The market capitalization of the stock markets in the U.S., U.K., and Japan accounts for 50 percent or more of their GNPs. In Germany the proportion is only 13.5 percent. It is an occasion for rejoicing when there is a new listing on the Frankfurt exchange.

The pickings are slim for investors. The government owns or has a major stake in 900 businesses, including the Lufthansa airline and Volkswagen car firm. As in the U.K., the government wants to denationalize some of its holdings, but its proposals are unpopular. Critics believe a government pullout could make it harder for troubled firms to raise new capital. Some are also concerned that sales of a number of the government's enterprises would simply transfer control from one monolith to another since the big commercial banks are expected to be the major buyers. Of the 2,000 incorporated companies in Germany (known as AGs, which stands for *Aktiengesellschaften*), only 450 are listed on a German exchange. The others decline to join either because bank loans are easy to get or because they are reluctant to unveil their finances and trade secrets to competitors or the public. Another deterrent is the heavy listing expense; including a fat fee to the sponsoring bank, it can total as much as $100,000, more than at any other European exchange except Paris (up to $150,000).

Furthermore, Germany has 300,000 GmbHs (*Gesellschaften mit beschränker Haftung*—privately owned companies with limited liability), most of which are too small to seek an exchange listing. Many are small handicraft companies with few employees. "The German mentality is to build up a business for children and grandchildren, with the intention of keeping the business in the family at least until the year 3000," says Karl-Oskar Koenigs, chairman of the Frankfurter Börse. "In North America people will sell their business if the price is right or go to the market and raise capital, but Germans want to retain their independence."

The poor performance of the German market is another disadvantage. The bond market has a consistent, albeit unspectacular, track record, but stocks performed dully between 1962 and 1982. "There was nearly no increase in stock prices during this period and thus no music in the market for investors," says Karl Hauser, director of the Institut für Kapitalmarkt Forschung (Institute for Capital Finance), which does research on the capital market in Germany. He also heads the economics institute at Goethe University in Frankfurt. "There were many years during the 1970s when more money was paid out in dividends than newly invested in stocks."

Investor interest was enlivened in 1983 and 1984 by anticipation of outstanding company profits in 1984, and the Frankfurt stock exchange's share price index set several records in late 1984. But during 1985, mirroring the weakening of Germany's economic growth, stock prices rose less meteorically.

Compounding the market's flaccid performance are several other factors that have handicapped the exchange in attracting more investors. Some are historic; others reflect the cautiousness of the populace in investing their money and the banks' emphasis on lending rather than underwriting new issues.

The English never mention the impact of World War II on their stock market, and the Japanese just allude to it. In Germany, although forty years have since elapsed, the stock market, like much else, still bears the scars. Only in the past few years has Frankfurt completed the reconstruction of its historic sites, including the Alte (old) Opera, with iron sculptures of winged horses on the roof, the town square, and the *Börse*, built in splendid neo-Renaissance style in 1879, which was almost entirely destroyed by a 1944 air raid. Bearing scars, too, are some executives who served in the German Army and were severely injured. Koenigs, the chairman, lost a leg, and Schlict, an arm.

The war also resulted in the flight from Germany, or the deaths, of many Jewish bankers who had previously constituted the largest segment at the exchanges. "Look at this photo of the Frankfurt exchange in 1880; two-thirds of its members were Jews and they continued to play a major role until the war," Michael Hauck, president of George Hauck & Sohn Bankiers, a major private bank, said to me as he pointed to a picture at the entrance to his office.

The Germans are parsimonious when it comes to the stock market. A popular German wisecrack is: Question—"How do you make a small fortune?" Answer—"By investing a large one in the stock market." Most Germans prefer to put money in bank accounts despite a substantially lower interest rate than in the U.S. "In New York it is not uncommon to hear a taxi driver discuss what stocks to buy or sell over his car radio with another cabby, but in Germany the market is not as popular with the average German," says Hansjürgen Müller, general manager of the Frankfurt branch of the Morgan Guaranty Trust Company.

In contrast with France and Italy, Germany has no foreign exchange controls, and residents can take any amount they want out of the country. The restrictions have goaded the French and Italians into devising ways of evading them, but the open-door policy does not tempt the Germans because of their devoted commitment to savings accounts. "I have been in the investment business for twenty-five years, yet I cannot convince my parents to place any money outside their savings account," Müller says—and he is a very convincing fellow. The loyalty to the banks is based on pragmatism. Customers readily obtain higher interest rates in return for banking large sums, a procedure that at U.S. banks must make its way through piles of red tape.

German residents sporadically go on binges of pulling their money out of Germany, but this is more for psychological than financial reasons. "Whenever tension intensifies between the West and the Soviet Union, there are concerns about keeping all one's money in Germany since the USSR is so close," Müller says. This happened, for instance, immediately after the West German government agreed in 1983 to the U.S.'s stationing cruise nuclear missiles in Germany.

Long memories of losing money in bad stocks and a lack of stern shareholder protection laws are a further depressant on German investment in the stock market. There are no "blue sky"* laws against securities fraud, and anyone can put an advertisement in a newspaper claiming investment in a certain stock will result in making a fortune. The Germans still bitterly recollect the losses suffered by those who invested in IOS (Investors Overseas Service), one of the all-time enormous international financial swindles.

IOS, founded in 1960 by Turkish-born, U.S.-reared Bernard ("Bernie") Cornfeld, was an elaborate mutual fund scam involving misrepresentation of the investment performance of the funds and illegal currency transactions. It flourished for ten years because the public eagerly lapped up IOS's promotional theme of bringing capitalism to the masses. Nowhere did IOS do better than in Germany. By 1969 Germany accounted for half the clients, salesmen, and volume of sales in IOS.

Germany was fertile territory for IOS since although the German economy boomed in the 1960s, stock prices did not and so the Germans steered clear of the market. They were left with a lot of money to invest elsewhere, and IOS happened along at this ripe time. The negative impact on investor confidence of the IOS scandal was worsened by its ocurrence just as Germany was basking in its economic recovery from the war. "People had bought a house and a car and

---

* *Blue sky* is a slang term for laws protecting the public against securities fraud. The term *blue skied* means a new issue has been cleared by a securities commission and may be distributed to the public.

finally had the money to invest in the market, and when they did, they got burned," says a senior manager in the securities department of one of Germany's biggest banks.

Some of the blame for the low rate of stock market investment belongs to its member banks for generally giving more attention to their other business areas. Traditionally the German commercial banks have derived only 25 percent of their business from their investment division, and the makeup of their management boards reflects this preference. Most executives are from the commercial rather than the investment end. For example, of the twelve managing directors at the largest commercial bank, the Deutsche Bank,* ten are commercial managers and two are investment ones.

The banks are followers, rather than leaders, in the current drive to increase listings on the exchange. The *Börse*'s members are thrilled that twenty-six companies listed in 1983 and 1984. However, the impetus for their joining was given by a small Munich portfolio management firm that is not a member of any exchange. After a two-year waiting period to see how this upstart outsider fared, the Deutsche Bank became the only member of a German exchange to follow suit. Many more months elapsed before the Dresdner Bank, the second-largest, underwrote in 1984 its first new listing in fifty years. In contrast, the New York Stock Exchange in 1983 alone added twenty-four new listings.

Germany's thirty mutual fund companies show the same aversion to risk as the typical German individual. According to the Commerzbank, the number three commercial bank, about 80 percent of the mutual funds are in bonds, an even higher proportion than the 65 percent average for the nation. The mutual fund companies have been doubly prudent since 1983, when they rushed to establish high-technology funds and stubbed their toes. The public responded eagerly to these funds, with ADIG Investment, a mutual fund owned partly by the Commerzbank, for example, raising 200 million marks in only two weeks. Unfortunately half the money was invested in U.S. high-tech stocks just two weeks before they plummeted in value.

As with everyone else in Germany, institutional investors prefer being safe to taking risks—and if that means being regarded as less

---

* Despite the similarity in names, there is no connection between the government-owned Deutsche Bundesbank and the private-enterprise Deutsche Bank.

sophisticated than U.S. fund managers, so be it. After all, the firing rate is high among the "sophisticated" American managers if they do not produce instant big gains on investments. In Germany, where firms are content with steady returns, the managers are not in jeopardy to the same extent.

Even if the managers were inclined to high risk, government restrictions prevent any wild speculative digressions. Insurance companies are prohibited from investing in options or futures and from placing more than 5 percent of their portfolios in stocks. Also, corporate pension funds, normally a big source of investment money in the market, are much smaller than in the U.S. In Germany the money is kept in-house instead of in the market. This inflates the liabilities side of corporate balance sheets since the item "provision for pensions" often is as much as shareholders' equity.

This practice stems from the aftermath of World War II. As the Germans rebuilt their economy, Konrad Adenauer, who became chancellor in 1949, faced a dilemma: How could workers benefit from the restoration of companies' financial strength without sapping the firms of their capital? His solution: Pension money would remain within the companies and not be invested in the stock market. Later an onerous codicil was added: If a company goes bankrupt, all other firms must guarantee its obligations to its pensioners.

This clause has an ironic twist since competitors can wind up footing the bills for collapsed rivals. A foremost instance occurred in 1983 when Siemens, the country's largest telecommunications equipment manufacturer, contributed 30 million marks toward the pensions of its troubled competitor AEG-Telefunken. While Adenauer's solution worked in the short term, there is increasing apprehension that the system could cause the funds to run dry.

Potential German investors can turn to three types of banks when they become interested in the stock market. First, there are the full-service commercial banks, for which the investment business is only one spoke on the wheel (they also engage in loans, deposit taking, and foreign exchange dealing). The Big Three banks in this category—the Deutsche Bank, Dresdner Bank, and Commerzbank—were split up after World War II, but a 1956 law restored their original form. The trio have their head offices in Frankfurt, in a triangular layout a block apart, with the Deutsche, perhaps symbolically, at the apex of the triangle. The Dresdner's headquarters features an unusual amenity for employees—a swimming pool on the top floor for use in the evening.

The Dresdner Bank was the center of unwelcome attention in 1984 and 1985. Its chairman, Hans Friderichs, was alleged to have accepted bribes in his previous position as Germany's economic minister in the so-called Flick Affair—political payments to various members of the Helmut Kohl government by the Flick Company, Germany's largest private holding company. Friderichs and his successor were charged with taking bribes in return for awarding Friedrich Flick, head of the family-controlled empire, a tax break on the 1975 sale of his shares in the Daimler-Benz car company. The trial, originally scheduled to start in January 1985, was postponed until late August 1985 and was expected to last more than a year.

Under West German law, political contributions by corporations are not illegal, but the recipients were tarnished because the present Flick's late father played a key role in financing Adolf Hitler's rise. That their chairman was involved in this scandal was humiliating to Dresdner Bank and employees, who felt it hurt their bank's image. They privately expressed a desire that he would resign. He did so, effective March 27, 1985.

The second set of banks to which investors can turn is the savings banks. Originally these banks concentrated on collecting savings from the public, but they gradually spread into the same areas as the commercial banks. The third choice is the private banks, the oldest group in the German banking system. Specializing in portfolio management and securities issues, they are either sole proprietorships or, as is becoming the trend in both Germany and Switzerland, limited partnerships. An eagerness to reduce personal liability and the hope of increasing capital through accepting new partners triggered the switch.

The private banks are minnows compared to the commercial banks. The combined assets of the top twenty private banks are only one-fifth those of the Deutsche Bank. In terms of branches, the private banks also are vastly outnumbered. Most have fewer than 5; the Deutsche has close to 1,400. The private banks have no foreign offices; the commercial banks are worldwide, with the Deutsche, for example, having offices in fifty-three countries.

The private banks are more influential than their size would seem to indicate. Their strength comes from their concentration on portfolio management—especially for the very wealthy. Up to 75 percent of their business is derived from commissions charged for the sale or purchase of securities for individuals. Commissions are fixed in Germany at 1¼ to 1½ percent of the value of the deal. Although each private bank unblinkingly maintains its bank is absolutely *the* only one without financial criteria for potential clients, most private banks stress that their less egalitarian competition demands at least 500,000 marks.

The private banks can afford to be choosy since they have been around for years and have kept generations of the same prosperous families happy by fattening their portfolios through astute investments. Twenty of the eighty-three still in existence were established before 1800. A visit to a German private bank is a return to the stately, opulent ritual of business that flourished in past centuries. The exterior may resemble a mansion complete with courtyard and have a family crest above the entrance gate and door knockers shaped like eagles, as at the Bethmann Bank, founded in 1748. Or it may be a small, plain office building with a discreet nameplate.

Whether the outside is impressive or plain, inside, the atmosphere breathes rarefied refinement. Passage to the offices is blocked by a porter, usually middle-aged, whose obsequiousness is overlaid by a veneer of snobbishness. Visitors are ushered into a corridor of private offices so that their identities are not revealed to other clients also wanting anonymity. There is a public waiting room, but it is empty as customer and banker are closeted in a private room, much as confessor and priest meet away from the public eye. These rooms are not bare-boned cubbyholes; instead, they are furnished with the sort of delicate antique chairs on which hefty people hesitate to sit; exquisite gold French antique clocks; and massive portraits of past generations that headed the bank, with pictures of the founder and his wife at the center.

Some private banks are now subsidiaries of big commercial banks, a connection downplayed to the point of secretiveness, so clients will not be alarmed that the intimacy of dealing with their private bank has vanished. Such is the case, for instance, with the historic Bethmann Bank. There still are a Bethmannstrasse (Bethmann Street), on which the bank is located and which leads to Frankfurt's town square, and a Bethmann Park. But since 1982 the bank has been wholly owned by a Munich bank, Bayerische Vereinsbank. Previously the Vereinsbank had owned half of the Bethmann Bank for many years.

The universal banking system which distinguishes German private banks from British merchant banks is disappearing as U.K. merchant (and commercial) banks buy brokerage houses in advance of the 1986 Big Bang in London. The two countries' financiers still diverge on the importance they attach to corporate financing, which figures more prominently in the U.K. than in Germany. As with many elements in Germany's financial system, the reason for this attitude dates back to the country's recovery period after World War II, when companies could readily obtain loans from their "house" banks. Thus most firms were in no hurry to be listed on the exchange; those that were did not automatically issue new shares to obtain funds since bank loans were so available. Takeovers, which generate much of the activity on U.S. markets, are rare in Germany.

The chairmanship of the *Börse* is unofficially reserved for the head of a private bank, but the power to appoint him resides with the Big Three banks. This was made evident in early 1984, when Ferdinand Graf (Count) von Galen was whisked out of office after the private bank he headed, Schröder, Münchmeyer, Hengst & Company, nearly collapsed. The bank's troubles arose from loans von Galen made to a tottering German construction machinery firm. The loans were more than ten times the legal limit for credit to a single borrower, and Schröder, Münchmeyer would have gone into bankruptcy if Germany's other banks had not stepped in to rescue it. They did so to forestall what would have been the worst banking disaster in Germany since World War II.

Lloyd's Bank International took over the good parts of Schröder after it had been shorn of its credits to the ailing equipment firm. Lloyd's purchase included a strong securities division, which competitors regard as one of Germany's finest. In 1985 the West German government charged von Galen with fraud and breach of trust.

When the scandal erupted, some of the mud splashed on the *Börse:*

guilt by association. It acted quickly to scrape the mud off. The representatives to the *Börse* from the Big Three banks held a telephone conference and decided, as they later wryly put it, to "exchange" von Galen for his predecessor, Karl-Oskar Koenigs. Von Galen was ousted within days, trading was not affected, and the *Börse* continued as if nothing at all had happened.

It was unscathed largely because Koenigs is highly regarded by the financial community. Although his goal is early retirement so he can farm (farming and banking are part of his family's heritage), Koenigs agreed to serve as chairman at least through the *Börse*'s 400th anniversary in August 1985. He is one of two outside partners at the blue-blood Bankhaus B. Metzler seel Sohn & Company. The bank is in its twelfth generation of family ownership, under President Friedrich von Metzler, making it the oldest bank in the world still to be in the hands of its founding family. Its research staff includes the prince of Hanover, a cousin of Queen Elizabeth II of Great Britain. The Metzler bank has guided the destiny of the *Börse* for years. Friedrich von Metzler's father was the *Börse*'s chairman for ten years, and Koenigs held the post for fourteen years until von Galen succeeded him.

To North Americans, accustomed to the separation of the banking and securities business, there would seem to be a conflict of interest in the German universal banking system. Not only do the banks underwrite corporate issues, but they frequently also invest in shares of their clients, and senior officers of the banks and of industry sit on one another's boards. Under German law, the banks must declare in their annual reports those companies in which they hold 25 percent or more of the capital, although they do not specify precisely how much. This close relationship makes it possible for the banks to ascertain early if a firm is in trouble. In such instances, they not only could but also have dumped their shares in advance of public awareness of the problems.

The U.S., Canada, and Japan have laws keeping commercial banks from doubling as underwriters of new issues to prevent such situations. But the West German and Swiss governments are content to rely on the banks' sense of ethics in performing their dual functions. There is no "Chinese Wall"—an invisible wall on the scale of the Great Wall of China—separating the investment and corporate financing sides at the German banks. Analysts in the investment department are frequently caught between informing investors and protecting loyal corporate customers against painful disclosure. They do it by implying between the lines that a company is in trouble.

The head offices of the big banks determine the investment strategy and stock price analysis for Germany and the rest of the world on the basis of reports from the branches. They then distribute the information back to the branches. For instance, each Monday the Dresdner Bank sends to its worldwide offices a telex detailing an investment strategy for major markets. It circulates valuations of individual stock prices and profit estimates every two months. However, financial analysis remains underdeveloped in Germany largely because until the market began to move in 1983, there was little of interest to follow. It is estimated that there are only 150 financial analysts in Germany; in the United States, there are around 20,000.

German banks can manage with so few analysts because of a technical analysis publisher, Hoppenstedt Company, located in Darmstadt, a fifteen-minute train ride from Frankfurt. Established in 1926, the family-owned firm has a staff of 300, who produce a wealth of business reference books and graphs on stock market performance that the banks purchase and then supply to clients. The material includes domestic and international data on corporations: assets, revenue, products, date established, number of employees, and senior management. There are separate books covering 3,000 machinery manufacturers, 21,000 listed and unlisted industrial firms, 455 insurance companies, 1,500 banks and financial companies, 2,500 brewers in Western Europe, 50,000 leading personalities in the German economy, and 45,000 in middle management, plus the 2,000 largest companies in Austria.

Hoppenstedt also publishes a slew of charts on foreign currency exchange rates (every two weeks), high and low share price performance, and monthly highs and lows for domestic and foreign companies on German exchanges and key companies on foreign exchanges. Its annual epic is a five-year summary, published each December, containing stock market performance, primarily in Germany, but also including some information on foreign stocks and currencies. Hoppenstedt's prices are reasonable, the five-year charts selling for 134 marks prepublication to subscribers and 168 marks subsequently; the banks find it more practical to buy from Hoppenstedt than hire staffs to prepare similar material.

In the U.S. new stock market listings seldom rate more than a yawn or a passing glance by investors unless the newcomers are considered highly promising. Germany is aglow over the listing of a little more than thirty companies between 1982 and the end of 1984. In conservative German financial circles this was regarded as a boom, especially because only twenty-one companies were introduced into the German stock market between World War II and 1977.

The credit for this accomplishment largely belongs to a maverick Munich firm, Portfolio Management. PM, as it is known, was established in 1967 as the first independent German portfolio management company of its kind. It is not a member of any German exchange and is located apart from Germany's financial community. Its offices in a renovated brownstone, with door handles shaped like doves, are near the university, about a ten-minute subway ride from the central railway station.

The Munich site is due to happenstance, but PM's president, Bernd Ertl, says that in an age of speedy telecommunications PM's location is unimportant, although half the companies it has taken public are in the Munich area. PM specializes in the listing of small high-tech companies, and the Munich vicinity is similar to California's Silicon Valley. Siemens, as well as several other electronic companies, are near Munich, and as happened at the same kind of U.S. concerns, employees left these older firms to start their own enterprises.

The bushy-haired Ertl, who is in his early forties, is a man with a mission. His goal is to convince German companies of the necessity of an exchange listing for raising funds and their profiles and to get Germans to invest more in the market. His success prodded the Frankfurter Börse into organizing a second market to reroute the newcomers from the less regulated over-the-counter and telephone markets to which most head. On the investor side, Ertl admits the new listings have attracted regulars more than novices. According to him, about 70 percent of the shareholders in the newly listed companies already invested in the market.

Ertl's crusade has also benefited Portfolio Management. Half its revenue now comes from new issues business. PM charges an average commission of 5 percent, and another 2 percent goes to its banking partner in underwriting. Ertl will not divulge total commissions, but a fairly accurate calculation on the companies it listed between 1981 and 1984 is somewhat more than 6 million marks. On the portfolio side PM manages a total of 400 million marks. PM's success is abundantly displayed to visitors. The office walls are lined with an extensive art collection, and the oval boardroom table is of expensive gray marble. The table centerpiece is somewhat unusual: a glass bowl, shaped like a huge brandy snifter, filled to the brim with cigarette packages.

Ertl began musing about why there were no new issues in Germany while working for the Frankfurt branch of the large U.S. broker Bache & Company, after graduating from university with a degree in economics. He could see that Bache and other U.S. brokers did well in new issues business in the U.S. and decided that what worked there could be transplanted to Germany. Ertl joined PM in 1969 and soon began making his pitch to German banks and companies.

His enthusiasm fell on deaf ears. "I told everyone that a lot of money could be earned, but the whole German financial community said it was impossible. Their argument was that it would fail because Germans traditionally had not been risk-oriented in the stock market. I maintained that was due to their not having the choice. I also said that if nobody else is doing something, that is when entrepreneurs should reach for the opportunity."

Unable to enlist the German banks, Ertl decided to pursue his cause on his own. His exhaustive blitz began with his culling the newspapers for names of rapidly growing companies. He wrote a "few hundred," and close to 20 percent responded—a high rate for direct mail campaigns. However, only 2 percent asked for a sales presentation. Ertl followed these up with letters every three months. He also embarked on a lecture circuit to chambers of commerce, wrote article after article for financial publications, and attended electronic trade fairs in Munich and Cologne to buttonhole people and give his familiar spiel.

Besides convincing companies, Ertl had to line up a bank willing to participate in underwriting the new issues. As he foresaw, and as is now PM's practice, PM would handle 40 percent of the new issue and the bank (or banks) the rest. Achieving this was as difficult as persuading the companies to list. Most banks were wary since the companies Ertl collected were small, with profit of under 100,000 marks, and young. The banks feared such firms might not survive and their collapse would smear their reputations, causing clients to desert. The banks also believed they would lose esteem if the prices of stocks they brought to the market were to drop.

Because no German bank would agree to be a counderwriter, the tenacious Ertl approached the Swiss subsidiary of the famous London-based N. M. Rothschild & Sons banking house. The Rothschilds had made their money in large measure through new issue business; consequently, its Swiss manager readily agreed to be comanager of PM's first new issue. Despite the Rothschild connection, the big commercial banks and elite private banks in Frankfurt remained aloof. Ertl resorted to two small Hamburg banks. His first choice, the Robert Mayerling Bank, turned sour when the bank went bankrupt. The second choice, Bank Marcard, has worked out.

By the time PM was ready to take its first candidate public in 1981, the market had gone flat. Nevertheless, Ertl decided to proceed on the ground that "growth companies can do well even if the market is poor." Of the ten companies PM listed between 1981 and 1984, the average share value climbed by 40 percent, and the share price of the most successful, Electronic 2000, more than tripled. But one of the ten became bankrupt a year after its listing, and another was on the verge only a half year after it had gone public.

It is an unpleasant but not unusual fact of life that companies listed on a stock market sometimes fail, but such incidents stand out more in Germany for the very reason that there have been few new listings. The blame was assigned to PM, even though it had distanced itself from the troubled companies. "When we took all the companies to the market, we emphasized they were high-risk," Ertl says. "Even companies with thirty million marks in revenue can have problems." To shore up its reputation, PM reacted by tightening its standards for accepting candidates. It quintupled the minimum earnings requirement to 500,000 marks and raised the number of years a firm must be in business to five years from three.

That some companies brought to the market were as much as seven times oversubscribed did not escape the notice of the banks that had sat on the sidelines when Ertl sought their assistance. The first big bank to follow PM into the field was the Deutsche. Although the Deutsche is portrayed by rivals and self-described as the most cautious of the Big Three banks, its actions belie this reputation. Back in the 1970s when his was a voice in the wilderness, Deutsche's senior vice president with responsibility for its securities business, F. Wilhelm Christians, preached the necessity of enlarging stock exchange listings.

The Deutsche has good rapport with the German populace because of some adroit footwork in the 1970s. During that period leftists were decrying the power of the banks, accusing them of controlling Germany by sitting on boards of corporations as well as being their lenders. Placed on the defensive, the banks were saved by a piece of good luck. Concurrently with all the furor, Middle East interests wanted to buy a major portion of Daimler-Benz, the luxury car manufacturer. Daimler-Benz is regarded as one of the pearls of German industry, and there was the same sort of consternation that would occur in the U.S. if General Motors were the target of a foreign takeover. At the height of the uproar the Deutsche Bank sprang to the rescue by purchasing a sizable stake in the car firm. It was a public relations coup. Newspapers that the day before had been howling over the banks' power did a complete reversal and hailed the Deutsche Bank as the savior of Germany. Ever since, talk of the banks' having a conflict of interest has ceased to be a major issue.

Just as it had kept a watchful eye on its opportunities in the Daimler-Benz affair, the Deutsche Bank observed the success of Portfolio Management with more than casual interest. It was attentive for two years, long enough to learn from any mistakes Portfolio Management made. Because PM's smallness restricts its ability to bring big firms to the market, the Deutsche Bank concentrated on such companies. Among those it has attracted to the market are Wella AG (the hair products firm), Porsche AG (the sports car builder), and Nixdorf Computer AG (a major computer manufacturer). None of the Deutsche's listings has failed, but only a few are huge successes.

For all the excitement over the new offerings, they lack a prime ingredient to snare shareholders. In order for the companies, many of which are family-run, to retain control, they put very few shares on the market and generally restrict them to nonvoting status, thereby emasculating the power of outside shareholders. Even so, the big names of Porsche, Nixdorf, and Wella were oversubscribed by as much as ten times, often more for emotional than for investment reasons. This was particularly true of Porsche, whose name has a certain magic with sports car fans. Buyers offered more than the market price just to get one share.

The success of the new listings campaigns by Deutsche Bank and Portfolio Management should not obscure the cold reality that it is only a small, first step. The combined trading volume of the new listings is just over 1 percent of all trading in Germany. Although Ertl optimistically forecasts that 100 more companies will join the market by 1989, he tempers his prediction by pointing out that in theory *1,000* companies are eligible for a listing.

That same reserved attitude could also be said to be the general prognosis for the Frankfurter Börse—not exactly rooted at the status quo but not wildly rushing to change either. The revamping at other major exchanges may eventually seep into Frankfurt, but for now the *Börse* is content to amble along in its conservative fashion rather than change for the sake of change.

New York

(New York and American Exchanges; also NASDAQ)

New York is the only major financial center with two rival stock exchanges. At 11 Wall Street is the New York Stock Exchange, established in 1792. Called the Big Board,* it chalks up 60 percent of world trading and 85 percent of U.S. volume. A few blocks away, behind Trinity Church, burial place of Alexander Hamilton, the first U.S. treasury secretary, is the American Stock Exchange (Amex), the third-largest floor-based exchange in the United States and one year younger than the NYSE. Both exchanges are almost as old as the United States is as a nation.

But a growing piece of the pie is going to a nationwide electronic floorless exchange headquartered in Washington, D.C., the National Association of Securities Dealers Automated Quotation System (NASDAQ). Founded in 1938, it lists over-the-counter securities—those not listed on the regular exchanges. NASDAQ has become the

---

*The term *Big Board* has nothing to do with the NYSE's volume. Instead, it dates back to when giant annunciator boards were attached to the side walls of the trading floor. These were covered with flashing lights, each with a number on it for a broker. The clerks at the telephone booths around the perimeter of the floor would signal their brokers to come for orders by flicking switches to activate their lights on the boards.

second-largest securities market in the United States and the third-largest in the world. At its current rate of growth it could exceed share volume on the NYSE by the end of this century.

NASDAQ's 1984 volume was up four times over 1980; the Big Board's doubled in that period. NASDAQ now averages daily volume equal to 75 percent of the NYSE's, but on occasion it has surpassed the Big Board. Just six years ago NASDAQ did only 45 percent of NYSE volume. Since NASDAQ share prices average one-fifth those on the NYSE, narrowing the gap in dollar value will take longer. NASDAQ claims 600 of its listed companies are the size that the NYSE accepts for listing. The Big Board, using different criteria, says only 300 do. Over the past decade NASDAQ's listings have ballooned by 60 percent, but the NYSE's have shrunk by 1 percent and Amex's by one-third.

"The U.S. now has two national markets," commented Roger Birk, recently retired chairman of Merrill Lynch and immediate past vice-chairman (until May 1985) of the NYSE. "One is the unlisted NASDAQ market, which has been making much progress. The other is fragmented, with lots of stock exchanges and the related options market among which there probably will be networking and joint venturing."

Thirty-five percent of the 326,000 people in the $37 billion U.S. securities industry work in the square quarter-mile area of Wall Street, making *Wall Street* a generic term for the investment community. Wall Street views itself as a pioneer, a beacon to the world's securities industry, the place with all the answers, where the swiftest, the toughest, the winners congregate. Yet there are signs that it has rushed into uncharted waters without regard to the possible negative consequences. The only place seemingly immune to the commotion and change is Wall Street's most popular hangout, Harry's at Hanover Square, a restaurant with a huge mahogany bar staffed by six bartenders and supplied from a 100,000-bottle wine cellar. Its owner, Harry Poulakakos, who runs similar establishments in the Amex building and near City Hall, was formerly a beekeeper in Greece.

Behind the symbols of success—the fat cigars, thick carpeting, profusion of flowers, walls covered with paintings, guards at the visitors' desks, secretaries who have secretaries who have secretaries—there is deep concern and perplexity about the future. Besides de-

The New York Stock Exchange floor vibrates with activity on a typical afternoon.

With headquarters in Washington, D.C., NASDAQ, a nationwide floorless exchange, lists over-the-counter securities not listed on regular exchanges.

bating whether the floor or the computer box is to be the exchange of tomorrow, Wall Street is wrestling with whether twenty-four hour global trading would be a boon or just an added expense at a time when it is trying to learn to curb costs. Securities houses also wonder who will control Wall Street—themselves or newcomers, such as banks, insurance companies, and department stores—and what impact the new arrivals will have on government regulation and profits. So far, the synergy at these patched-together behemoths is poor and their creation has not helped—and has sometimes damaged—profits. Wall Street is also concerned that it may have overwhelmed the public with too many financial products.

What happens is of paramount importance to American shareholders, who invest more in the stock market than the people of any other nation. Nearly three-quarters of the U.S. population own shares of corporations—either directly or indirectly through pension plans, mutual savings, bank accounts, and life insurance policies that are invested in the market.

The NYSE and NASDAQ represent warring ideologies. The NYSE is an auction, order-driven system the linchpin of which is the middleman called a specialist. Past specialists include Jacqueline Kennedy Onassis's father, John Bouvier, and several members of his family.* Specialists are exclusively assigned up to six stocks each. They must risk their own capital by buying and selling for their personal accounts to fill gaps in supply and demand and thus artificially create an approximation of what a true auction market would be if there were sufficient participants. The specialist also serves as a broker's broker, executing limit orders (requests to buy or sell at a specified price, or a better one) for brokers who want to proceed to other transactions and not wait until the price reaches that level. Specialists receive handling fees based on the number of shares and prices of the stocks. Critics of the specialist system claim these fees cost investors an unnecessary $100 million annually since specialist intervention occurs in only one out of ten transactions.

NASDAQ has a dealer system in which competing price quotations of market makers (brokers who can both fill clients' orders and trade for their own accounts) are the driving force. They can partic-

---

* Joseph P. Kennedy, Sr., President John F. Kennedy's father, was the first head of the Securities and Exchange Commission.

ipate in as many stocks as they want, provided they meet NASDAQ's capital requirements of fiscal worthiness. NASDAQ insists on at least two market makers per stock; on average there are seven, and one firm, the MCI Communications Corporation, a large telecommunications company, has forty-nine. Market makers must enter both a bid and asked quotation and be good for at least 100 shares on either side. Clients pay no handling fees over and above the regular brokers' commissions. When a market maker trades for his own account, his profit comes from the difference (spread) between the bid and asked price.

Filling an order in an auction market versus the dealer market is the difference between the horse and buggy and the race car. At the auction market the brokerage house telephones an order to buy or sell to a phone clerk in its booth on the exchange floor located near the trading post. The clerk writes out the details on a piece of paper: "Buy 100 XYZ at the market." (XYZ is the symbol for the stock, and *at the market* refers to the prevailing price or better.) The clerk hands the paper to a floor broker, who takes it to the space, known as the trading square, at the trading post where that stock is traded. Other traders (the crowd) shout price quotations as at any type of auction.

If a deal is struck, the seller fills out a form in triplicate with parts for himself, the buyer, and exchange personnel, who time-stamp it for the exchange's daily record keeping. The trader throws his order slip on top of a heap of others, contributing to the floor's garbage dump appearance. He gives his copy of the confirmation to the clerk, who notifies his office, which in turn tells the client. In the case of limit orders ("Buy XYZ at ¼"—the full price is omitted), the broker leaves the order with the specialist, who puts it in his limit order book to execute when that price is reached. At one time specialists wrote these orders in notebooks; in recent years electronically generated display screens have replaced pencil and paper.

The NASDAQ system is less cumbersome. By pushing a few buttons on a computer terminal, rented from NASDAQ, a buyer or seller obtains the latest bid and asked prices each of the market makers offers in a stock. The best price is listed first; if several offer the same best price, the first to offer it is given top spot. If it is for under 500 shares, the trade is completed through NASDAQ's electronic small-order execution system introduced in 1984; otherwise, deals are consummated by telephone or teletype. In 1982, at the behest of the Securities and Exchange Commission, NASDAQ expanded its automated quotation system from merely providing bid and asked prices to encompass the latest price, high and low prices for the day, and volume. This "national market system" put NASDAQ on the same footing as conventional stock exchanges in information supplied to the public.

Wall Street is uncertain whether the NYSE or NASDAQ will win in their slugfest, but there is no problem in pinpointing the loser—the American Stock Exchange. Squeezed between the NYSE's appeal to companies with upscale pretensions and NASDAQ's appeal to the types of smaller companies that used to switch to Amex, Amex is becoming increasingly redundant. The big question is whether Amex can continue existing for long.

Although it has set records in volume in recent years, Amex's hold on total share volume in the U.S. is down to 7 percent, and its dollar volume proportion is only 3 percent. Between 1979 and the end of 1984 Amex listings declined from 931 to 796. Since its listing requirements are lower than the Big Board's, Amex traditionally was the market for younger, growing companies.* But NASDAQ companies are now resisting moving to either Amex or the NYSE, despite recruiting efforts by both exchanges.

With its niche in the marketplace preempted by NASDAQ, Amex looked for alternatives and decided to become a leader among stock exchanges in the trading of options. It has accomplished this goal, but its achievement has further overshadowed its original role as a stock market. Now Amex is in danger of losing some of its share in the options market to the newer entrants—the Big Board and NASDAQ—which are both lavishing attention on this popular trading product.

The NYSE has cultivated an image of being to the stock market world what having ancestors who arrived on the *Mayflower* is to the

---

*The NYSE requires minimum net assets of $16 million. Minimum pretax income must be $2.5 million for the most recent year and $2 million for the two preceding years or an aggregate of $6.5 million for the three fiscal years, including a minimum of $4.5 million in the most recent year. Amex requires minimum net assets of $4 million and minimum pretax income of $750,000 in the preceding fiscal year. The NYSE also requests a total of 1.1 million publicly held common shares and Amex, 500,000.

social set. Only 7 percent of U.S. securities firms are NYSE members, but they employ 77 percent of the industry's work force. But like many blue-blood, snobbish families, the NYSE has a skeleton in its past. In 1938 Richard Whitney, who had served five terms as president, admitted embezzling funds entrusted to him by the exchange and the New York Yacht Club; he had also misappropriated funds from his father-in-law's estate, and it was for this that he was tried and sentenced to Sing Sing Prison. Three years earlier reformers at the exchange who were incensed by his do-nothing attitude had ousted him. Until then Big Board presidents wishing another term were automatically reelected.

The Big Board's style is to be seemingly inactive while other exchanges trailblaze with new rules and equipment, then suddenly to adopt what competitors have initiated or embellish on their innovations and through its size to gain once more the upper hand. The NYSE was much like an exclusive men's club until 1967, when Muriel ("Mickie") Siebert, who had started on Wall Street as a $65-a-week analyst, was accepted over stiff objections from many members. She went on to become the only woman to own an investment house in the United States.

In the spirit of good neighborliness the exchange accepted Canadian firms as members in the 1960s; other foreigners were barred until 1977. A Japanese firm, Nomura Securities, was not admitted until 1981. Members expected Nomura's entrance would spur the Tokyo Stock Exchange to accept foreigners; as of summer 1985, this had yet to happen. "We joined because of the prestige of a membership and to increase the morale of the Americans working for us," explains Yoshio Terasawa, New York-based chairman of Nomura Securities. "I hadn't realized how important it was to the Americans until they began dropping by my office, one by one, to say how happy they were we had become a member." Practical economic considerations also influenced Nomura. "We also can attract more sources of revenue. If we give an institutional fund manager a thick report on a Japanese computer firm and he buys IBM instead, he gives part of the order to us as a token of appreciation. As a NYSE member we can now execute that order."

Until 1970 the exchange held the peculiar position of not allowing its members to be publicly listed, even though its business was the trading of stocks. The threat by a big member, Donaldson, Lufkin & Jenrette, Inc., to resign and join the third market (an informal market run by nonmembers for large orders of listed stocks), prompted its change of heart. "We were Peck's bad boy, although many members were sympathetic," Chairman Richard Jenrette recalls as his courtly southern drawl and surroundings of exquisite eighteenth-century Americana form an incongruous backdrop to his fighting words. "It was ridiculous for the exchange to espouse public ownership of corporations while remaining a private club itself."

Similarly, the NYSE opposed the electronic Intermarket Trading System linking the regional exchanges with the two New York exchanges and NASDAQ. ITS display terminals show the current quote in a trader's market and either the current quotes at the other exchanges or the best price available. If another exchange has a better price, the trader uses ITS to access that marketplace. There is no fee to investors; ITS is funded by the exchanges, which receive income based on volume of business. The NYSE feared it had everything to lose and the regionals everything to gain from ITS. The exchange gave way because institutional investors, from which it derives most of its business, might have gone elsewhere. It need not have worried: Trading with the regionals still involves communications delays and despite big gains—1,100 listed firms, compared to 11 at its April 1978 birth, and 1 billion shares annually compared with 235,000 between April and December 1978—ITS is dwarfed by the 23 billion shares in 1984 at the NYSE.

In response to NYSE lobbying, Congress suggested the SEC include a clause ensuring that ITS would be an auction market. The SEC ignored this directive because, as Richard Ketchum, director, division of market regulation, says, "We didn't feel everybody should be forced into one shoe box of either the traditional or electronic method of trading."

Since John Phelan, a thirty-year veteran of the exchange (first as a member and then as president), became chairman in May 1984, he has moved swiftly to make his own imprint. Sometimes, though, he seems to be marching to a different tune from many members. This is most apparent in the way he has embraced twenty-four hour trading and linkages with domestic and foreign exchanges for joint trading of stocks. A small step in this direction occurred at the end

of September 1985, when the NYSE advanced its opening time to
9:30 A.M. from 10:00 A.M. The impact on other exchanges of what
the NYSE does was amply demonstrated when other North American exchanges quickly adjusted their opening times to match the
change at the Big Board. In 1986 the Big Board is expected once
again to advance its trading start—this time to 9:00 A.M.—and again
the other exchanges will do the same. The Pacific Stock Exchange
members' trading day will then begin at 6:00 A.M. local time, which
PSE president James Gallagher wryly says "will cause sociological
problems in California." Several major U.S. corporations are already
traded internationally on the London and Tokyo exchanges. Phelan
believes greater global interest would develop in NYSE stocks if NYSE
members could transfer their capital to other marketplaces when it
is not in use in New York, and he has begun talks with London and
Tokyo. Despite its size and record volumes, the NYSE believes such
arrangements are necessary to compensate for its slowing year-to-year
growth rates and fewer foreign listings than in London.

This could be accomplished, for example, if the NYSE had satellite branches in such places as Tokyo and London. Alternatively, NYSE
traders would pass on their orders to the other markets, just as a ba-
ton is passed from one relay runner to the next. Phelan is convinced
twenty-four-hour trading is essential for the NYSE to retain the business of U.S. institutional investors and prevent off-floor trading by
members with overseas offices. The Big Board's prohibition against
this applies only within the U.S.

His enthusiasm is not contagious. NYSE members generally
maintain Phelan's scheme would necessitate hiring more staff for the
extra shifts at a time when their profitability is already squeezed. They
further argue that longer hours do not guarantee more volume. (There
was little increase in volume from Europe in response to the initial
expansion of the NYSE's trading day in September 1985). For these
reasons, member firms on the exchange's committee on international and capital markets unanimously opposed twenty-four-hour
trading. Yet a week after the committee's rejection of twenty-four-
hour trading, Phelan publicly announced the exchange was considering how this could be done.

The securities industry was not pleased. "The public isn't clamor-
ing for this since it likes to go to sleep at night," Securities Industry

Association Chairman Robert Shapiro, also chairman of Wertheim & Company, remarked dryly. Added the securities industry analyst Perrin Long, Jr., of Lipper Analytical Distributors Securities Corp., Inc., of New York: "The NYSE should keep in mind that there is little to be gained from twenty-four-hour trading since seventy-seven percent of NYSE-listed shares is held by U.S. institutional investors, who would be more involved than individuals in twenty-four-hour trading. Since these investors live in the U.S., what is to be gained by 'round-the-clock trading, especially as institutional managers are not going to work 'round the clock? The reasoning seems to be that the exchange is now only utilizing its facilities for one-fourth of the day, and if it is open longer, there will be more business. But will it be profitable business? After all, it costs money to stay open longer."

Like other exchanges, the NYSE is owned by its members, and they believe this entitles them to the final say over policy. Phelan's disregard of their views on twenty-four-hour trading infuriated many. Robert Towbin, vice-chairman and senior managing director of L. F. Rothschild, Unterberg, Towbin, did not mince words: "What John Phelan thinks is meaningless because he is like a chamber of commerce president in that he has no power. It is the member firms that have the power since their membership is essential to the exchange's existence."

Even if members approved twenty-four-hour trading, the exchange would require SEC approval. SEC officials are skeptical about the necessity and worried that lack of standardized global regulations could provoke abuses. They also are concerned that an oligarchy would result.

The NYSE started in humble circumstances—members met under a buttonwood tree—and so did the American Stock Exchange. Amex was first known as the New York Curb Exchange (the Curb) because brokers stood on the curb to conduct their business. Descriptive hand signals designating stocks and the quantity wanted originated at Amex, as did the brightly colored jackets floor traders wear. To watch for the signals from their clerks the brokers leaned over the windows of nearby office buildings, and the jackets served as quick identification. In 1953 the Curb was renamed the American because it traded mostly American stocks. Initially its directors se-

The American Stock Exchange stands opposite historic Trinity Church in lower Manhattan.

lected the National Stock Exchange but reconsidered after the NYSE had objected that the name implied the Big Board was not a national institution.

Just as the NYSE has its black sheep—Richard Whitney—so too does Amex. In the 1950s many scandals rocked Amex, culminating in the disclosure that a known stock manipulator had paid a gambling debt for the exchange's president, Edward McCormick. Reformers among the membership forced McCormick's resignation and replaced him with thirty-eight-year-old Edwin Etherington, a lawyer and former NYSE vice president, who cleaned up Amex's image.

If exchanges were ranked by pioneering rather than volume, Amex would be well ahead of the Big Board. It accepted female members two years before the NYSE. It was eight years ahead in launching options and in 1985 became the first U.S. market to trade options on gold bullion. It was the first U.S. exchange to introduce touch screen technology for high-speed order execution. In 1985 it took the lead in allowing a television network (Cable News Network) to transmit live market updates from the floor and in forming an overseas electronic trading link. The connection enables British investors to trade directly in some Amex options.

Securities firms, upset at the cost of belonging to two places so near each other, have frequently suggested merging the NYSE and Amex. The larger NYSE has been reluctant to do so. Not until 1976 did it allow members to trade Amex stocks, and in 1977 it backed out at the last moment from a proposal that would have placed all stock trading at the Big Board and all options at Amex.

Speculation about a merger flared briefly after the May 1985 hiring of Amex's president, Robert Birnbaum, as president of the Big Board. Such an arrangement would bring the NYSE more listings, along the lines of the second-tier markets in Japan and Europe, at a time when takeovers among member companies are shrinking the total number of corporate listings, a trend that could very well continue. Also, Amex has the attraction of a much bigger options business.

In contrast with the NYSE and Amex, NASDAQ could be characterized in dramatic terms as the Horatio Alger of the stock market, the little exchange that by dint of ingenuity and hard work climbed out of obscurity. But that would be wrong. NASDAQ has actually grown in spite of itself. Much as the fiercely proud NASDAQ officials would hate to admit it (considering their barely disguised contempt of the NYSE as archaic), NASDAQ has exhibited similar reluctance to accept change. Indeed, it owed much of its success to changes congressional and SEC actions foisted upon it rather than to its own initiative.

With no trading floor the National Association of Securities Dealers (NASD), which runs NASDAQ, has no need to be headquartered in New York, where the brokers are. Instead, it is a short subway ride from the SEC. Congress established the NASD to oversee the OTC market under the 1938 Maloney Act amendments to the 1934 Securities Exchange Act, making it the sole U.S. stock market legislated into existence. Only 16 percent of the total 30,000 OTC stocks traded in the U.S. are on NASDAQ, but they account for 85 percent of all OTC volume. The other 15 percent is traded via so-called pink sheets, a daily printed list of price quotations.

The SEC browbeat the NASD into setting up its automated quotation system in 1971. Previously dealers in over-the-counter stocks could never be sure if they were getting the best price since there was no quick, centralized way of checking for it. Brokers were only obligated to compare prices of three NASD firms and to take the best one; deals were made via telephone. Pink sheets were unavailable until the next day and covered only one-third of the stocks. Dealers often did not adhere to their pink sheet quotations. As early as 1964 the SEC stated it wanted a nationwide computerized electronic system providing buy and sell price quotations to assure more accurate and rapid distribution of information. Many NASD firms stalled, fearing loss of business if customers could easily and quickly identify who offered the best price. Instead, the accurate, fast information increased confidence, and hence volume, in the market.

Implementing the system was the first task of Cleveland broker Gordon Macklin, who became the NASD president in 1970. Homespun, Macklin is a salesman to his toes, but he knows when not to push. While the NYSE's Phelan irritated the London exchange by initially exaggerating the status of linkage discussions, Macklin was low-key. "London has an enormous agenda to address in a very compact time frame, and therefore, it is not timely to put more items on its plate," Macklin said shortly after Phelan's approach to the London exchange. He could afford to be statesmanlike; London officials had visited NASDAQ in Washington a week after Phelan announced his initiative. Plans for an electronic link between London and NASDAQ are much farther along than talks between London and the NYSE because of the compatibility between the automated systems at NASDAQ and London. The NYSE has just developed a screen trading system geared to global trading, with London targeted as the first international partner.

Macklin is a management-by-objectives man, who, with his staff, spells out problems and potential solutions in blanket detail in a thick manual brought out annually. For example, 1985's assessment called for increased competition. The solution: Increase NASDAQ's visibility by encouraging more newspapers to list NASDAQ in their stock pages, a campaign that is gaining momentum.

Macklin believes the automated system will assist NASDAQ in building up international ties in its race against the NYSE to develop global alliances. Already there are 8,000 NASDAQ quotation terminals located in thirty overseas countries. In addition to the London exchange, Macklin is wooing the Eurobond market, which, like NASDAQ, operates from traders' offices rather than a floor, and the Swiss exchanges. However, Nicolas Bär, president of the Zurich Stock Exchange, says his exchange has no concrete plans for a hookup, although it would be interested in an international arrangement in options trading. Australia and the Middle East are also high on Macklin's shopping list because "one of the beauties of an automated system is that places which might not seem like logical contenders can be."

The SEC also persuaded NASDAQ to introduce the national market system in 1982 and recommended that only those stocks with at least 100,000 shares worth $5 each be included. About 2,500 stocks, representing 75 percent of NASDAQ's volume, qualified. Macklin says the increased visibility the expanded reporting provides has helped NASDAQ retain companies eligible for NYSE or Amex listing. Through the display of last sale prices, rather than merely the advertised prices at which market makers are prepared to buy or sell, the system also seeks to stop what critics allege is the practice of some market makers to quote only their prices rather than those of competitors—a violation of the multiple market maker rule that is the crux of NASDAQ. This last trade information enables clients to determine whether their NASDAQ broker, when involved as a market maker in a stock, quoted the best price available.

The national market system and NASDAQ's new small-order execution system also benefit the NASD financially. Its automated quotation system is stipulated as a not-for-profit service, in line with the association's tax-exempt status as a disseminator of trading information. This constraint does not apply to any other systems it develops, and consequently, for these two new systems NASDAQ is charging rates that yield a profit. This money goes to research and development of electronic systems, and any surplus is rebated to members. In 1984, $1.4 million was returned.

Today NASDAQ is the toast of the securities industry. But at the outset of the 1980s it had a life-threatening emergency on its hands. It had taken over its central computer processing facility (located in Trumbull, Connecticut, a seventy-five-minute train ride north of New York) from the Bunker Ramo-eltra Corporation, with which it had contracted to build the system. Unfortunately NASDAQ was ill prepared since it lacked both the staff and the organization necessary to keep the system functioning smoothly. Equipment and programming were deficient, and computer uptime was below 95 percent, causing irate members to scream they would take their business elsewhere. At the very time NASDAQ was poised for big gains in volume, its reputation was suffering from deserved criticism that it had one of the country's worst on-line systems.

To bring order out of the chaos, Macklin handpicked a two-man team with divergent backgrounds. He named Frank Coyle, formerly vice president of consumer banking data processing at the Chase Manhattan Bank, as vice president in charge of systems operations. Macklin wanted him because of his proved skill in producing service quality. As vice president, systems engineering, Macklin hired Randall Sampietro, who had developed and installed New York State's computerized welfare management system. The two men were ordered to enlarge NASDAQ's handling capacity, a priority if NASDAQ was to achieve Macklin's goal of handling 200 million shares daily by late 1985. (In 1981 it was doing only 35 million shares daily.) Coyle and Sampietro doubled the size of the Trumbull facility and installed a second power generator so the plant can operate without oil for a week. NASDAQ now plans a second data center in Virginia as a backup site in case of a major power failure in the northeastern United States.

Listings are the lifeblood of an exchange, and the battle for them is hotter than ever. NASDAQ could have been a greater threat to the NYSE if it had included listed securities when it established its automated quotation system. It chose to exclude such stocks because it thought it more important to automate the over-the-counter stocks which were its primary business. Also, fewer than 2 percent of the original applications for NASDAQ listings covered listed securities.

Technically NASDAQ members can trade stocks listed on an exchange under the Intermarket Trading System. Originally just the country's seven exchanges were involved, but in 1982 the SEC decreed that NASDAQ be added. It has got little business as the result of a NYSE rule forbidding off-floor trading by its members.

In early 1985 the SEC allowed two regional exchanges—Boston and the Midwest—to trade NASDAQ securities. A subsequent SEC decision could further blur the demarcation between NASDAQ and the listed markets. The commission authorized the NYSE, Amex, Philadelphia, Pacific, and Boston stock exchanges, as well as the Chicago Board Options Exchange and NASDAQ, to trade options on some of NASDAQ's most heavily traded stocks. The ramifications could damage NASDAQ. The SEC is permitting the exchanges to trade the underlying stocks along with the options, a reversal of its 1973 prohibition of such side-by-side trading, which it maintained could spark manipulation. The danger to NASDAQ is that the exchanges could drain away business in these popular stocks and then seek to trade more unlisted ones. But this problem may evaporate because the exchanges face a daunting situation: member companies might refuse to pay the exchanges' high listing fees; or they might depart if under the new system, rival firms on NASDAQ were also traded on the exchanges without having to pay for a listing. The dilemma of the NYSE and Amex, which earlier vociferously opposed side-by-side trading, could deepen if the big Chicago Board Options Exchange wins SEC approval to trade the underlying stocks of the options it now trades.

It is unlikely NASDAQ will gain any NYSE companies through their delisting from the Big Board since tough rules make it virtually impossible for a company to leave. Two-thirds of a company's shareholders must approve such a decision, and only 10 percent can be actively opposed. Even when this hurdle is surmounted, the exchanges will not let go. Recently an Amex company had to go to court to obtain an order for Amex to allow it to delist and move over to NASDAQ.

The NYSE has held its market share in listings as a percentage of those that qualify, and it has attracted new ones. But its grip is precarious because takeovers and mergers among members are diminishing listings. This slippage places the exchange in a dilemma over the violations of its prohibition against issuing shares of unequal or no voting power. Some of the NYSE's biggest members have recently issued new shares of this nature as a defense against unwanted acquisition bids, but the exchange is reluctant to delist them lest they scurry over to NASDAQ, which so far has no restriction against weighted shares. Thus the Big Board is reconsidering its ban, though the maneuver further dilutes the already weak position of minority shareholders.

For its part, to hold on to its momentum, NASDAQ has been ladling out tender loving care to its member companies. In 1976 it established a corporate advisory board of chief executive officers of NASDAQ companies. Four years later it appointed a group of corporate consultants—NASDAQ companies assigned the task of recruiting more firms. Then, in 1985, NASDAQ created the position of senior vice president of company services, whose task is to coddle member companies. On the principle that the best person for this job would be someone from a member company, NASDAQ President Gordon Macklin chose John Guion, formerly a life insurance president and a member of NASDAQ's board. "My job is to relate the benefits of being on NASDAQ to member companies and to make certain they know what services it can offer them," Guion says.

Since stroking the companies may not be enough, NASDAQ offers rock-bottom listing fees. The maximum charge, unchanged from 1974, is $5,000, and Macklin says there are no plans to raise it. The NYSE's assessment is based on the number of shares issued by a company, and the minimum fee is $12,700 per million shares for the first 2 million. There is also a one-time listing surcharge of $31,700. NASDAQ's maximum annual fee is $2,500; the minimum at the NYSE is $12,700. Unlike the exchanges, NASDAQ does not have disclosure or reporting regulations in addition to those of the SEC.

All this has garnered NASDAQ ardent admiration among analysts, brokers, and corporations. "Shortly after John Phelan became chairman of the NYSE, I was sitting on a dais with him and asked why a company should list on his exchange," recalls Sanford Robertson, president of the San Francisco investment house of Robertson, Colman & Stephens. "He replied that it is a wonderful experience. For the corporation, he said, it is like receiving the *Good Housekeeping* seal of approval. It is also a wonderful experience, he went on, for the wife of the corporation's president because the president receives a tie clasp and his wife a white orchid when the first symbolic trade is made. The chairman hosts a luncheon in their honor and gives them a speech in his office on the virtues of free enterprise.

"But there is no true economic justification for a company to be listed on a conventional exchange. The electronic market is the market for the future. Amex mostly has marginal stocks, and NASDAQ outperforms the NYSE in liquidity. So we don't encourage clients to go to New York."

NASDAQ's chief corporate cheerleader is William McGowan, chairman and chief executive officer of MCI Communications, the size of which qualifies it for NYSE listing. "Amex has no liquidity or big spreads and is more interested in options," McGowan told a meeting of NASDAQ companies. "As for the NYSE, think of its image—stodgy, large capitalization stocks. People like it because they can park their money there."

Longtime securities analysts favor NASDAQ, too. "In the old days there were good reasons for listing on the NYSE because it facilitated the dissemination of information about what was happening at a company and the prestige involved helped in raising equity," says analyst Perrin Long, Jr. "But all that has gone by the board with the rise of NASDAQ. Getting listed on the NYSE is now just an ego trip, and many companies are listed that shouldn't be because they're not traded much. When a pair of shoes gets old and scuffed, you throw them out. You would think the exchange's management would similarly want to upgrade the quality of companies listed, but any management likes to say its outfit is the biggest and the exchanges are no different."

Robert Towbin of L. F. Rothschild, Unterberg, Towbin hangs out black crepe for the exchange: "The NYSE is a thing of the past; it has no real meaning anymore. Before there were instant telecommunications, the exchange provided a central marketplace where you could determine the real value of a stock, but that is no longer necessary. The exchange could have killed the NASDAQ system off at the beginning, as well as private computer systems giving quotes of listed stocks, since it had a system of its own it could have used. But instead, it chose to fight these systems. The only role left to the exchange today is a self-policing regulatory function over its members, but one could debate whether self-policing is better than government regulation. Now that the technology is here, a floor is no longer needed; the NYSE's could be turned into a basketball court."

Recognizing that its stock listings were unlikely to grow, the Big Board branched into futures in 1980 and options in 1983. Neither is yet profitable. The New York Futures Exchange (NYFE), set up as a subsidiary because futures fall under Commodity Futures Trading Commission (CFTC) regulation and options and stocks under the SEC, has only about a 2 percent market share. In options the Big Board has only a 1.1 percent share; Amex has 26 percent.

Critics blamed the NYSE for believing it would do well in futures simply because it was the Big Board and futures were booming. "The exchange was determined to be in the business but didn't know what it was getting into," a close observer of the situation, who requested he not be quoted by name, told me. "It spent money like a drunken sailor, but money doesn't always solve a problem. There is too big a staff, and its budget is way overboard. Here it is, the nation's sixth-largest futures exchange in terms of volume, and it can't make money." NYFE also suffered from starting with products similar to those at the big Chicago futures exchanges, even though the conventional wisdom is that the first exchange with a product does best.

In early 1985 the NYSE entered into negotiations with the New York Cotton Exchange to shift NYFE from facilities near the Big Board over to the World Trade Center, where most of the city's commodities exchanges are located. The talks followed similar discussions with the Commodity Exchange Inc. (Comex), the third-largest U.S. commodities exchange. Comex, a gold market, was interested because its attempt to launch financial futures had failed. It thought the deal was all but consummated, but NYFE preferred the Cotton Exchange since its only request was that its traders have access to NYFE's contracts, whereas Comex wanted 50 percent of NYFE.

In the case of options the NYSE could claim that its entry was delayed by the SEC's 1977–1980 moratorium on the establishment of new options exchanges or new contracts. The SEC used the time for studying the implications of the explosion in options trading after the start of the Chicago Board Options Exchange in 1973. A former senior CBOE executive, Ivers Riley, heads the NYSE's options division, but progress is hampered by a lottery system which assigns options exclusively to an exchange. As long as multiple trading of options on the same stocks is prohibited, the NYSE can never be a big player, primarily since there are only about two dozen desirable listed stocks left on which options are not traded. "The other exchanges trading options are content to live with this cartel arrangement because it has protected them from the NYSE," explains Joseph Sullivan of The Options Group.

"The smaller exchanges believe this arrangement has saved them from being devoured by the two largest exchanges trading options, the Chicago Board Options Exchange and Amex. In turn, the CBOE and Amex are so fearful of the NYSE they have curbed their greedy tendencies to make off with what the Philadelphia and Pacific exchanges have. The CBOE and Amex also realize that an out-and-out war between them could be devastating to both."

Not all of the NYSE's options problems are traceable to outside forces. Because it was much slower than the CBOE in establishing options on stock indexes, a popular product, the CBOE has the lion's share. In addition, the Philadelphia Stock Exchange has demonstrated that newcomers to options can do well. Founded in 1790, Philadelphia, the oldest U.S. exchange has been housed since 1982 in a unique environment for a U.S. exchange: on the ground floor of an atrium in an office building. Glass windows enable passersby to observe the action.

President Nicholas Giordano credits options as "the most significant contributor to our growth over the last ten years. They now account for sixty percent of our variable income and were the motivating force behind our moving into our new building." The revenue also bankrolled the launching in 1985 of a Board of Trade in financial futures.

In 1982 the Philadelphia exchange became the first in the U.S. to trade foreign currency options. That bold move lifted it into third place in options business, ahead of the NYSE. Foreign currencies gave Philadelphia international stature, and it capitalized on this by becoming the first U.S. securities exchange to open an office in Europe, in London. In 1985 it notched another first, beating runner-up Amex by a few weeks and NASDAQ by several months, in establishing an over-the-counter index option based on NASDAQ's most popular stocks.

Options were Philadelphia's last hope for survival. It had picked up some extra business through mergers with exchanges in Baltimore, Washington, and Pittsburgh during the 1950s and 1960s, but not enough to halt its downhill slide. It saved itself from extinction by offering discount rates to institutional investors before the NYSE did so in 1975. "It is important for a stock exchange to meet the demand for more diversity from the securities industry," Giordano explains. "The risks in financial instruments are greater than ever, forcing financial institutions to hedge against potential loss from price fluctuations." Aware of the warning example of NYFE's me-tooism, Philadelphia wanted to carve out its own niche.

The idea for foreign currency options was originally floated by Arnold Staloff, now president of Philadelphia's Board of Trade, when he was in charge of computer operations at the NYSE from 1978 until 1980. He was certain of its success because "more trading occurs

Glass walls enable passersby to observe the action on the floor of the Philadelphia Stock Exchange, which is housed in the atrium of an office building.

in foreign currency than in stocks, gold, or commodities." To his disappointment, his idea got mangled in the bureaucracy. "Trying to get anything going at the NYSE is almost impossible due to its structure," Staloff says. "My suggestion was gaining acceptance until it got into the hands of several of the exchange's committees. Anything new that the NYSE does, it has copied from other exchanges."

Staloff's idea was warmly received by Giordano, who wanted to turn a disadvantage—Philadelphia's position in the shadow of New York—into an advantage. "We could exploit the New York market more easily and cheaply than the Chicagoans, and as a result, a lot of people on our options floor are transplanted New Yorkers." But first Giordano had to overcome the impediment of options on currencies being under the jurisdiction of the CFTC since Philadelphia, as a stock exchange, is under the authority of the SEC. He persuaded the SEC to give the go-ahead on the ground that foreign exchange was not necessarily included or excluded in the 1934 Securities Exchange Act, which established the SEC.

The success of NASDAQ places the NYSE in a quandary. It has to gauge the extent to which it can counter NASDAQ by employing NASDAQ's technique of automation without at the same time destroying its own cornerstones of the floor and the role of the specialist. Its record of revising trading methods in response to marketplace pressures indicates it will do whatever it believes is necessary to survive.

A century ago stocks were shouted out on a roll call basis for bidding, similar to the *criée* system still in existence in Paris and Switzerland. As listings multiplied and members became impatient for a stock's name to be called again, the NYSE went to a continuous system of trading all stocks simultaneously. As communications improved, the Big Board progressed to stock tickers, installed in 1867, with trading information transmitted by printed tape; later the overhead moving electronic ticker came into use.

Today many members ignore the specialist despite the exchange's Rule 390 stipulating that all members' orders must be done on the floor. Large block transactions (10,000 shares or more) are mostly done *upstairs* (off the floor) and then formally completed on the floor to comply with the rule. A big chunk of NYSE volume is affected since about half its business comes from blocks, more than double the amount ten years ago. The upstairs traders do not use the specialists to smooth out imbalances in supply and demand because only one-third are regarded as sufficiently well capitalized to fulfill their role in all market conditions. With the NYSE averaging daily volume of 90 million or more shares, at about an average of $35 a share, few specialists have the millions of dollars to back their positioning.

The third market normally operates when the NYSE is closed or when a trading halt is called before or after a news announcement that could substantially affect the price of a stock. In 1983 the exchange requested the SEC to outlaw such transactions, and when the SEC refused, the exchange curtailed its trading halts to three hours. If the NYSE had acquired the Pacific Stock Exchange, resulting in the PSE's trading all Big Board stocks, the third market, the leading participant of which is a Los Angeles firm, could have lost much of its appeal.

To preserve the function of the specialists and satisfy their voracious need for capital in today's big-volume market, in the spring of 1985 the NYSE relaxed its rules to allow all-purpose brokerage houses to own specialists. The NYSE had maintained its rules prevented conflicts of interest resulting from the specialists at a brokerage tipping the trading side about competitors' moves, but full-service houses argued that such breaches would be avoided by a "Chinese Wall" between the divisions. The NYSE was equally, if not more so, persuaded by the need to squelch competition from the Pacific and Boston exchanges, which already allowed brokers to own specialist firms.

Many big "retail" brokers that deal with the public are eager to buy specialists so as to retain the commissions they now pay them. But the big institutional-oriented houses, such as Goldman, Sachs, Morgan Stanley, and Salomon Brothers, are vehemently opposed. They have reservations about the effectiveness of the "Chinese Wall." Also, the new broker/specialist combination of the retail firms might be able to handle the large trades now done upstairs by the trading desks of the institutional houses.

In terms of automation, Wall Street has journeyed far from 1968, when what the industry called the great paperwork crunch in documentation covering transactions forced the NYSE to curtail trading by two hours daily and then by one day a week for many weeks. The crunch was caused by daily volume equivalent to only 25 percent of what the exchange now handles easily—thanks to the installation of $100 million worth of automating systems. Up to 60 percent of transactions can now be done electronically; that means bypassing the specialists the exchange is otherwise attempting to preserve.

Because the equipment also could eliminate clerical trading floor positions of several hundred exchange employees, the employees threatened to strike in 1985, largely over the issue of job security. However, they were in a no-win situation because the exchange's automated systems would have prevented the strike from having a major impact. The walkout was called off just minutes before its scheduled start. It would have been only the second strike in the exchange's long history.

Much of the automation has been a defensive effort aimed at forestalling further off-floor execution of orders by members. When the SEC ruled in 1976 that orders of 100 shares or less need no longer go to an exchange floor but could be done in-house by brokers, the two largest retail brokers—Merrill Lynch and Dean Witter Reynolds, Inc.—grabbed the opportunity. They maintain they save their clients time and money. Since a transaction is done instantaneously, via computer, while customers are on the telephone, they no longer run the risk of the price rising as they wait several hours for the trade to be done on the floor.

If there is no offsetting request from another client to buy or sell, transactions are done from the broker's inventory. Customers no longer have to pay the specialist's handling fee of one-eighth of a *point* (dollar) on odd-lot orders. (If the stock were trading at $17⅞, the client would be charged $18.) "Putting a fee on top of the commission just for making the trade is a rip-off," asserts H. Hanford Smith, Jr., senior vice president, transaction services of Dean Witter.

Smith says it took time for the concept to catch on even at his firm because account executives were reluctant to yield their personal contacts with clients. "Account executives are fat, lazy, and overpaid. Give them something good, and they won't read the memo. It took them awhile to realize it allowed better utilization of their time." Now business is coming in a tidal wave, with 90 percent of Dean Witter's eligible odd-lot business performed this way. The 1985 volume of 18 million shares (the average odd-lot customer buys 30 or 40 shares) was double the 1980 volume.

That is vastly surpassed by the NYSE's average *daily* volume of 92 million shares in 1984, but the Big Board wanted to prevent further erosion. Its answer was the R-4 program—Registered Representative Rapid Response—introduced in 1982 and covering orders of up to 600 shares in 68 popular stocks. The specialists feared potential big losses in business, but R-4 handles only 300 trades a week and the SEC had said 200 stocks could be covered.

Another new system, called Super Dot 250,* electronically connects member firms to the floor and returns reports in up to 1,099 shares in market (current price) orders and up to 30,099 shares in limit orders. Expansion to larger orders is under consideration. Super Dot was introduced to offset the regional exchanges' gearing their computer programming to orders of this size.

The specialists are more in dread of equipment capable of squeezing them out of large block orders, especially since these orders account for half the NYSE's current volume, compared with 17 percent a decade ago. The best-known and most successful producer of such programming is New York-based Instinet (Institutional Networks Corporation). Buy/sell execution is done in thirty-five seconds through an electronic network among brokerage houses, eliminating the need for the specialists on the trading floor. A received order is entered into a computer terminal in a brokerage house's trading room and then routed via a series of linked computers in brokerage firms across the nation to the trader offering the best price. The computer rotates orders if prices are identical.

Since both the NYSE and the Amex prohibit off-floor trading by members, Instinet does not include their stocks. That is less of a handicap than it may seem because many NYSE and Amex stocks are also listed on the regional exchanges. These exchanges have installed Instinet or let their members do so, even though they, too, prohibit off-floor execution. They simply exempted Instinet from the regulation since getting increased order flow took precedence. About 4,500 listed and over-the-counter stocks are on the Instinet system. Its annual volume of 100 million shares slightly exceeds the NYSE's daily volume.

---

* The letters *DOT* stand for Designated Order Turnaround System; the 250 refers to a goal of handling 250 million shares a day. A daily record of 236 million shares was set in August 1984, and the exchange now has capacity to process 400 million shares daily.

Brokers like Instinet because it gives instant access to market information, can handle large orders of up to 1 million shares, and eliminates the cost of a floor operation. Institutional investors like it because they do not have to pay the specialist's handling fee and can do large trades easily. Eighty of the nation's largest institutional investors are subscribers.

In many ways Instinet is an automated offspring of the third market, so it is not surprising to find among its key personnel the leaders in the third market during the 1950s and 1960s—Donald and John ("Jack") Weeden. Donald, from 1979 until the summer of 1985 a partner in Moseley, Hallgarten, Estabrook & Weeden, Inc., a New York securities house, is a director of Instinet, and Jack is senior vice president and treasurer. The Weedens' maverick streak was inherited from their father, who took his firm, Weeden & Company, public in 1927, when no exchange allowed members to be publicly owned. Weeden & Company became a third market firm to survive.

In the 1970s the brothers Weeden helped develop the nation's first automated electronic exchange in Cincinnati. The very concept of the Cincinnati exchange dictated that all trading be done upstairs. As Jack Weeden explains, he and his brother believed "the marketplace need not be a geographic center, but a computer in which buyers and sellers could meet more efficiently and economically and in which there would be fewer errors" because far fewer people and far less paperwork would be involved. When Weeden & Company went out of business in 1979,* a victim of the discount commissions that the third market's success prompted, Merrill Lynch, always a supporter of greater automation, briefly replaced it. Merrill's Roger Birk said the firm withdrew since "not enough other strong participants were attracted." But industry scuttlebutt says Merrill's purpose of forcing the NYSE to automate more had been accomplished. In any event, Merrill recognized the parallels between Cincinnati and Instinet and bought a minority stake in Instinet in 1984. Smaller portions were purchased by Dean Witter, Shearson Lehman, and the E. F. Hutton Group.

Instinet President Fredric Rittereiser and Merrill Lynch's former executive Vice-President and Chief Administrative Officer Robert

---

* Donald Weeden recently started his own firm under the same name.

Rittereiser* are brothers, but fraternal ties had no bearing on Merrill's investment decision. Instead, it reflected its enthusiasm for automation. "Merrill Lynch is driven by the concept of taking Wall Street to Main Street and the vehicle to do that these days is electronic technology," said Rittereiser, whose background is in computer systems development. With IBM, Merrill Lynch is devising computer programming that encapsulates information for investors on today's vast range of financial products (many of which Merrill initiated).

Because Merrill does 13 percent of all transactions by Big Board members, the exchange is at least listening to its proposal that Instinet terminals be installed on the NYSE floor. Instinet has held "cordial," albeit unproductive, discussions with the exchange about obtaining a NYSE listing. An Instinet subsidiary, the INC Trading Corporation, is a member of the Cincinnati, Boston, and Pacific exchanges, and both Instinet and INC are members of NASDAQ, on which Instinet is traded. NYSE specialists have thundered that Instinet will come to the NYSE only over their dead bodies. However, Rittereiser argued that their hostility is diminishing as they realize they may actually benefit. "If the specialists are good, they will survive," Rittereiser maintained. "They resisted Super Dot because it eliminates their handling fee, but the trade-off has been that order flow has increased. Instinet could do likewise."

All U.S. exchanges have vastly different constituencies from twenty-five years or even a decade ago. In 1960 securities firms were partnerships or privately held corporations; today half the 7,300, including eight of the ten largest, are publicly owned. In 1960 they were highly specialized by function, such as stocks, bonds, or commodities; today many sell up to 240 financial products, including insurance and real estate. Since their debut in 1975 discount houses have gained 20 percent of stock market business, and according to some forecasts, their share could rise to 35 percent. Institutional investors have supplanted individuals as the major source of business.

Securities executives believe capitalization of at least $1 billion is necessary to survive in this era, and to get the money, they are selling to outsiders. The new owners include a department store, a credit

---

*The interview with Robert Rittereiser for this book was conducted before he became president of E. F. Hutton in June 1985.

card firm, and several insurance companies. Sears, Roebuck & Company, the world's largest retailer, has bought Dean Witter Reynolds. Dean Witter estimates that up to 40 percent of its accounts were opened at financial desks in Sears stores and that four-fifths are first-time or reactivated accounts. The average household income of clients is $36,000, the same as that of customers at conventional brokerage offices.

American Express has acquired Shearson Loeb Rhoades, and Lehman Brothers Kuhn Loeb, and eight insurance companies have purchased minority or whole interests in brokers, led by the Prudential Insurance Company of America, which acquired Bache Halsey Stuart Shields of New York. The others include the Equitable Life Assurance Society (Donaldson, Lufkin & Jenrette of New York); the Kemper Group (Loewi Financial Services Limited of Milwaukee, Bateman Eichler, Hill Richards, Inc., of Los Angeles, and Prescott, Ball & Turben of Cleveland); the John Hancock Mutual Life Insurance Company (Tucker Anthony and R. L. Day of Boston); and the Hartford Insurance Group (Thomson McKinnon, Inc. of New York).

If these new superpowers overcome their problems in meshing their disparate components, they could "potentially make the NYSE obsolete" predicts Richard Jenrette, chairman of Donaldson, Lufkin & Jenrette and immediate past chairman of the Securities Industry Association. "The NYSE is an ideal vehicle for small firms to bring their business to a central market, but if ten firms wind up doing ninety percent of the business, they may start acting like mini NYSEs through internalizing their orders." The top ten securities houses now have a 60 percent slice of total industry revenue.

Continues Jenrette: "If just six internalize, you can say, 'Good-bye, NYSE.' Already our Pershing Division [which executes and clears transactions for regional securities firms, banks, and other financial institutions] does as much volume as the NYSE did seven years ago. By the year 2000 Wall Street's superpowers could conclude that since they are doing most of the trading, they don't need the NYSE except perhaps as a computer center."

As for the securities firms, they are threatened by the rise of discount houses and by the increased incursion of the banks. More than 600 discount operations have sprung up since the SEC ordered the NYSE to change to negotiated commissions on May 1, 1975—"May

Day" to the industry. Only one NYSE member firm, the then smallish Quick & Reilly, Inc., became a discounter. It took sixteen months for another member to follow suit. "It was a gamble that worked, with the phones ringing constantly," President Leslie Quick recollects. The firm now has forty-two offices across the U.S., and Quick and his family have become worth around $100 million.

Discounters charge up to 70 percent lower commissions than full-service houses. They do not have the cost of providing analysis and investment counseling and can save money by having austere offices. Quick & Reilly shaves its rental costs by disdaining sidewalk quarters because, Quick says, "There is insufficient pedestrian traffic to warrant them." Most orders are by telephone.

Many Wall Street firms had protested that "May Day" discount rates would ruin the industry, and the NYSE's then president, James Needham, threatened a lawsuit to block their advent. Undercapitalized firms did die, but today industry profitability is up substantially.

Now Wall Street is concerned it may lose control of the marketplace to the nation's banks. Citibank and BankAmerica have greater combined assets than all 409 NYSE member firms dealing with the public. The securities firms possess only 1 percent of the $5 trillion consumers have in financial assets, compared with the banks' 35 percent. Nine out of ten Americans have bank accounts, but only one out of ten has an account with a broker. "It's like pitting guns against spears," says Robert Towbin.

The banks' push to be in the securities business is a step backward in time. Until the 1933 Glass-Steagall Act banks were involved in the issuing of corporate securities to the public. Congress excluded them in 1933 because it believed the collapse of many banks after the 1929 stock market crash had contributed to the depression. Department of Justice officials now think this was a misreading of events and that the act is anticompetitive. At first the banks tested the waters for a return to the securities business by opening discount operations; 2,000 banks (one-seventh of the total) now have them. They also want reentry into the lucrative area of underwriting.

For its part, Wall Street edged into banking via cash management accounts (CMAs), introduced in 1977 by Merrill Lynch on the ground that its basic business was not securities or options or commodities but as a depository for clients' money, just like a bank. CMA clients use their accounts as if they were bank accounts and, like bank customers, receive checkbooks and bank credit cards. The difference is that their money is placed by the investment dealer in a high-interest-earning money market fund. Merrill now has 1 million CMA clients. Its success upset the banks because the money invested in CMAs would normally have gone to them. The banks struck back by demanding that Congress dismantle the Glass-Steagall Act.

Later, some brokers circumvented the legal definition of a bank as a financial institution that both accepts deposits and makes loans by doing only one or the other; their ventures were dubbed nonbank banks. They carefully selected state banks that are not members of the Federal Reserve System since they are exempt from the Glass-Steagall Act.

A bank already belongs to the NYSE: Brown Brothers Harriman & Company, the oldest private bank in the United States. Founded in 1818 as an investment and commercial bank, it ditched its investment banking side when the Glass-Steagall Act was passed because 65 percent of its business was commercial, and only 35 percent underwriting. It could continue underwriting government bonds while acting as a broker for investment clients.

The blurring of the distinctions among banks, brokers, and insurance companies has resulted in an overlapping of government regulations. Three agencies—the Office of the Comptroller of Currency, Federal Reserve Board, and Federal Deposit Insurance Corporation—cover the banks. The SEC oversees the equities and options business except for options on futures over which the CFTC has authority. Insurance companies are not directly regulated by the federal government. The growing school of thought is that regulation should be along functional lines. A broker's banking operations would fall under the banking agencies, and a bank's brokerage activities would be established as a separate division and come under the jurisdiction of the SEC.

For Wall Street to be in fighting shape, it will have to stop hiring droves of people when times are good and firing them when times are bad. Employees account for 60 percent of operating expenses, including the $1 million—and occasionally more—in salary and compensation received by some chief executives. "The industry has been legitimately criticized for not controlling costs," concedes Edward

O'Brien, president of the Securities Industry Association. "This is partly due to its heritage as a private partnership business in which partners believed they had an absolute right to do with their money as they saw fit. Also, ours is a very unpredictable business as we can't anticipate volume in advance and schedule production like the car industry."

Executives at private partnerships counter that they are not profligate. "We don't let our costs get out of control in the good years," says Richard Menschel, a senior partner at Goldman, Sachs & Company, one of Wall Street's most profitable partnerships. "We don't hold many parties and have limousines or a company plane. Other people in this industry use the excuse that it is tough to budget expenses, but we find we can do so by using share of market and commission fees as yardsticks. Traditionally the industry hasn't done this because of its desire to retain its entrepreneurial spirit."

Brown Brothers Harriman, another profitable private partnership, is delightfully down-to-earth. It curbs costs by putting profits ahead of visibility. "Many brokers that have gone to Europe offer unprofitably low commission rates even though it costs more to do business abroad; by contrast, we tell overseas clients that if their business is unprofitable to us, we will drop them," says William Moore III, Brown Brothers' vice president in charge of foreign investment.

"Much of the industry has given away profitability through astronomical salaries to attract star analysts and high commissions to salespeople. We never pay on a commission basis; instead, we give a salary plus performance-related bonus. In great years most firms pay out whatever they earn so that in bad years they have to reduce their staff. We have had no layoffs in the twenty years I have been here, and staff turnover is low because employees know they're not going to be fired if business turns sour. Products we introduce are brain-intensive rather than people-intensive. Nor do we put costly tombstone announcements in the paper about securities issues we handle."

Other brokers differ with Moore, saying diversification is a cushion against the cyclical nature of their business. Shearson Lehman owned by American Express (credit cards, travel service, property and casualty insurance through the Fireman's Fund), has one of the best earnings records on Wall Street. "A broad mix reduces reliance on any one segment," says Jeffrey Lane, Shearson's vice-chairman and chief operating officer. "We also avoid exuberance when business is at the top or despair at the bottom to prevent the tremendous human disservice of layoffs."

Conversely, Merrill Lynch (stocks, Visa credit cards, mortgage insurance through the Family Life Insurance Company, residential real estate sales, corporate relocation, and a state bank charter) reported sharply lower profits in 1984, compared to 1983 (although the last quarter of 1984 showed an upturn). It laid off many of the 6,000 people it had hired in 1983.

Merrill's problems cannot be pinned solely on diversification. It suffered from unrelated bad judgments, including its costly, ill-timed purchase of part of Sun Hung Kai, the Hong Kong broker, and a write-off of $83 million in annuities it sold on behalf of a company (Baldwin United Corporation) that collapsed. In fact, in 1984 its real estate and insurance revenue offset decreased stock market commissions.

"In some respects, diversification added more to our costs than we would have liked, but if we hadn't offered new products, we might have lost customers," Robert Rittereiser reasoned. He contended that the brokerage industry faces unique marketing problems because "something that is not in vogue for years may suddenly have a mad run for popularity." He also asserted critics should remember that other industries which underwent deregulation, such as transportation, have had problems adjusting "in spades."

As the NYSE and Amex near their bicentennials (the NYSE in 1992, Amex in 1993) and NASDAQ approaches its fiftieth anniversary in 1988, they are locked in gladiatorial combat. The significance of their battle lies not only in the spectacle of a struggle between titans for supremacy but also in what sort of trading system—the floor or the box—will triumph. Neither system can rely on its member firms to rally exclusively to its cause because the members are far more concerned about their survival and what form that survival should take.

Epilogue

Longer trading hours, increased emphasis on automation, and national and global linkages are the trends at the world's major stock exchanges. But engrossed with modernization, the exchanges seem to be overlooking their stated purpose: to provide individuals with opportunities to increase their capital while funding the growth of private enterprise. With institutions dominating most marketplaces, the individual appears forgotten.

Perplexed by the confusing jargon and the constant stream of new, hard-to-understand products, the general public is concerned that investing is high-risk and low-return. It is distrustful because some securities firms have been found guilty of fraud. It is wary of escalating insider trading. And it is discouraged because it gets little say at shareholder meetings.

The public also has a hard time placing much faith in brokerage houses' analysts since so-called screwball investment theories often work as well as the traditional tools of statistics, graphs, and charts. The favorite unusual indicator: If a National Football Conference team wins the Super Bowl, stock prices rise; if an American Football Conference team does, prices fall. Perhaps awareness of this omen has made it self-fulfilling, but the omen has been accurate in all years but one since the first Super Bowl in 1967. For those who prefer fashion to football, there is the hemline theory that rising skirt lengths are a forecast of ups in the market and longer ones of downs.

Contradictions on the extent and implications of electronization and internationalization abound. Many would argue that as trading floors become more automated, the next logical step would be to dispense with the floor and switch to the computer box, the way NASDAQ already has. Trading electronically has proved cheaper in several respects. Customers are able to buy instantly before the price changes; on the floor by the time the congestion is penetrated the price may have risen. Furthermore, the box eliminates the specialist's extra fee and the broker's expense of floor operations. Fewer people involved should decrease the chance of errors.

An electronic market is suited to this age of home computers. Even now it is possible to transmit an order electronically from a personal computer to the broker's. The rules still call for orders to go through brokers, but conceivably customers could contact the automated network directly through their computers. That, of course, would jeopardize the future of brokers.

If electronization spreads, one national market per country or time zone could handle trading in stocks of national and international interest and regional exchanges would shrink to handling only local stocks. It may be difficult to arrive at one national market since each prominent exchange would likely feel best suited to represent the entire market. The United States already has two nationwide markets: NASDAQ and the Intermarket Trading System. The NYSE tried to form a third by its overture to the Pacific Stock Exchange. Superpower brokers could supersede all these markets by trading electronically among themselves. Merrill Lynch's and IBM's investor information program lays the groundwork for their starting such a system; and Reuters, Dow Jones, and AT&T also have the capacity to establish worldwide financial trading networks.

Europe is inching toward its own electronic link under pressure from European Commission officials who believe such an arrangement is essential for Europe to be competitive against the strong U.S. and Japanese markets. "There is a perceived drift of trading in European securities to the U.S. market, with the volume in some exceeding that at home," explains Christopher Cruikshank of the Commission's securities market division. "Trading in Europe is now divided into compartments that are insulated from one another. People involved in arbitrage know what is happening in the various markets and what the best price is, but the ordinary investing public doesn't."

Under the electronic Interbourse Data Information System (IDIS), exchanges will share final price information in the 140 blue-chip stocks quoted on two or more European Community (EC) exchanges. Because Reuters and Dow Jones news services supply the same figures, EC officials regard IDIS as more important in its ramifications than in its function. "Now that the exchanges are tackling something in common, it lays a small seed that could lead to other things, if there is the right political backing," Cruikshank says. However, the formation of a single European exchange is unlikely. Aside from patriotic pride, there are the obstacles of clashing currency exchange controls as well as differing regulations and trading methods. Outside events could force these exchanges to a compromise. Some companies are bypassing the exchanges in favor of raising money off the trading floor through the *Euromarket* (an umbrella term for international money and capital markets developed since the 1950s by European banks) and distributing their shares to traditional Eurobond buyers.

Almost 400 foreign stocks are already traded in American Depository Receipt form in the U.S., and about 200 U.S. companies on the NYSE are also listed on one or more overseas markets. Some $15 billion in U.S. pension money is invested outside the U.S., and U.K. investment in foreign equities has increased more than sixfold since 1975. Raising money in more than one market is gaining popularity among corporations as the scope of their underwritings surpasses what they can obtain domestically. Transactions done in the U.S. in foreign companies' shares have jumped more than fifteen times in value since 1970. The success of European second-tier markets, with their less stringent listing requirements for smaller companies, may inspire other world exchanges to establish similar junior markets as a way of increasing listings. As corporations rely more on overseas markets, international partnerships among brokers will probably proliferate, or brokers will have to have offices in all major world trading centers.

The internationalization of trading is intensifying competition among markets because of readily available alternatives for investors. At the same time joint projects in the trading of interlisted stocks are apt to multiply since no exchange can afford to be entirely independent in an electronic age that enables orders to be given quick attention anywhere. Unfortunately for shareholders and potential investors, the drive for worldwide twenty-four-hour trading appears to be outpacing efforts to protect investors. The quantity and quality of market information vary widely; simultaneous trading could cause major price disparities, especially if the same stocks were traded in different currencies; and listing, reporting, and regulatory differences are abundant.

The behavior of the U.S. Securities and Exchange Commission as a quasi-international stock market policeman displeases many foreign countries. While they recognize that the rules in the U.S. are much tougher than theirs, they point out that these rules have not prevented a great many violations and instances of fraud. Many also view American accounting principles, with which all foreign firms seeking a U.S. exchange listing must comply under SEC regulations, as too rigid and detailed. The SEC has hinted that it may agree to reciprocal criteria for listings because its restrictions place U.S. markets at a disadvantage in the global trading arena (far fewer foreign companies are traded on U.S. exchanges than U.S. ones on overseas markets). Under a reciprocal arrangement, documents accepted in one country would be regarded as sufficient for listing in another country.

But as yet, there is no central forum to encourage coordination, although three organizations are campaigning for standardization of regulations: the Brussels-based European Commission, the Paris-based International Federation of Stock Exchanges (Fédération Internationale des Bourses de Valeurs—FIBV), and the International Association of Securities Commissions. Each has made limited progress. The International Association of Securities Commissions, founded in 1975, did not become truly international until 1984. Until then only North and South American countries were involved.

The International Federation of Stock Exchanges was founded in 1961, and thirty-one exchanges from around the world are members.

The FIBV wants to harmonize international clearing and settlement of securities; share information on communications, technology advances, and international taxation; and promote cooperation in quelling insider trading. It is not truly representative of global trading since its membership rules are erratic. In most cases a country's largest or two largest exchanges belong. But although trading volume in the U.S. is much higher, only two American exchanges are members, in contrast with three Swiss. The FIBV has also been unsuccessful in devising a standard formula for members' annual trading statistics. This does not bode well for more crucial matters.

Only four of the twelve European Community nations—the U.K., Netherlands, Denmark, and France—have accepted EC directives pertaining to shareholder disclosure and listing requirements. The exchanges are reluctant to submit to universal rules because they may not fit the local situation. They resent government interference and prefer to handle such discussions through the Committee of European Stock Exchanges, formed in 1974. Their hostility has not halted the commission's planning directives on insider trading and intentions regarding a takeover by a person or firm that acquires 10 percent of a company. The only EC countries with an existing rule are the U.K. and France. In the U.S. the trigger point is 5 percent.

In their desire to keep up with the times, the exchanges are relinquishing their unique personalities. The axis of power is shifting to member firms and listed companies. Because exchanges are desperate to keep both constitutents happy in this era of fierce global competition, their officials are no longer dictating to these groups but instead bowing to their demands. Even the mighty and proud New York Stock Exchange is having to advertise in distant as well as local publications.

The blurring of the distinctions among stock, commodities, and options exchanges, as each trades the others' products, is adding fuel to the increasingly hot rivalry and forcing rethinking of the need for separate jurisdictional agencies and regulatory rules. With electronization as a common denominator, it is not inconceivable that the exchanges could coalesce into a federation, a sort of United Nations of stock, commodities, and options markets, with trading conducted via satellite. There would be no Colossus, no grand marketplace, as the

NYSE now is, although the United States as the leading center of institutional investment, would likely continue to be the world's paramount trading arena.

This ultramodern new trading world beckons with its dazzling promises of speed, efficiency, and reliability, but it could drain away the color, individuality, and spontaneity of the trading floors—where the excitement at big price gains and pain at big losses are the heartbeat of the world's major exchanges today.

Index

INDEX

252

Hamilton, James Dundas, 32
Hammering, 44
Hanover Stock Exchange, 186
Harris, E.B. (Everette Bagby), 77, 78
Harris Bank, 79
Harry's at Hanover Square, 208
Hartford Insurance Group, 234
Hauck, Michael, 193
Hauck & Sohn Bankiers, George, 193
Hauser, Karl, 192
Hedging, 64–66, 67
Heiwa Real Estate Company, Ltd., 5
Henry, Charles, 70, 82, 104
Henry Ansbacher Holdings, 51
Hercus, Barry, 7
Heusser, Charles, 176
High-technology options index, 108
High-technology stocks, 111–12, 183,
    195
Hill Woolgar, 55
Hitler, Adolph, 162, 197
Hoare Govett, 48–49
Hodgson, Robin Granville, 55
Hoffman-La Roche S.A., 165
Honda Motor Company, 5
Hong Kong, 17, 48, 49, 157
Hong Kong and Shanghai Banking
    Corporation, 45
Hong Kong Futures Exchange, 58
Hoppenstedt Company, 201–2
Hughes Tool Company, 86

IBM, 5, 18, 19, 233, 240
INC Trading Corporation, 233
Indonesia, 17
Industrial Bank of Japan, 13
Insider trading, 108, 159, 181–82, 243
Instinet (Institutional Networks Cor-
    poration), 52, 88, 231–32, 233
Institut für Kapitalmarkt Forschung
    (Institute for Capital Finance),
    192
Institutional trading, 21, 36, 42, 128
  in France, 150
  in Germany, 195–96

  in Japan, 9, 10, 26
  in the Netherlands, 60
  in Switzerland, 182–83
  in the U.K., 39, 40
  in the U.S., 43, 87, 96, 107, 115,
    150, 163, 182–83, 195–96,
    214, 216, 229, 232, 233, 244
  See also Insurance companies;
    Pension funds
Insurance companies, x, 37, 45, 119,
    126, 161, 172–73, 183, 196
Intel Corporation, 111–12
Interbourse Data Information System
    (IDIS), 241
Inter-Finance, 149
Intermarket Trading System (ITS),
    87, 96, 111, 115, 214, 222, 240
International Association of Securities
    Commissions, 151, 242
International Federation of Stock
    Exchanges (Fédération
    Internationale des Bourses de
    Valeurs–FIBV), 17, 88, 242–43
International Futures Exchange
    (Intex), 113
International Monetary Fund, 60, 78
International Monetary Market
    (IMM), 76–77, 78–79, 81
International Options Clearing
    Corporation, 61–62, 132
International Telephone & Telegraph,
    18
Investment Dealers Association of
    Canada, 120, 131
IOS (Investors Overseas Service), 194
Italy, 22, 176, 177–78, 193
IU International, 18

James Capel & Company, 45, 50, 51
Japan, 49, 50, 165, 172, 183, 191
  collective decision making in, 25, 26
  economic health of, 2, 17
  exchanges in, 8–9, 17, 22
    Tokyo. See Tokyo Stock Exchange
  foreign banking activity in, 26